THE SPY WENT DANCING

THE SPY WENT DANCING

Aline, Countess of Romanones

G. P. PUTNAM'S SONS/NEW YORK

G. P. Putnam's Sons
Publishers Since 1838
200 Madison Avenue
New York, NY 10016

All interior photographs are from the personal collection of the author.

Library of Congress Cataloging-in-Publication Data

Aline, Countess of Romanones, date.
  The spy went dancing.

  1. Aline, Countess of Romanones, date.
  2. World War, 1939–1945—Secret service—United States.
  3. World War, 1939–1945—Secret service—Spain.
  4. Spies—United States—Biography.   I. Title.
  D810.S8A44   1990   940.54'8673   89-24393
  ISBN 0-399-13509-X

Designed by Rhea Braunstein

Printed in the United States of America
4   5   6   7   8   9   10

For Alvaro

For Alvaro, "El Abuelo,"
For Alvaro, my son,
For Alvaro, my grandson

The importance of securing good Intelligence is apparent + need not be further urged. All that remains for me to add is, that you keep the whole matter as secret as possible. For upon Secrecy, Success depends in most Enterprises of the kind, and for want of it, they are generally defeated, however well planned + promising a favorable issue.

—GEORGE WASHINGTON
Letter to Colonel Elias Dayton, 26 July 1777

Author's Note

Writing a nonfiction espionage book is difficult and delicate. Many people dislike being connected with espionage, partly because they feel espionage is dishonorable, though in my opinion it is one of the most necessary and probably the cheapest weapon any country can have. Because of that reticence, however, and to protect descendants and relatives of the guilty, I have been obliged to change names, some dates, and to disguise the identity of some of the figures in my story. Nevertheless, the story is true. The people are real. Some of the missions I have disclosed in this book have been known to many, and others have been handled in very great secrecy and are known to very few.

Those of us who work in intelligence do not always learn the answers to all the questions we have, and it may seem extraordinary that two missions over such a long span of time could be connected. However, life, I have found, is full of coincidences, and sometimes even more so in the world of espionage.

A few dramatic moments have been left out, as well as some insignificant events, in order to make the book move smoothly. With the limitations I have mentioned, I have attempted to give my reader the clearest possible picture of these intelligence operations in which I was involved. I have studied archives, old letters, spoken to people who are still alive and who also took part. I have researched newspapers and magazines of the periods. Conversations have been re-created, of course, but always with an effort to reflect as exactly as possible the personality of each character and event.

Many brave people were involved in this story, whose names I am unable to mention. They also contributed to the security of our great country, and it is to them I dedicate this book.

Prologue
MADRID, FEBRUARY 1966

I t was the coincidence that began it for me—two such long-ago echoes coming on the same day. If it had been either one alone, I could have said no. But together they proved irresistible—and nearly fatal.

Danger was far from my mind, however, as I paced about my house that morning, surveying the preparations for a black-tie dinner my husband and I were giving for the Duke and Duchess of Windsor. It was one of those Spanish winter days when the sky seemed unnaturally clear, the colors nearly scalding. The sky was so blue it was almost purple, and a magical sun cast glints of gold all over the city of Madrid. The perfect weather for riding, I thought, as I looked out the window. That afternoon I would exercise my horses, and then go to tea at my mother-in-law's . . .

I looked at my watch. I'd better stop daydreaming and return my attention to the dinner. It had to be perfect. The Duchess was an old friend, but she was also a brilliant hostess and would notice every detail. Our entire household was involved in getting ready for the occasion. The smell of freshly baked pastry wafted from the kitchen. Damask cloths were being starched and pressed in the laundry. Tables and chairs piled up as they emerged from the cellar, and, outside, workmen hammered and rapped as they enclosed the terrace to provide more room for dancing. Then, above all this chaos and racket, came the voice of my maid announcing a telephone call. The minute I heard the name, I knew something was up.

John Derby, code-named Jupiter, had been the OSS's chief of Secret Intelligence for the Iberian Peninsula during World War

Two and was currently a high official in the CIA. He had also been my boss in espionage ever since I had started to work as a spy for the United States government over twenty years before.

I'd seen him on and off over the years since the end of my wartime missions, but not for quite some time, and somehow I suspected this was not a social call. When I picked up the phone, however, the warm familiar voice carried the tone of an old friend merely interested in saying hello.

"Aline, I've just arrived in Madrid and I'd love to see you."

That sounded innocent enough. I relaxed and told him how delighted I was to know he was in town and suggested he come to my dinner for the Windsors that night. He accepted but insisted, "Aline, I must see you alone first. It's a matter of major importance."

That's when I realized my qualms had not been imaginary. Most of Derby's life seemed to be spent on a plane. He never discussed his activities and I knew better than to ask. I'd been in the business too long not to understand the unwritten laws. And now he had "a matter of major importance" to discuss with me.

Nevertheless, as soon as he was announced that afternoon, I rushed downstairs and gave him a big hug, glad to see again the nice Irish face which always looked as though it had just been scrubbed. The last time I had seen Jupiter had been several years before at the Madrid airport, where my husband and I had been waiting for a plane to Morocco. He'd been haggard from lack of sleep, his suit wrinkled, and he'd held a bag slung over one shoulder—unusual for the impeccable spymaster. He looked like a man who had lived out of a suitcase for too long, and our greetings that day had been rushed and vague. I had worried about him during that flight and even that night as I lay awake in the home of our Moroccan friends. It seemed strange and unfair that, while my husband and I enjoyed the leisure of peacetime, Jupiter continued to live as though the war had never ended.

That bright February, however, John Derby seemed hardly changed from those first days when he had recruited me into the OSS twenty-three years before. It still amazed me that I had met him on a blind date. At the time I had been a twenty-year-old model for Hattie Carnegie. I was just four months out of a Catholic women's college and desperate to join my older brothers in the war effort overseas. But every organization I had applied to—Jacqueline Cochran's Flying Training, the WACS, the WAVES—had refused me because I was too young. That first evening I had mentioned my frustration to John Derby, along with the fact that I loved adventure and risk. He had surprised me by saying he might be able to help. The next month I had found myself at a spy school outside of Washington, D.C., where I learned the skills of espionage, from codes, weaponry, and self-defense to parachuting. In December of 1943, I was sent on my first secret mission to Spain, beginning a lifetime of spying for the United States.

That afternoon the flecks in Jupiter's pale blue eyes seemed to sparkle more than usual as he took a seat on the red damask sofa under the large Goya painting my husband had inherited from his grandfather. At first Jupiter talked about banalities: these new Constellations, only twenty-two hours from New York to Madrid, and the changes and prosperity Franco had brought to Spain. "Those highways and the traffic. I remember when not even the rich could get a car!"

But abruptly he paused, changed position, and leaned forward, with hands on his knees, speaking in a lower, softer tone. No one was nearby, but this hushed intonation had become customary with him when discussing the trade. His first words didn't surprise me.

"Aline, we have a job for you."

I laughed. "Oh, John, not again. You know I can't do any more jobs for you. My husband made me promise the last time I wouldn't get involved ever again."

Although I had fully intended to give up espionage when I married, I hadn't been able to resist the opportunities afforded by my new status as a grandee of Spain. After all, my specialty had always been my ability to penetrate the upper echelons of Spanish society without arousing suspicion, and now I was permanently lodged there! Wherever we traveled, my husband and I were invited to interesting homes where we met aristocrats, chiefs of state, and important international figures. Having been trained as a spy before I became a countess, I found the old habits difficult to forget.

When my husband had learned a few years before, however, that during one of our many trips abroad I was actually scanning our circle of acquaintances for a Soviet spy, he had put his foot down. I was endangering not only my own life, he claimed, but the lives of our three children as well. Moreover, I was a threat to the reputation of his family, which spanned eight centuries. He had made me promise to give it up, and since then I had kept my word.

"But this one's different," said John Derby. "Your husband worries about his country and his family, but this has nothing to do with Spain. And the job's tailor-made for you."

"I don't even want to hear about it. The answer is no."

"You used to be more patriotic than that." The remark stung, but before I could react, he waved it away wearily. "I'm sorry, Aline. That wasn't fair. It's just that it's been a very difficult case. Look, let me explain a little bit of it to you. Then you'll see how important it is, and maybe it'll make a difference." He looked at me for permission and, taking my silence for acquiescence, continued. "Needless to say, everything I'm about to tell you is confidential." He paused, and I nodded. He went on. "It concerns NATO. A mole in the Paris headquarters. Somehow the Soviets are receiving top secret information about America's contingency plans to meet a Soviet attack. It's compromising our defense systems everywhere."

Jupiter paused again and, finding that I was listening intently, continued. "You remember the SIOP affair in '61?" I nodded. In 1961, a Sergeant Johnson, on duty alone Saturday nights at Orly Airport, had photocopied the American Single Integrated Operation Plan and passed it on to the Soviets before being caught. Derby's tone was solemn. "Now it seems that someone else is passing on that same kind of information. We believe it's someone inside NATO, because plans from the French and British have also been included. And it has to be someone high up. An agent of ours inside the Soviet General Staff—this is not for anybody else's ears, Aline!—tells us they receive information often only a week after our people forward it from Washington."

"That's terrible," I cried, forgetting for a moment that all of this was far removed from me. Drawing back, I added, "but of course there's no way I could be useful in an operation so far from Madrid."

"Yes, you could. Thanks to one of our best agents, we know a few things about the mole. She really felt she had a lead. But now we can't use her anymore." John Derby kept his eyes on me while he spoke.

I knew he was studying my reaction. Though I feigned indifference, in fact I was intrigued. "Why? Why can't you use her anymore?"

"Because she is dead." I felt my breath catch. "She was a close friend of yours."

A jab of fear went through my stomach. Who this time?

"It was Magic. She was found dead last week."

My heart sank. Magic had been my roommate at the spy school outside Washington. Her life had been a series of tragedies. Her father, a famous concert pianist, had died in a concentration camp in 1943. Her husband of one year had disappeared after the Nazis had picked him up. She had dedicated her life to espionage for the United States—at first against the Nazis, but later in any capacity where she could be useful.

Such a difficult life had jaded her, of course, yet in some ways she had remained surprisingly naive and vulnerable. In her letters to me she had confessed that she wanted to get married and have children. Then she wrote that the perfect man had entered her life and that she was about to get married. Soon after, someone informed me that the scoundrel had skipped and taken her life savings with him. That happened twice, that I knew of. The drinking problem she developed may have had something to do with these unfortunate love affairs.

Because of my fondness for Magic, Jupiter's news about her death was a blow, yet I wasn't so naive myself as to think he had brought it up by accident. He was an artist at convincing me or anybody else to comply with his wishes, but this time it wasn't going to work. Nevertheless, I couldn't help musing how everything had seemed to go wrong for Magic. My own life in comparison had been a series of fortunate unexpected blessings. She had been born into a wealthy family and had lived in a palace in Berlin and then lost everything. I had been born into a family with few luxuries and had only dreamed of houses like those I had today, ancient and large enough to have ghosts and uninhabited wings where a child could get lost. I thought of my charismatic husband and our three healthy sons—Alvaro, Luis, and Miguel. Mine was a fairy-tale existence. It didn't seem fair.

"John, naturally I'm upset about Magic, but whatever I do won't bring her back to life. And you know very well that I will always do what I can for my country, but this time it's impossible. I've promised my husband. It wouldn't be fair to him. No, I'm sorry, you'll have to find someone else."

For a moment, silence enveloped us. The workmen's hammers

and children's boisterous shouts in the garden had ceased. The streaks of late afternoon sunlight dappling the hand-loomed carpet with shadows of gold had vanished, too. I stood up to switch on a lamp.

"Magic herself asked me to get you to help with this mission," John Derby said quietly. "I didn't ask you, because I thought she could do the job alone, and I knew your husband would be against it. She'd learned that the person providing the material was well-known in Paris society. That's your strength, Aline. Magic knew that you could meet people in Paris that she could not. The guests of honor at your dinner tonight are just an example."

"John, it's preposterous to think that because I have friends like the Windsors, I can pick out an enemy agent. It would be like looking for a needle in a haystack. I can't move to Paris. And even if I could, I wouldn't know where to begin."

"You wouldn't have to move to Paris. Just make a trip now and then, as you do anyhow. And I'll tell you how to begin. We're sure the man we're looking for is American. From the information he's passing on, it's apparent he's connected with the American European Command. Unfortunately, we lost the Frenchman Magic got her information from at the same time we lost her. The Soviet surveillance team must have discovered he was living with her. They eliminated both, of course."

Jupiter shook his head and sighed long and slow. "We're almost starting from scratch again, but we have more than enough to get you going. We know that if you go to Paris, there's a good chance you could run into the mole at some party. You're accustomed to this sort of job. There are thousands of NATO employees, but few who circulate with the Windsors and the social elite of Paris. Magic had a hunch that many of your friends attended the same parties as our traitor. That alone gives you a start."

I shook my head. "Not at all. There's so little to go on."

Really, I thought, this was all from an earlier time of my life, one which was over. Now I was a mother, a wife, and an active member of Spanish society. My husband was right—espionage was completely inappropriate in a life such as mine.

"No, there's more. Listen. I can even give you the names of some suspects. And we have a few other leads." He grabbed my arm. "For example, we know the mole was out of France for a few weeks during the month of January. The regular reports coming in to the

Soviets were interrupted during that time. But he was in Paris the night of February first. The night Magic was murdered."

Magic! I felt my emotions begin to rise again. Magic had been so devoted to her work and had always been willing to take chances. It seemed unjust that this should be her reward.

Steps were approaching. He stopped speaking. The next second the butler entered the room to declare that the florist was waiting to discuss table decorations. His news, coming like an omen, brought me back to my real life to save me just in time. I felt relieved, as if I had just peered into the window of a dark and ominous house and then been told I did not have to enter.

We both stood up. "John, I'm really sorry I can't help you this time. Right now I'm hectic with the preparations for the party tonight. But I'm still expecting you to come."

"I'd be delighted, but look, Aline, don't make up your mind yet. Have lunch with me tomorrow, at Jockey. We'll talk some more." Before the door closed behind him, he added, "And remember Magic. This could be your chance to avenge her."

That evening during the dinner when the footmen began serving the almond gazpacho, I glanced across the room at my husband's table. He and the Duchess of Windsor were laughing, probably at one of her jokes. She was wearing the canary diamond clips, the ones she called her "very ripe pears," and of course the ring to match. The diamonds on her bracelets sparkled. All those jewels and her embroidered blue satin Givenchy dress made her glow in the flickering candlelight. One of the few women who got better-looking with age, I thought.

We had met the Duke and Duchess in the winter of 1947 in New York, during our long honeymoon throughout Europe and the United States. That summer in Venice, we'd become friends with Elsa Maxwell, the American society hostess, and when we'd arrived in New York, she'd invited us to her fabulous parties. The Americans we met were intrigued with Luis and me, because we were the first titled Spaniards to visit New York in a decade, due to the Spanish Civil War and then World War Two. Besides, exit visas for Spaniards were almost impossible to obtain at that time. We soon found ourselves in the social whirl of New York.

At a dinner given by Elsa's friend Charlie Cushing, the Duchess of Windsor was seated on his right, and I on his left. I happened to comment to the Duchess about the sensation a Hollywood actress was creating on the other side of the room.

The Duchess leaned across Charlie Cushing to speak to me. "My dear, I'll show you how you can generate the same excitement without having to be a movie star." Returning to Charlie, she said, "I'm going to ask Aline to point out three men she doesn't know at your party. Then after dinner I want you to casually say to those three, without the others knowing about it, of course, that Aline said something very complimentary about him. Let's see." She fingered her gold bib necklace imbedded with rubies and emeralds. "To one, what about saying Aline finds him the most handsome man in the room. To the other, tell him Aline wants to meet him—he looks so intelligent. And to the other, say . . ." She giggled. "Well, Charlie, I think a rogue like you will know what's most appropriate to say better than I."

The Duchess looked at me again. "And now, my dear, just wait until the stampede begins."

I laughed, considering her suggestion simple social banter, and forgot the incident. That is, until the rush began. The three men pursued me relentlessly, not only that night, but at every other party for weeks after. Two of them sent flowers almost daily. My husband was furious.

The Duchess was delighted when we met her at another party soon after, and I told her the results of her little experiment.

"Don't complain," she said. "You've learned an important lesson, which if you take heed, can serve you well in life."

My eyes widened.

"Compliments received through a third person are always more effective," she said. "When you want to make an impression on anyone, do it that way."

That incident initiated our friendship. That summer we kept meeting, at the Hotel du Palais in Biarritz where we both spent the month of August, and later in Paris at the same parties. Having American wives and sharing an admiration for Americans helped our husbands to become friends. Several years after the Windsors had moved from an apartment into their house in the Bois de Boulogne in Paris, they invited us to stay with them, and they came to visit us in Spain. Despite the difference in our ages, for almost twenty years now we had been friends.

I looked toward the table at my right. Of course, for the Duke and Duchess I had made a point of inviting the most glamorous members of Madrid's social world. Ava Gardner had the Marqués of Deleitosa enthralled, as I'd figured she would, but her familiar tic of moving her lower jaw in circles made me aware she was nervous and dying for a drink. When I had invited her several weeks before, she had vowed not to take a drop, and so far she had kept her promise. But I worried that it might not last long. She was always the most beautiful woman in any room but, plagued by an insecurity difficult to understand, she never realized it. I'd placed the handsome King Simeon of Bulgaria on her other side. I hoped his attractiveness would distract her from the glass of wine she was caressing.

John Derby was striving to entertain the Duchess of Alba, who seemed more interested in something Franco's son-in-law was saying. Carmen Franco, on the other hand, was dutifully listening to the elderly governor of the Bank of Spain. All in all, things seemed to be going as they should, and I directed my attention to the Duke, who was chatting with King Simeon's wife, young Queen Margarita. And that's when the past assaulted me again.

"We both fell in love with the painting," he was saying. "Because it had a little yellow cairn terrier in one corner that reminded us of Slipper, the first dog I ever gave the Duchess."

His words rang a bell from long, long ago. Of course it couldn't have anything to do with Operation Safehaven—that was twenty years ago. In fact, I might not even have thought about it if Derby hadn't shown up that day, but the Duke's mention of a painting with a yellow dog brought back memories of that unforgettable period at the end of World War Two. It couldn't hurt to ask.

"Sir," I interrupted. "By any chance was that painting by Cézanne?"

His Highness chuckled. "Oh, I hardly think that possible. The price would have been higher. It really wasn't anything important. Quite small, in fact. We wouldn't have noticed it if it weren't for the little dog."

"Where was the little dog? In the left- or right-hand corner?"

"Let me see now," said the Duke. "Left or right? Silly of me, but I don't remember." He turned toward me with a smile. "We'll ask the Duchess after dinner."

Somehow we never did, though, and when my husband and I went to bed that night, instead of commenting on the usual ups and downs of the party, I talked about the Duke's amazing reference to a painting with a yellow dog in the corner.

"Are you listening?" I asked him. "Remember the yellow dog?"

"What yellow dog?"

"The one in the Cézanne painting I was looking for during the last year of the war. The reason I was so interested in Impressionist paintings. You have to remember. I think I told you all about it."

"Oh, that! But that was so long ago."

"Yes, about twenty years. When I think about those times, I realize what a miracle that . . ." But he wasn't listening; he was already asleep.

I was in a state of confusion. The coincidence of Jupiter showing up unexpectedly and the reference to a painting of a yellow dog, both occurring the same day, kept me awake for hours. That Cézanne had held the secret to one of the most tantalizing unsolved enigmas of my espionage career. And, I realized suddenly, it had been the last time I had ever seen Magic alive. Magic . . .

When I finally fell asleep, my dreams were a jumble of images from those times. The scenes came to me like nightmares. Again I stood horrified looking down at the white pillow in my bedroom, at the woman's head with the black hole in her temple, the stream of dark blood marking an ugly line across her face. Then the night of the Country Club Ball. I struggled for breath as an assassin's hands tightened on my neck and I searched in the dark for my pistol. The dreams were as terrifyingly real as if they had taken place only yesterday . . .

PART ONE

Chapter 1
MADRID, JANUARY 1945

M adrid was windy and cold, but the sky was sharp blue and cloudless that January morning of 1945. I was late, and running to the OSS offices hidden on the top floor of the American ambassador's residence on the corner of Eduardo Dato and the Castellana. Phillip Harris, code-named Mozart, the station chief for American espionage in the Iberian Peninsula, was waiting for me. The day before, he had left a note on my desk in the code room. "Tomorrow morning at nine in my office, urgent." He was like that: no unnecessary words, abrupt, mysterious. And, for me, always a bit terrifying. Was he going to fire me or ship me back to Washington? After one whole year I still couldn't figure him out, and I never felt at ease with him.

I'd arrived in Madrid a little over a year before, recently graduated from college and with only a few months' work modeling in New York City as experience. It had been New Year's Eve, and the last thing I'd imagined was that I would come face-to-face with an assassin. My training in self-defense from the spy school outside Washington had served me unexpectedly well. But what was up now? The war was far from over. It had been a bad Christmas, with the Germans giving us a scare in their surprise attack at the Battle of the Bulge, and the recent Japanese victories in the South Pacific. The last three months had been unusually calm and I feared the chief might have decided that my services were no longer necessary.

Still running, I reached the Calle Eduardo Dato and skirted past an old man wrapped in a long brown cape, which also covered half his face. Spaniards of his generation believed dangerous *microbios* entered the body through the mouth on days with frosty gales like these. Across the street, just in front of the embassy, a carriage-taxi was parked waiting for passengers. The old horse was skinny, but then so were most of the 900,000 human inhabitants of the city. The Civil War had ended in 1939, the same year World War Two had erupted in Europe, so Spaniards were still poor. For all that, they were still exceedingly warm and generous with their friendliness.

"Vaya usted con Dios, señorita," called the milkman as he filled the embassy maid's pail from one of the metal cans on his donkey cart. Normally, I would have chatted with him. But today I merely waved and ran through the huge iron gates, up the narrow stairway to the door on the third floor. There in huge black letters was the name of our cover for espionage in Spain, the American Oil Mission.

I knocked and a booming, masculine voice told me to enter. Phillip Harris sat hunched over an enormous desk, which except for a small rectangular photograph in a silver frame, telephone, and blotter, was void of other objects. He had been my boss since I had arrived in Spain on New Year's Day a year before. During the past year he had proved to be brilliant and untiring in protecting our small group of ten American agents. Not a very imposing force, considering that the Gestapo had over six hundred spies operating inside the country. My mission had been to uncover Himmler's special agent in Spain, and instead I had found a double agent in our midst. It was a discovery which had nearly cost me my life. Mozart's face was massive, big-boned yet angular, and his eyes, shiny brown beads minuscule in that enormous face, always avoided mine. I sat down in the only other chair in the spare room. Sealed shutters blocked out the sunny morning and the noise of the braying donkey in the street below.

He stood up after a brief salutation and went to the window. A silent moment passed before he turned around again.

"Miss Griffith," he began. He rarely used my code name, Tiger. "I've asked you to come here because we have a new mission for you." Without looking at me directly, he continued. "Not an easy one. And probably dangerous. Are you interested?"

A tingle of anticipation ran up my spine. Though my first mission had left me drained and somewhat shaken, for several weeks now I'd been yearning for the excitement of working on something special. To have a mission was to be obsessed. Normal everyday living had become dull in comparison. I hoped Mozart couldn't detect my nervousness when I asked him what it concerned.

"There's a large operation going on now in collaboration with the rest of the Allies. It involves uncovering assets that have been looted by the Third Reich and by individual members of the Nazi government. Gold, jewels, art. Assets stolen from governments, private persons, and companies. Often from wealthy Jews whose effects were confiscated or who were tricked into paying a ransom for a freedom they never enjoyed."

He lumbered back to his desk, and the wooden swivel chair groaned as Harris' massive frame overflowed into it. The arms he crossed in front of him on the desk top made the room and the furniture seem minute. Suddenly we faced each other for just a moment. Then he lowered his gaze and picked up a yellow pencil, which he twirled in his fingers.

"Just because we're talking about art, don't think there's anything genteel about it. Behind this looted wealth is a ruthless gang of cutthroats. They operate like a multinational corporation, they pay exorbitant bonuses for secrecy and murder, and they are accumulating fortunes that could change the direction of the world. We even have indications that the Nazis are employing these looted funds to finance research on a supermodern bomb which could still influence the outcome of the war. Swiss bank accounts are being opened in names we must uncover. The loot is being shipped out of Europe to safe havens in South America. That's why we call it Operation Safehaven."

He paused while we both listened to steps on the barren wooden floor outside his door, until the sound faded away. I sensed that this was not the moment to interrupt. Top Hat, my Mexican OSS colleague during the past year, had told me months ago, "Keep your mouth shut with him. He does everything his own way." Mozart went on quietly. "We have many agents working on this—teams in Holland, Belgium, France, and Switzerland. But in Spain, the work will be more delicate." He leaned closer. I could smell the stale odor of cigar tobacco on his breath.

"The stuff goes by train from Holland and Belgium across France to Bordeaux. From there it's shipped across the Bay of Biscay to Bilbao by boat. Right now, Madrid is the hub of the wheel for all exports from the war zones. For Nazis trying to escape, too."

Mozart tapped his barren desk with the yellow pencil. "One of our agents in Holland saw a large shipment of French Impressionist works destined for Spain. He was in the warehouse while it was being packed and was able to provide a description of one of the paintings. His report states that it was a Cézanne and depicted a couple picnicking in a woods with a shaggy little lap dog in the lower left corner of the canvas. A yellow dog, the report specified. Probably one about so big . . . ."

He held his hands about a foot apart and looked at me.

"I hate those little mutts," he confided. "You know, the kind that are always yapping and biting your ankles."

I stifled a laugh, unaccustomed to such a human remark from my normally austere boss. But his change of personality didn't last. Without a smile, he continued.

"Our cryptoanalysts have discovered that the head of the organization is here in Madrid. He is referred to in the enemy cables we are intercepting as El Guapo, the handsome one." No inflection betrayed his voice, I was still wondering what part of this mission had to do with me when he pointed a fat finger.

"You, Tiger, are going to find that man. You have the best qualifications here. Unfortunately."

My shock must have been apparent, but I hoped he was unaware of the wave of incompetence I was experiencing. In my last mission, I had had the collaboration of others. Where would I begin on this one completely alone? What special attributes could I have? I was the youngest in the office. It didn't seem logical.

"You will uncover El Guapo through the looted paintings. Some may be gracing the walls of those grandee palaces you frequent, and if so, I expect you to discover their source."

His words sounded overly optimistic. After all, I had been invited to only a few homes of Madrid's grandees so far. I also couldn't understand why this would be more perilous than my previous missions. This was an outside enemy at least: much less dangerous, it seemed to me, than my last assignment, which uncovered a double agent in our midst.

When he spoke, it seemed he was reading my mind. "The risk," his words were uttered slowly, without emotion, "is greater for a number of reasons. The Japanese are assisting the Nazis in this operation, and they're fanatics. Right now their pilots are volunteering as Kamikazes, on suicide missions, flying planes into American aircraft carriers and combat ships. If the Japanese became aware you are trying to uncover their agents, you would be eliminated without consideration. Your tender age, your sex—none of this would make any difference."

"But why would I be chosen for this job instead of Jeff, or Top Hat?"

Jeff Walters worked with me in the code room. He was the fastest code clerk in the business and also operated his own chain of agents. Top Hat was a colleague with whom I had worked closely during the past year.

"As a matter of fact, you will be working with Top Hat," said Mozart, "but aside from your ability to operate in Spanish high society, you have one excellent qualification for this mission. I've mentioned the Japanese. Apparently, El Guapo uses the Japanese legation as a cover for his transactions. And you know the one man in Madrid best capable of penetrating the Japanese legation."

The news rendered me speechless. I scanned my memory for the person Mozart could be thinking of.

"He's a Spanish national," he continued, "and he already holds the top job a Spaniard can have inside the legation."

"No." I shook my head. To my surprise, I discovered that under my low chignon, my neck was damp, although Mozart's office was quite chilly. "There must be some misunderstanding, Mr. Harris," I said. "I don't know anyone inside the Japanese legation. If I did, I most certainly would have said so."

"Yes, you do, Miss Griffith." For the first time, a tinge of amusement, a different pitch, toned his voice. "Don't you remember, before leaving Washington for Spain, requesting permission to take a gift of money to Madrid for a friend?"

Yes, of course I did. Jose, the tailor at Hattie Carnegie, had asked me to deliver some money to his niece, a woman named Concha Pombo, but what did that have to do with the Japanese?

Mozart continued. "We had the niece investigated. We discovered she was married to a Spanish journalist who had lived in Tokyo for six years and recently returned to Madrid."

"The Washington office never told me that. My orders were to deliver the money, but to avoid any friendship with Concha Pombo. It wasn't easy. She called repeatedly. Why didn't you ask me to help before?"

"We didn't know the husband would be working in the Japanese legation later on. When we did, you were already deeply involved in Operation Bullfight. You were also too inexperienced then to have been able to handle this job, and you might have caused more damage than good. I think that's changed now." He paused. "At least I hope so." He coughed. "You may remember what I told you a year ago, Miss Griffith—I do not enjoy involving you or anybody else in a mission that might be dangerous. It's just an unfortunate part of my job." The next instant he lowered his tiny eyes, himself again, his shell closed.

As I staggered back to the code room, I thought about my astounding interview with the chief. My doubts about being up to the new mission were enormous. But it was reassuring that Mozart considered my contacts in the upper echelons of Spanish society useful for our work. When I'd first arrived in Spain, I'd been aware that Operation Bullfight—the name of my mission then—necessitated my being accepted into Madrid's social world. But to me such a feat had seemed an impossibility. Even now it still amazed me, for it had been less than a year since I had arrived in this country a complete unknown. Nevertheless the process had unrolled as smooth as silk. Edmundo Lassalle, code-named Top Hat, who seemed to know everyone, had introduced me to Casilda Avila and Carola Lilienthal, girls my age belonging to important Spanish families, and from then on, one invitation came after another. I was a new face in Madrid and was invited everywhere. Even Juanito Belmonte, a bullfighter who quickly became my suitor, was useful. He was at the height of his popularity, the toast of Madrid, and without realizing it presented me to precisely some of the people who turned out to be most useful.

As I sat at my code board transcribing a long coded message from Whitney Shepardson, the Secret Intelligence chief in Washington, I continued to ponder over my meeting with Mozart. I was excited to have a new mission and pleased to be working with Top Hat. He was fearless and a bit unscrupulous as well, but I couldn't help liking him. I also felt I could count on his fondness for me. Top Hat had unlimited advantages for our work. Women of all ages fell for the tall sleek Mexican and they loved to confide in him. Perhaps it was his mustache or the sly black eyes or his smooth feline movements; whatever the reasons, he was the proverbial lady-killer and knew how to take advantage of his special charm. Not even his weakness for titles and beautiful clothes nor his dangerous habit of kleptomania detracted from his being a superb spy. He had a faultless memory, took mere seconds to unlock doors in the dark, and above all, was without par in using a knife, when the order of the night was to kill silently.

Chapter 2

At nine-thirty that evening the large square barroom of the Hotel Palace was a rumble of mixed languages, each table packed. The thick pungent smell of black tobacco almost made me choke as I wove my way to the far corner table where Top Hat was waiting—a delicious confection of warm brown skin, dazzling white teeth, and slick black hair. He stood up as I approached. The fine line of his Pancho Villa mustache gave his smile a sly smirk as the long caramel fingers lifted my hand to his lips. As always, his greeting was stagey.

"*Divina,* you're ravishing." He stood back to appraise my black faille suit piped in red silk over a raspberry satin blouse. "On you, that Balenciaga is sensational. I see my protégé has become the best-dressed woman in Madrid."

I sat down. He slid onto the leather banquette with that catlike grace, the kind of slinky movement that had made his tangos famous.

"I've just returned from Portugal. A few weeks off now and then from the grind of this spy business is indispensable." He sighed. "My pet, you can't imagine how dowdy the women in the casino in Cascais are these days!" In another theatrical gesture, his cigarette outlined an arc in the air. "Life has been such a monotony since I saw you last."

That had been over a month ago and his explanation that he had been on a vacation all that time did not fool me. A vacation in the middle of a war for a man who lived for danger and intrigue was ridiculous. I indicated my skepticism with a shrug.

While the waiter took my order—it was always a problem for me to think of something in a country where there were few fizzy soft beverages other than plain soda water—I noticed that my companion was anxiously concentrating on the door. In a moment I saw why. The chic, auburn-haired Princess Renata von Walperg's green eyes were scanning the room. She was Top Hat's prime target at the moment. He had even dared to invent an excuse for courting her. In a written report to Mozart, he had declared that she was an enemy agent. When Edmundo had handed me that particular report, he'd even had the nerve to tell me not to take seriously what he said about the German princess.

"She's really anti-Nazi," he had confessed. "But business is slack lately, and I have to keep Mozart happy. There's always the possibility he might fire me, you know."

As a result, Princess Renata von Walperg was now on the OSS blacklist—which made her much more interesting, of course. Tonight she was dressed in a navy silk suit, green satin blouse and cuffs, a round chignon supporting her tiny navy pillbox hat. An extremely unattractive man accompanied her: Fritz Waldner, supposedly an attaché at the German embassy. Edmundo and I knew Waldner to be the Gestapo chief. As Renata passed our table, Top Hat received a wink, hardly perceptible to anyone else.

"Edmundo, I'll bet anything you were in Portugal with your favorite princess." I nodded toward her retreating back. Because he treated me like a younger sister, I didn't want him to think he could fool me.

"What do you expect, my pet? She pursues me, and after all it is part of my work, you know. Renata gives me the inside track to Gestapo gossip. She may not be a Nazi, but she knows them all. The trouble is, she's getting serious. Can you imagine—she's thinking of marriage! I should have someone read my cards. I do want to know if I'm going to be in the *Almanack de Gotha,* where all those European aristocrats are listed. That would certainly improve my seating at these Spanish dinners."

"Edmundo, you must really be in love. Marrying Renata won't give you a title. German titles cannot be passed on to husbands. But if you married a Spanish woman with a title, you could become a marquis or a count or a duke, whichever you preferred."

"You're right. Maybe I'd better reconsider. And I'm getting tired of waiting for a deposed queen to float into town." His tone was facetious, but I knew he was dead serious about wanting to improve his social standing.

"What happened to Renata's husband?"

"She never had one."

"She looks a bit old never to have been married."

"That's because you're so young." Edmundo shook his head in a gesture of tried patience. "She's probably in her mid-thirties, a woman's most seductive age." He sighed. I surmised he was recalling moments of their last encounter. He ordered another *combinación*. "Oh yes, Renata's lineage is unbeatable, absolutely—"

Edmundo jumped to his feet. The cause was a tall radiant blond woman entering the room, a slinky silver fox stole draped languidly over one shoulder. She was followed by a short, slim, bespectacled man. Edmundo stretched out his hand to her and briefly introduced her as Princess Ada, although some weeks before I had heard her referred to as Señora de Fribourg. She received Edmundo's greeting with a devastating smile, while the man accompanying her, who turned out to be Señor Fribourg, looked on without any readable expression. He barely saluted Edmundo, although when introduced, he was polite enough to me and mumbled a few timid words. Edmundo continued to talk with Princess Ada, while Klaus Fribourg stood uncomfortably, waiting. Slight of frame and with thinning hair, the only thing remarkable about him was his plump and very pink lips. They seemed too big for his otherwise small and colorless face. Finally, he nervously nudged the gorgeous Ada to move on. Before doing so, she exchanged a few pleasantries with me and expressed a fond farewell to Edmundo. When Top Hat sat down, his black Aztec eyes were shooting sparks.

"That Fribourg. Did you see how he ignored me?" Edmundo's voice trilled with indignation. "He gets invited to places only because of his wife's beauty. And, I suppose, because he's rich, too. He doesn't admit it, but I think he's Jewish. I hear he's a benefactor for Jewish children orphaned in the war. Isn't that nice? But even that doesn't make up for his pretensions as far as I'm concerned. I'm told he's working for us. Little do I care." Edmundo shrugged. "I don't know why she married him."

"His money," I suggested.

"I don't think so. She's an unusually sensitive and kind woman. I'm more apt to think she married him out of gratitude. She told me herself, just the other day at Carmen Yebes's cocktail, that Klaus helped her when she was down and out. Yes, I'll bet that's it."

By now my colleague was concentrating on others. His glance

scanned the room. "Look around, my pet, at the enemy camps represented in this room."

I followed his gaze to the open double door. The press attaché of the German embassy, Hans Lazaar, had just come in. He stood for a moment—obviously trying to locate someone. The monocle squeezed between his pudgy cheek and overhanging brow reflected light from the elaborate chandelier like a glaring bulb in his sinister bald head. Lazaar and I had had many a run-in during my last mission, and his presence still unnerved me.

Top Hat was saying something about a French agent who was sitting at the next table, when I noticed Klaus Fribourg was back, standing next to us, his hand outstretched.

"Come on, Lassalle, I'll give you a fresh pack if you're so in need. But I'd like my cigarette case." His former quiet manner had disappeared entirely.

To my amazement, Top Hat lifted a silver box out of his pocket and handed it to him. "Maybe you'll be more civil in the future, Fribourg." He chuckled flippantly as Fribourg turned and walked away.

I was indignant. As soon as the little man was out of earshot, I reprimanded Edmundo.

"You know, it's very embarrassing to be working with someone who steals. One of these times your victim may think I did it."

"Don't flatter yourself, *Divina.* It's not easy."

"Every time I go to someone's house with you, I worry about what you may have taken. Remember that porcelain vase you put in your pocket at Mimosa's reception?"

Top Hat, unruffled, waved for the check. "Don't nag, my pet." He put his hand into his pocket for his billfold. "When next Señor Fribourg and I meet, I bet he'll treat me with more respect."

A few moments later, we were waiting on the front steps of the hotel for a taxi—Edmundo was taking me to dinner, where he said there was someone important named Paredes he wanted me to meet—when an elegant Cord convertible entered the circular drive and stopped at the farther end of the driveway. I couldn't see the fellow's face, but a well-built young man dressed in a beige trenchcoat, with a white silk scarf hanging from his shoulders, jumped from the driver's seat. I continued toward the taxi and was about to step in when a familiar voice called out.

"I say, Aline, hold it a moment." Turning, I faced the driver of the Cord, a man I hadn't seen in some time. It was the Count of Quintanilla, the good-looking beau of my friend Casilda. I some-times remembered with amusement my arrival at the Palace Hotel that first day in Madrid, when he had carried my bags to my room. Because he had light-colored hair and pale green eyes, I had thought he was a German agent. He had chatted agreeably in a marked British accent as the elevator climbed to my floor, but I hadn't dared utter a word. When I'd reached my room and shut the door behind me, I had been filled with relief. Casilda and I had laughed many times over that story, for in fact, Luis Quintanilla was the only son of one of the best-known families in Spain.

"I'm meeting Casilda," he said. "Is she inside?"

"She's in the rotunda with Carola Lilienthal and Pucho Gamazo," I told him.

"What a pity you're just leaving," said the Count of Quintanilla. "I always seem to miss you. Casilda tells me the Oil Mission keeps you very busy."

I sensed Edmundo shifting beside me and mumbled some re-sponse. I was eager to divert conversation from my supposed job. Trying to account for my long hours and frequent disappearances was always a chore.

Quintanilla looked at Edmundo and smiled. "I know," he said. "Why don't you both join us for dinner at Chipén? I've ordered a paella. The chef is from Valencia and it's his specialty."

"I'm afraid we can't this evening," said Top Hat. "We're meet-ing friends at Horcher's."

The Count bid us good night and continued up the marble steps. I watched him ascend, and when he looked back from the top, I waved. I turned back to Top Hat and was surprised to find him smirking.

"Sorry to have spoiled your evening, *Divina,*" he said, winking suggestively.

I regarded him with amazement. "What's the matter with you?" I asked, as we settled into the worn leather seat of the ancient cab. He was silent while the coke-fueled vehicle bounced across the Plaza of Neptune, past the Hotel Ritz toward the Calle Alfonso XII. Then, in order to be heard over the racket of the noisy taxi, he shouted, "I guess I'm worried that you'll marry a grandee before I do."

"Don't be ridiculous, Edmundo. I hardly know Luis Quintanilla.

He's practically engaged to Casilda, my best friend. The families are planning the wedding already, and he adores her."

"My pet, the person who should marry the Count is yourself." Edmundo carried on. "He's a grandee and the most eligible bachelor in the country. You can't remain a spy forever, you know."

"You're the limit, Edmundo. Don't think everyone is as impressed by titles as you are."

"Too bad for us then," he said, sliding out of the cab to open the door for me. "This young count could be useful for our work. He knows everyone, and his family's homes contain precisely the kind of paintings we might be looking for."

That gave a different complexion to the matter. As we walked into the restaurant, I decided I would have to see more of Luis Quintanilla.

Chapter 3

Horcher's was crowded, yet only the tinkle of crystal and the soft murmur of voices could be heard. The thick carpet and padded red silk walls absorbed all sound. The maître d' led us to a corner table where starched red damask and silver candelabra sparkled in the glow of fluttering candles.

Enrique Paredes, a massive overweight man in a black suit, had a puffed face and a long thin nose. He stood up as we approached. After kissing my hand, he introduced me to his wife, Mitzi, and Edmundo and I sat down. As I did so, I wondered how a girl so young and attractive—she appeared to be about my age—could have married a man so unattractive and obviously much older.

Facing us, seated at a round table a few feet away, were Princess Ada and Klaus Fribourg with the Duke and Duchess of Lerma. I took a second look at Fribourg, wondering if he and Edmundo would have any new reaction to their recent experience with the cigarette case. But along with the others at his table, Fribourg nodded in a friendly enough manner, before returning to study the menu in his hand. Also at his table was Carola's father, the charming, barrel-chested Prince Niki Lilienthal.

Prince Lilienthal was one of the most famous aristocrats in Europe. His renown dated back to the early twenties, when his name had hit the front pages of newspapers around the world for having saved the life of a French ballet dancer. The young woman had jumped from one of the bridges over the Seine in a suicide attempt, and the prince had happened to pass in his car at that moment. The picture of "The Prince of Princes," as the papers referred to him, pulling the girl to the river bank had made him a celebrity because of his title and good looks.

Less well-known was the fact that Prince Lilienthal was one of the OSS's most valuable agents. Due to his wealth and holdings in Central Europe, he knew many Nazi leaders, and only a few months before had helped us locate the double agent who had so bedeviled us at the Oil Mission.

Paredes' chair creaked each time he changed position, as he gazed at the table next to ours. "I wonder if the Duke and Duchess of Lerma know the real story of the lady they're dining with," he said.

Edmundo's eyes brightened. "Princess Ada? Oh, do tell us."

"The full story would take us through the last course, but I'll concentrate on the important points." Languidly, Enrique took the menu being handed him, and not until he had ordered each course with a gourmet's detailed precision, did he begin to tell the story.

"The ravishingly regal Princess Ada . . . is not regal at all. In fact, she began life as the daughter of a blacksmith in Berlin and became a hairdresser, if you can believe that. The way she met her first husband, a German prince named von Lorentz, was when she went to his family's castle to coif his mother. Well! It was love at first sight. Needless to say, his family did not approve of his marriage to Ada, and as the young prince also didn't want to fight for Hitler, the young newlyweds moved to Zurich at the beginning of the war. Alas, it didn't work out. Prince von Lorentz was considered a traitor by his family and it weighed heavily on him, and maybe that's why he became an alcoholic and practiced all the sins, as they say. But that's how Ada happens to have a title." Enrique sighed profoundly. "Eventually, the nobleman left her. And, the sad part, for Ada, that is, was that he left her for another hairdresser." Again the dramatic heave. Paredes slowly sipped his wine.

I thought he had finished recounting Princess Ada's history. But when he put the glass down, he added, "But this time," he spoke slowly, "the hairdresser was a man!" Paredes laughed heartily. "Also, extremely good-looking, they say."

"That story is hard to believe." Mitzi Paredes spoke for the first time in a small shy voice. "Enrique, you never told me that before. I am surprised. She looks so—so distinguished. And I thought that little thin fellow with his back to us was the husband."

"My dear, he *is* her husband. Today she is the Señora Fribourg, no more. Fribourg's also one of the wealthiest men in Switzerland—estates all over Europe, or at least until this war began. But

I believe the Nazis took all that. Today he still has a gigantic income—from a Swiss chemical company. Founded by his grandfather, I believe. But he's not clever—a terrible businessman. His fortune was inherited. I heard, to get rid of him, his brothers sent him to Spain with the excuse of opening a branch office."

Our conversation was interrupted by two waiters carrying gleaming silver platters of crayfish in dill sauce. Then the wine waiter, dripping gold braid and attentions, served the wine. Comments turned to discussions of the Casino in Estoril where Enrique and Top Hat had been the week before. The men left us women out of the conversation entirely. Mitzi sat by in meek silence, and when I tried to break through her shyness, I realized she was accustomed to letting men dominate the discussions.

The delicious venison, which Enrique Paredes informed us was prepared "like in Berlin before the war, with cranberry sauce," appeared with the usual ceremony. Several waiters attended the ice buckets and wineglasses at the same time.

Dinner continued with apple strudel and cream for dessert, and a Portuguese port. About twelve-thirty, Paredes looked at his wife and informed us they would have to leave. His Thursday night poker game awaited him at home.

As soon as they had gone, I plied Top Hat with questions.

"Who is this terrible man? He looks like a bowl of gelatin dressed in a suit and tie."

Edmundo's high-pitched snicker made the people at the next table look up. "You're wrong," he said. "Paredes is brilliant. He's sort of a wheeler-dealer in the Madrid financial world: a representative of a Swiss pharmaceutical company, owner of an important insurance company, shareholder in one of the largest banks. Has a finger in every pie. That's why I wanted you to meet him."

"And what about those poker games? Who would begin to play at twelve-thirty A.M.? Not serious businessmen?"

"Precisely businessmen, or other rich men for that matter, sometimes until five in the morning. Paredes' games are famous for their high stakes, and guests have to be very special to be invited. He doesn't need to worry about office hours. He has a string of administrators who take care of that, but the brain behind everything is Paredes himself."

Edmundo ordered a cognac. "I'd like to know who is present at tonight's game. Enrique doesn't take sides in this war and makes a point of broadcasting that fact." He slid a look over to me. "Even the head of the Gestapo is one of his regular players."

When we got up to leave, Prince Niki Lilienthal invited us to join his table for a nightcap. Chairs were moved around and I was squeezed in between the Prince and Fribourg.

Lilienthal spoke to me as I adjusted my chair. "Do you miss your own country, Aline? Spain is so old-fashioned in comparison to the United States. Last time I was there, I was most impressed by the great number of filtered swimming pools. Here there's not one pool in the whole city. In fact there's not even a stream. I really was amazed when I first saw the Manzanares, which the Madrileños dare to call a river—it's as dry as a desert."

"You can't trust anyone these days," Ada Fribourg was saying on the other side of the table. "Do you know some Jewish friends in Holland gave their paintings to a neighbor for safekeeping so they wouldn't be confiscated by Goering, and then the neighbors went off with the paintings themselves? I despise people who make themselves rich by robbing others' belongings."

"I agree with you, my dear." Klaus Fribourg blotted his plump lower lip for the second time. "The Nazis' confiscation of the Goudstikker collection in Amsterdam is disgusting, as reprehensible as the Bolshevik corruption."

Edmundo glanced my way, but the mention of paintings had already alerted me. Fortunately, by now I had become expert in carrying on one conversation while listening to another. I continued to chat with Niki Lilienthal. The conversation had aroused his interest also.

"My friends," he announced, "it is a fact that Germany appears to be lost, but wait and see. Even when Hitler's dead, his devotees will be living like kings, thanks to him."

"What do you mean by that?" asked Fribourg. The voice was flippant, but he didn't fool anyone. At the table, silence reigned.

Niki Lilienthal explained. "Isn't it obvious, my dear Klaus, that quite a few Nazi crooks have money in safekeeping outside Germany? We may even know some of them, those who will now begin to live in luxury." His sarcasm created a ripple of discomfort.

"Now, now," blustered Pepito Lerma, rubbing his mouth with the damask napkin. "Who needs to be a friend of Hitler to enjoy lavish living? All one must do is stay in Madrid. Here we all live well. What about that *merluza* tonight! A treat for kings, I'd say."

At first I found it difficult to lead Fribourg into conversation. He responded to my comments about Switzerland in monosyllables, but finally, he lost his earlier reticence and spoke to me in a thick German accent.

"I'm ashamed of my own country," he told me, rubbing a pale hand over his thinning hair. "Switzerland closed their borders to Jews when it looked like the Nazis were winning. Fortunately, at that same time, Franco ordered his consulates all over Europe to give Jews visas and whatever assistance they needed." I liked him for that, but then he launched into a long, boring explanation of the importance of his wife's birth, as if it had been her birthright, avoiding mentioning that it belonged to her first husband, and I concluded that he was simply a snob. Edmundo ignored Fribourg and it was clear they would never understand each other. By now, a half-hour had gone by, and it was time to leave. As we all rose, Prince Lilienthal leaned over and murmured to me alone, "Don't get taken in by some of the lies going around this table." Startled, I tried to ask what he meant and who he was referring to, but he just winked and left.

Once in the street, Pepito Lerma insisted that Top Hat and I join them for flamenco in Villa Rosa in the Plaza Santa Ana. I was aghast. It was already one A.M. and I had to be in the code room at the American Oil Mission at nine. Flamenco sessions could last until dawn. But refusals were not accepted and I found myself seated in Lerma's old Peugeot. As the car swung around the Plaza de Independencia, Pepito pointed to the huge arch. "Has anyone explained to you, Aline, that that arch commemorates the date Napoleon's troops were ousted from Spain?"

As my eyes followed the direction of his finger, my view fell upon a pale, low-slung Cord convertible that I recognized immediately. Top Hat was saying, "And if you look up to the second floor of the building beyond, you'll see where Paredes' poker game is in full swing."

I couldn't tell at that moment, and much less ask, if Top Hat had also recognized the car parked smack in front of Enrique Paredes' door. But I had learned one more thing about the Count of Quintanilla. He played poker for high stakes.

Chapter 4

S everal days later, I rushed to Balenciaga for a fitting on a
black strapless cocktail dress, snug and simple, with a tiny
long-sleeved bolero jacket. Strapless dresses in Madrid were
popularly called *palabra de honor* dresses, meaning "word of honor"
they won't fall down. They were considered very daring and definitely "in," just the thing I needed for Madrid's night-club evenings and for the elegant receptions in the old palaces. As Felisa
directed me to a fitting room, Ada Fribourg emerged from another.

"Aline, what a coincidence! I didn't have your number and
wanted to invite you to a surprise birthday party I'm giving next
week for Klaus."

Since my fitter was already waiting, and it appeared that Ada
wanted to continue talking, I suggested she join me in the fitting
room. She was delighted and settled on a chair in the small room,
making light conversation. But as soon as the fitter left, she spoke
in a confidential tone that also carried a note of preoccupation.

"You know, Aline, we are both foreigners in this country and
maybe that's why I feel I can talk to you. It becomes difficult not
to have a sister or a childhood friend one can confide in sometimes.
Don't you feel that way too?"

Before she could continue, the fitter returned, and not until a
half-hour later when we were both seated in the lobby of the Hotel
Ritz having a cup of tea, did I manage to assure her that I would
be delighted to fulfill the role of sister.

It took a bit of prodding, but when she finally spoke freely, her
story was heartbreaking.

"You know, I am one hundred percent on the Allied side in this horrible war, Aline. How could I not be? One of my brothers died fighting for a cause he didn't believe in, and my other brother is now on the Russian front. Of course, against his will."

She spoke nervously, quickly. "You probably realize that many Germans hate Hitler. How many attempts have already been made on his life? Only yesterday I received a letter from my mother, so pathetic that I haven't slept a wink."

Ada struggled to keep tears from her eyes. I had time to wonder how strange life could be. Here I was taking tea with a woman whose brothers were fighting against mine in a brutal war being waged only three hundred miles away.

"Both my parents live in Berlin. There is no water, no meat, no basics whatsoever. People are starving. When will this war end?"

I told Ada that almost every day I felt guilty to be enjoying luxury and peace when so many were suffering the atrocities of war not far from Spain's border.

"What do you mean 'peace'?" scoffed Ada. "There's plenty of danger right here. Frankly, I can hardly swallow my food most of the time, I'm so frightened." Without moving her head, the huge blue eyes rolled from one side to the other. She was even more beautiful in the bright light of the Hotel Ritz hall—the skin was flawless, and the cheekbones and small chin gave her face a heart shape. But as she spoke her perfect forehead creased in deep wrinkles.

"That's not all," she said, more nervous and jumpy than before. "What makes me still more upset are the things going on right here in Madrid."

"What's that?" I asked.

She took a deep breath. "As you may know, my husband was once very wealthy. His most valuable holdings were in Berlin, and of course the Nazis took everything. Not just paintings, but valuable pieces of signed French furniture and precious porcelains. Of course I never saw any of this, but he reminisces about his beautiful things still. Oh, it's too painful . . ."

I was beginning to wonder if the story had a point, or whether she simply needed to talk.

She leaned very close and whispered. "Five days ago . . ." her long slim fingers restlessly clasped and unclasped one knee, "I was wandering along one of those narrow streets off the Calle del Prado. You know, where those small antique shops are?" She sighed deeply. "Well, you can't believe what I saw. There in the window—for sale—was a Ming vase, one that belonged to my husband. I stood and looked at it for the longest time. I was so confused. It was one of a pair he had. One, he managed to get out of Berlin. It's on the entrance table in our apartment here in Madrid. The other, I'm certain, is in that store. I can't tell you what I felt—the horror of seeing my husband's stolen possessions for sale in a shop here. I ran away, I couldn't stay there, I was too frightened!"

The plush of my chair was sticking to the palms of my hands. Feigning a nonchalance I was far from enjoying, I leaned back in a relaxed posture in the roomy armchair. If it was true that the vase was a Nazi-looted treasure, then this information could be of great importance. I struggled to contain my impatience.

"Where was this shop?" I asked.

But Ada wasn't listening. She was looking at the white tablecloth and rubbing the sleeves of her blouse as if she were cold. "I went home and told Klaus," she said. "He was furious, of course, but said that we should do nothing. He said these people are dangerous. That the vase was gone and there was nothing we could do. He told me never to go back to that shop. But do you know what?"

She looked at me intensely. Now she had taken a handkerchief out of her bag and was twisting it between her fingers.

"What?" I asked, impatient for her to continue.

"I did go back," she continued, giving a frantic fleeting smile. "The very next day. My plan was to buy it at whatever price and give it to Klaus as a surprise. But the Ming vase was gone! When I went inside, the owner told me they had no such object, and had never carried anything like the one I had described. I could see the man was lying. He was a crook and probably knew I was a German. I began to tremble. Then he got a strange look on his face and asked my name! I ran away! I did. Without answering him. I've never been so afraid. Of course I didn't tell Klaus about that, but now every night I worry that those terrible people may come to our house to steal the other one. That they may harm my husband . . . my children . . ."

Her voice was high and wailing now, and a spot of bright pink stood out on each of her pale cheeks. A sigh of disappointment escaped me. Was Ada too unstable to trust? As if to confirm my suspicions, she continued.

"Last night I wondered if I could have imagined the whole thing. I mean it. Do you think that's possible?"

"It's possible," I said. "But relax and stop worrying. No one can hurt you or your husband here."

"Do you think it's possible that things the Nazis stole would be sold here in Madrid?" she said.

As she stared at me, her large eyes, two frozen blue and white pools of splintered ice, suddenly seemed to chill me. I was instantly on my guard. Who was pumping who here? Was it deception? Or was I just too suspicious?

"I suppose that's possible, too," I said cautiously. "But why don't you take me to the shop? We can look for it together. Or give me the address. I don't mind going alone, if it frightens you."

Ada paled. "Absolutely not," she hissed. "It was stupid of me to go back. I won't let you put yourself in danger."

It was getting late. The tea services had been cleared from the other tables. The large hall of the Ritz was now almost empty. I was disappointed and baffled. What had seemed, at one point, to be a promising lead, had yielded nothing more than the rantings of an hysterical woman.

When we emerged from the Ritz, the wind was cold and it was already dark. Ada embraced me quickly. "Forgive me," she said, "for boring you with my fears. I'm sure I'm worrying about nothing."

Yet as she turned to walk toward her apartment on Alfonso XII, her expression was again vague and distracted, and I knew she was anxious as before. She had been sincere and candid with me, I decided, and I regretted suspecting her and not having brought her more relief.

Chapter 5

That same week, I initiated the penetration of the Japanese
legation by telephoning Concha Pombo, the niece of my tailor
friend from Hattie Carnegie. Concha invited me to dine the
very next day. When I arrived at the shabby building on the Callie
Castillo, the elevator had a *no funciona* sign on it, so to reach the
Pombos' fourth-floor apartment, I was obliged to climb worn
wooden steps and follow a dark narrow passageway reeking with
the odor of fried unrefined olive oil. Obviously, the Japanese were
not generous in their payments. I calculated this might make my job
easier.

Short, beak-nosed Julio Pombo answered the door. An engaging
smile illuminated his dark Mediterranean face, which also featured
black-rimmed glasses, slick patent-leather hair, small sharp eyes.
Concha had a pretty round face, buck teeth, and a blue-eyed expression of constant amazement and, when she spoke, made no sense
at all. Her husband didn't seem to mind and happily took the
responsibility of supplying the conversation—discussing bullfights,
flamenco, Spanish politics, and the war with a speed that left me
dizzy. He referred frequently to his wife in a way that made me
realize he was still amazed that such a beauty had married him and
that he considered her a feather in his cap.

Before I got around to inquiring about his work, Julio had already told me not only that he worked in the Japanese legation, but
he also was a radio broadcaster and wrote a column for several
newspapers as well. He invited me to take part in his radio program
the following week. I wondered if he knew that we sent messages
to our agents in southern France through songs that were broadcast

on the air. Perhaps he was indicating a willingness to collaborate, but it was premature to broach such things.

At a surprising speed, our acquaintance blossomed into friendship, Concha and Julio working harder at it than I. After only two weeks I learned why.

During a dinner Concha must have spent the day preparing, Julio concentrated his black horn-rimmed gaze on me. Concha stopped speaking in the middle of one of her nonsensical sentences. I looked from one to the other. A current of anxiety passed between them. I put my fork down and waited. Finally, Julio found the right words.

"Alin-ay," he began in the special accent with which he pronounced my name. "We've wanted to ask you a favor for a long time." He wiggled nervously in his chair. "I'm not certain that you will consider us close enough friends, but I dare not put this off any longer."

I encouraged him to continue.

"You may have noticed that we live in no luxury." He gestured around the room.

Was he preparing to ask for a loan?

After an embarrassing silence, he got to the point. "I want to work in a country where I can make a decent living. I would like immigrants' visas for my family and myself to go to your country."

His request was too good to be true. My assignment now was simple. Cautiously, I suggested he might be able to obtain a visa if it were possible for him to provide information on activities inside the Japanese legation. I said that I would try to help him by speaking to the American ambassador, who might even be willing to pay for his collaboration.

Julio Pombo shook his head. "No, I don't want money. I want only immigrants' visas for my family, and I'm willing to do anything to obtain them."

"But this work might mean risking your life," I warned. "The Japanese would not take it lightly if they caught you divulging information about their activities."

"Concha and I are aware of that. We made this decision a long time ago, but I dared not be seen going into the American embassy. When we met you, Alin-ay, we realized this was our opportunity."

What a stroke of luck!

About a half-hour later, Señor Pombo took me to my apartment, and when we were at my door, I told him I would speak to the ambassador the following morning. "Most probably he will be interested," I said. "So we'll be seeing each other in a few days."

Pombo answered with what I always considered typical Spanish pessimism. *"Si Dios quiere, Alin-ay. Si Dios quiere."* If God so wishes.

God did so wish, and Julio Pombo became agent number 660, code-named Smokey, within a week. From then on, he regularly provided copies of cables and reports from the Japanese legation.

One day, he telephoned me at my office, rather imprudently, I thought, asking to see me urgently. "At the cafe on the Castellana in front of the Montellano palace," he said.

I got permission from Mozart and rushed out to meet him.

With both elbows leaning on the wrought-iron table, rubbing one hand restively in the other, more jittery than I had ever seen him, Smokey told me the extraordinary news he had just uncovered. While he spoke, his eyes darted from side to side, he hunched his shoulders repeatedly and bounced around in the old metal chair like a polliwog.

Smokey had reason to be excited, and I hastened to pass his news on to the boss. When I opened Mozart's door thirty minutes later, he returned my smile only fleetingly, his manner as formal as always. I was impatient to give him Smokey's information, but Mozart ceremoniously asked me to sit down.

Without recourse to further amenities, his voice quiet, controlled, without inflection, he said, "Tell me, Miss Griffith, was Smokey's tip worthwhile?"

"I think it was," I answered, trying to imitate his manner. "Someone from the German embassy telephoned the Japanese ambassador this morning to say that their local 'administrator' would be sending some valuable boxes for safekeeping to the legation. A short time after that, two large crates arrived. Smokey was present when the ambassador opened one of the crates. He saw him remove a painting and overheard comments between the ambassador and his first secretary which indicated that both crates contained important paintings. Smokey helped to place the boxes into a closetlike room which the Japanese use for guarding secret material."

I waited for the chief's reaction, but he remained mute, so I continued. "Smokey also overheard the ambassador remark that the shipment had originated in France and entered Spain at the Port of Bilboa and"—here was the part I couldn't wait to tell—"that El Guapo would have them picked up as soon as arrangements for their shipment to South America had been finalized."

Mozart's huge fingers tapped the table. He couldn't entirely hide his satisfaction.

"Advise Smokey to keep you apprised of any new deliveries and to recruit someone in whom he has complete confidence to help him to keep the Japanese legation under surveillance at all times. I don't think he'll take any chances with the person he hires, since his own life is at stake. If those crates are removed from the legation, we must know where they are delivered." He looked at me for just a second. "And be careful to be seen with Smokey as little as possible. Now that things are moving, if you're not cautious, any gesture could blow your cover."

Without further explanation, he stood up and thumped to the door, placing one hand on the knob. "And, Miss Griffith." I looked at him expectantly. "Don't trust Smokey completely."

No shadow, no change of expression crossed his face while he opened the door and ushered me out.

Chapter 6

About the second weekend in February, my bullfighter friend, Juanito Belmonte, telephoned to invite me to a weekend shoot at El Robledo, the *finca* of the Count of Yebes in the mountains of Toledo about two hours south of Madrid. Bullfighters were considered idols by Spaniards and their every move, in or out of the ring, was covered by the press. To me, he was simply Juanito.

"You must come. This shoot is one of the best in the country for big game, stags, wild boar, and roebuck," Juanito said. "All the best guns will be there, maybe even Franco, although he only likes to shoot partridge. And you'll meet my father at last. He's going, too." Juanito's father, Juan Belmonte, was considered the greatest bullfighter of all time. "You're going to enjoy this," Juanito spoke excitedly. "A shoot for big game in Spain is a magnificent spectacle. Bring sturdy boots and something that is comfortable in case you have to get on a horse . . ." His voice trailed off and the line cut. He rang back as if nothing had happened—we were all accustomed to the intermittent Spanish telephone service—and continued.

"Mules and country horses are supplied for those who are assigned posts high up in the mountains where it can be chilly. Wear warm clothes."

We left Madrid a few sunny days later in Juan's Italian Bugatti Royale two-seated roadster. He was very proud of it and went on about how only a few had been built with over 250 horsepower like this one. It was a type 41, he said, with an eight-cylinder, 12.7-liter engine. I understood very little of all that, but I nodded and smiled, aware that famous matadors needed powerful automobiles to enable them to travel fast during the height of the season. The highway was almost empty, the road ours, and Juanito took advantage of it, racing through the multicolored fields of the Castilian plain—a mosaic of reds, grays, browns, and greens. Beyond stretched the snow-capped Guadarrama mountains outlined against a deep blue sky. When, about an hour later, we reached the massive stone-walled fortifications and storybook turrets of Toledo, I thought this was the most beautiful day of my life. We skirted the walled-in city and took one of the fortified stone bridges across the Tagus River and up a potholed winding road into the brown hills beyond. I turned back to look down upon the city El Greco had made famous, in reality more breathtaking than any painting.

My friendship with Juanito Belmonte had begun almost the first day I had arrived in Madrid a year ago. He had seen me in a theater and sent me huge baskets of red carnations, chocolates wrapped in pink silk paper and even one of his richly embroidered "suit of lights." That was before I even knew who he was. I imagined that a matador would be tall and strong, something like an American football player, but when I saw Juanito I was more than a little disappointed. He was short, frail, and skinny with sallow olive skin, a beak nose, and an affected gait.

Yet, when I watched him march across the golden sand of the Madrid bullring, his shocking pink stockings moving in time to the music, his glittering green cape thrown over one shoulder, the exotic black matador's hat straight over his black eyebrows, I became aware that he was a great star.

His first bull, a gigantic black Miura bull, roared into the ring snorting like a locomotive as he stormed past my seat—wild, ferocious, racing around looking for a victim. And then fearlessly, Juanito appeared from behind a small enclosure, alone in the huge ring, lifting his bright red cape high in the air, swaying it to attract the bull. Like the crowd, I became breathless with anticipation. Then the animal attacked, ready to tear him to bits. But my friend stood motionless, even pulling the cape closer to his body just as the beast reached the heavy cloth. He twisted, wrapping the cape around himself, leaving the animal plunging into open air. He repeated this several times, with the horns just grazing his body, as he moved gracefully, almost in slow motion, turning at just the precise moment to avoid the needle-sharp points of the huge ivory-colored horns. Juanito's courage, cool control, elegance in facing danger, and his arrogant display of fearless disdain during every harrowing second of the spectacle won my admiration forever after.

I remembered that fight as I observed the slim brown fingers gripping the steering wheel, marveling that this was the same man who could take a sword and drive it into a wild beast five times his size and ten times his weight, who could face death almost daily, without showing a sign of fear, of nervousness—able to laugh with me the day before, and the day after, never commenting on the danger. I wanted to preserve our friendship, but his jealousy and old-fashioned ideas, like a suitor of a hundred years ago, had started to make our relationship difficult.

Juan made what seemed the hundredth screeching turn on the steep tortuous road. Suddenly, I saw two men with shotguns slung over their shoulders, in brown and green uniforms and classic wide-brimmed hats, standing on either side of a simple stone-columned entrance to a dirt path. Juan waved to them. "The family gamekeepers," he explained. We followed that country road a short distance until hundreds of black and white dogs, chained in pairs, crossed our path, obliging Juan to stop the car. "Those are the *realas,* dog-groups, for tomorrow's drive," he explained. "They'll rout out the game and drive it toward the line of guns. There'll be more than three hundred *perros* scanning the terrain tomorrow. Each group of thirty dogs is handled by one man, called a *perrero,* who has trained them all year for this purpose."

We sped by stony, rubble-strewn fields, thick underbrush, now and then some trees. After a while we came to several red-tiled stone buildings, where women in long black clothes and black head shawls stood watching us pass by. More uniformed guards indicated the path leading to the main house.

Juanito pulled up in front of the ancient rambling whitewashed shooting lodge. Jeeps, old Rolls Royces, and ancient Peugeots were scattered helter-skelter on the wild terrain surrounding the famous building. Next to us a chauffeur was removing luggage from an impressive car which Juanito told me was the Prince von Lilienthal's famous Hispano-Suiza, a V-12 cylinder town car, which, he said, was not only the most expensive car in existence, but could exceed one hundred miles per hour. Other uniformed servants were transporting shooting equipment, rifle cases, leather ammunition pouches, and fur-lined capes into the house.

Juan parked and turned off the engine. From the midst of the hubbub, a young man in tweed knee breeches and cap, a shotgun on his shoulder, walked toward us. We were facing west and the setting sun made it impossible for me to see his features, but when he spoke, I recognized the voice immediately.

"Bienvenida," he called out. The hand dangling some dead birds waved at us. He came closer. The green eyes smiled at me.

"Luis Quintanilla!" I cried, as he opened my door. "I didn't realize you would be here. Is Casilda coming too?"

"No, Casilda's in Madrid," he said, helping me from the car. "She's not fond of shooting."

I was glad to see him. I had always liked him, and it relieved me to have another person there who could offset Juan's tendency to smother me.

As the Count of Quintanilla and I walked toward the high-arched entrance door of the house, he explained that this property belonged to his uncle. Juanito caught up with us and, scowling, passed me the handbag I had forgotten in the car. He was glum as Luis and I chatted on our way to the house. I found myself more peeved than usual by his jealousy and regretted that Casilda was not here so that I could talk to her boyfriend without incurring Juanito's boring envy.

The three of us entered a high-ceilinged hall and then a room buzzing with conversation, where men and women in tweed suits were drinking whiskey or plain orange juice. Niki Lilienthal came over to say hello. Luis Quintanilla introduced me around—Juanito knew everyone—and while the butler prepared a drink for Juanito, Luis explained details about the plans for tomorrow.

"You'll see a lot of activity. We expect about forty guns for the shoot," he said. "Personally, I prefer shooting partridge, but it is impressive to see the amount of big game that will be moving across these mountains tomorrow." He went on to say that there would be few girls my age. His sister had been expected, but at the last minute couldn't come because a sore throat had kept her in Madrid.

"Not many Spanish girls shoot," he said, "but my sisters are both good shots." Hearing this made me wonder what his opinion of me might be. Was I too outgoing, too independent, or too rambunctious for his Spanish standards? If I wanted to do my job well, I had to fit into this world and be aware of its customs.

Newcomers were arriving and Luis stood up to greet them. The

Marqués of Villabragima, another uncle, came in—short, middle-aged, with a big nose and sharp blue eyes. He pummeled the men vigorously on the back and kissed the ladies' hands. When introduced to me, he stopped to make a few exaggerated compliments, but he did not kiss my hand. It was not correct to kiss the hands of unmarried women. Then the Count and Countess of Mayalde came in. They were cousins. The Count, I knew, had been Spanish ambassador to Berlin until a short time ago. He wore gray lederhosen, green wool knee socks, and a dark brown loden jacket. The Countess was in an olive-green long loden cape and a felt shooting hat, with what looked like large round silver coins pinned around it. Luis explained that these were emblems given when one bagged a trophy for the first time in someone's shoot. Each estate had its own design: A deer's head, or the antlers, or the design of a boar, sometimes a sketch of the castle or lodge. As with a coin, the name of the estate was carved around the border.

Guests continued to pour in amid a bluster of jolly salutations and high spirits. When Luis Quintanilla went to look for a servant to direct me to my room, I walked to a window and looked out at the wild country outside. Juan came to my side. "The least I can expect is that you speak to me!" he cried.

His jealousy annoyed me. "Please, Juanito, be reasonable. If you continue to behave in this way, I won't talk to you at all. What sort of guest would I be if I refused to talk to others or were rude to the host?"

Like a spoiled child, he walked away. As I watched him cross the room, I marveled that someone so poised and graceful in the ring could be so unpolished and insecure in life. I decided that unless his manner improved, this would be one of my last outings with the great bullfighter.

That night before dinner, red-faced, blue-eyed Prince Niki Lilienthal sat next to me in the large salon and began to chat. His large uneven teeth spoiled an otherwise handsome face. The fact that he was the father of my friend, Carola, made it easy to transmit messages without arousing suspicion, and tonight I sensed he had something to tell me. Mozart often reminded us, "Never risk being seen with someone you have no logical reason to know. If you're being shadowed, the enemy would know you were both agents."

As we talked, I marveled that I had once believed this courteous man to be cold and cruel. That was when I had first met him—the afternoon I had jumped out the window of his study and landed right in front of him. He had been holding a rifle in his hand, and the moment had been terrifying, since my purpose for being in his study had been to unlock his safe and to pry through his papers, searching for specific information Mozart had requested. It wasn't until later on that he became one of our agents.

Among other favors Prince Lilienthal did for our OSS office was to serve as Mozart's principal informant for inside information on German businesses and their Spanish associates. As soon as Niki felt the other guests were too far away to hear, he whispered.

"Aline, I have news for Phillip Harris. Tell him Monday to contact me the usual way." His eyes kept roaming around the huge room. People were warming their hands at the fireplace, others were seated in a corner sipping their drinks. Through the open doorway, we could see still more guests chatting in the adjoining room. "I may uncover something important this weekend," he continued. "It's quite a strange coincidence that you happen to be here."

I explained how I was invited. He rubbed a hand over the slight stubble of his white beard. "Certain facts indicate that the man we're looking for may be shooting with us tomorrow."

My expression must have alarmed him. "Don't look startled. Smile."

I did.

"That's better." he continued in his clipped German-British accent. "Keep your eyes open and your wits about you this weekend. We'll compare notes on what we've been able to pick up here next week." He continued. "I think I've got a lead on El Guapo, but I don't want to accuse anyone until I'm certain. I also believe it's safer for you not to know the name at this point. You may unconsciously act differently and arouse his suspicions." He looked at me for agreement, and I nodded.

The large room was filling now with guests. Although no one was near enough to hear our conversation, I knew Niki felt we should not prolong our conversation. "Just one thing, though. In case I don't get another chance to speak to you alone"—he lowered his voice—"please advise Mozart the minute you get back to—" A gust of wind and a commotion at the door in the main hallway caused us both to look that way.

Ada Fribourg, accompanied by her small husband and, what

astounded me, Edmundo Lassalle, as well, were all three literally being blown into the house. Edmundo was swathed in a long brown Portuguese cape with a black fur collar.

Niki's last word to me before he went to greet the newcomers was "Tell him to call me. And you be careful!"

Ada's glorious thick straw-colored hair whirled around her face and cascaded in shiny curls over the collar of her luxurious ankle-length chinchilla coat. She no longer looked depressed or worried, and the effect of the glamour she trailed in, along with the chinchillas, was reflected on the faces of those watching her.

Not only did Prince Lilienthal rush to her side, bowing and kissing her hand, but Enrique Paredes and Luis Quintanilla did so as well. I stood by, watching the salutations, wondering what Niki's message for Mozart would be.

While all the excitement about Ada's arrival was going on, Edmundo came over to me. Theatrically, he raised my hand to his lips. My colleague ignored the Spanish custom of only kissing married women's hands.

"How delightful to see you, my dear Aline. I had no idea you were among those who assassinate defenseless beasts."

Without more ado, he moved on to salute someone else who touched his fancy. Juanito stood leaning against the far wall, apparently the only one unaffected by Ada's grand entrée. I turned to him.

"I didn't know that Edmundo was fond of big game shoots," I said.

"That fop," grumbled Juanito, obviously still in bad humor, "hasn't the slightest idea how to shoot anything."

Fortunately, he didn't notice the amusement his words produced on me. If my colleague Top Hat could handle a gun as well as he did a knife, he'd probably be the best shot there. The image of a man facedown, a knife protruding from his black tuxedo, came back to me in all its ghastly color. That had been on my first night in Lisbon, before I reached Spain. And Top Hat, fop or not, had surely been responsible. I would never forget that frightening moment when I suddenly recognized the dangers I would face as an undercover agent in a foreign country.

"Your friend can't bear to miss anything that has a social aspect," continued Juan disparagingly. "That's why he's here. This is the most elegant shoot of the season. Always, a few guests come merely to watch the spectacle from some comfortable perch in the mountains." As Juanito spoke, I wondered if, this time, Edmundo's interest was purely social. All that cold wind outside and climbing mountains at daybreak didn't strike me as being his cup of tea.

Ada's low, seductive voice addressed those surrounding her. "It's not my fault we're late. These important businessmen!" Her huge blue eyes rolled scoffingly. "Can you imagine, Klaus kept me waiting for three hours while he attended to some boring affair in his office. And Edmundo made us wait another half-hour while he looked for his boots."

During the past weeks, the Fribourgs had invited Edmundo at least twice to dine, so I was aware Klaus's and Edmundo's original animosity had been overcome, at least to a certain extent. And knowing Edmundo's admiration for the beautiful Princess Ada, I knew he would relish the two hours' drive with her, even if he had to put up with the "insupportable husband," as he still referred to Klaus.

At dinner, over thirty people were seated at one large table. Only ten were women. To me, the men seemed especially handsome and interesting, or maybe it was the elegance of the casual country clothes and the exuberant atmosphere.

After dinner, Prince Lilienthal and Belmonte's father, who was especially charming and who had kept the table entertained with amusing anecdotes, retired to a small room with two other men to play the popular Spanish card game of *mus,* where the winner is the one who's best at chiseling and cheating.

Top Hat sat in a corner with two women and the hostess, the Countess of Yebes, a woman famous not only for her beauty, but for her intelligence as well. She held her little group enthralled with comments about Moscow in 1917 when, as the seventeen-year-old daughter of the Spanish ambassador, she had met Rasputin and many other personalities of that time. This was the group that did not intend to shoot the next day. Juanito and Luis Quintanilla and I were seated nearby. At one point, I heard Edmundo declare, "Oh, I could never use a gun to kill innocent animals." He sighed. "Just the sight of blood makes me sick." I stifled a gasp and dared not even look in his direction.

The house was made of stone, large and rambling, probably dating from over one hundred years before. The furniture, however, was Spanish seventeenth century, which fit well into the rustic ambience of a shooting lodge. On the whitewashed walls were large nineteenth-century oils of shooting scenes. Each room had at least one fireplace and there were brass braziers everywhere, even in the hallways. Their smoldering embers gave off more heat than the chimneys. One reason people did not dress for dinner was because there was no central heating, even in some of the large homes in Madrid. As a result, Balenciaga evening dresses, both short and long, were designed with long sleeves and made of wool.

The rest of the party was divided into small groups hovering around one of the two blazing fireplaces, talking, smoking, and joking. After a while, Luis Quintanilla and Juan went to check their ammunition for the next day and Ada came to sit on the circular bench next to me. Klaus was at the other end of the room, studying the map of tomorrow's drives. I made some remark about Klaus being as enthusiastic about shooting as the Spaniards. Ada said that, before the war, he had been one of the best shots in Europe. Then she confided that she considered herself especially fortunate to have been married to two such good men.

"My first husband was very handsome and we were deeply in love. Our world was crumbling around us, but we managed to find moments of wild happiness. He was the eldest of an aristocratic German family which has been entirely wiped out. Do you know, when he married me, a poor unknown girl, his parents, despite their disappointment, treated me like a daughter? None of them were Nazis, and although his brothers fought and died for the Fatherland, Anton—that was my husband's name—refused to fight, and we fled to Zurich. He was declared a traitor by the Third Reich and even though his family despised Hitler, they and his friends considered him a coward for not having stuck it out with the rest. That destroyed him and our marriage, too."

Ada's story about her first husband startled me. It was very different from Enrique's. Who was telling the truth? I could understand that Ada might try to improve her husband's image, but why would Enrique want to deface it? As she continued, I listened attentively.

"Anton was deeply affected by the loss of his family and his country and began to drink. We were really down and out in Zurich. And if it hadn't been for Klaus's help when my husband died, I don't know how I would have managed."

At that moment our host, Eduardo Yebes, approached and said

that numbers were going to be drawn for the posts for tomorrow's shoot. He asked Ada to pull them from the hat. As she read the numbers, there was no longer a trace of the frightened woman who had had tea with me a few weeks before. There were groans and cries of jubilation. Good posts meant a much more exciting day. Some butts were apt to have a chance at five or six stags and as many wild boar; others might not see any game at all.

Juan compared the number I had drawn to his. *"Maldito sea,* damn. Just my luck today!" he exclaimed. "We're not even on the same line of guns."

By this time it was after midnight. Spaniards, I knew by now, never seemed to need sleep. There was no purpose in waiting until the rest retired, so I started to look for the way to my room. The spacious hall to the entrance staircase was drafty and I hugged my jacket close to my body. Passing the game room, I bumped into Prince Lilienthal, and we walked down the hall together. I thought he might continue the conversation he had started before dinner, but before he had the opportunity, footsteps approached close on our heels and Niki began to tell me how he had won the game of *mus.*

I continued up the staircase calculating that Ada Fribourg, who had remained in the large room, would probably be among the ladies who would breakfast in bed the next day around noon. But I had only six and a half hours before the time we, who were attending the shoot, had to be up.

Gazing into the burning embers of the small fireplace in my room, I went to sleep wondering who among the guests might be El Guapo. I wanted to ask Top Hat's opinion, but I realized I would have to wait, probably until we were both back in Madrid.

The next morning, a maid awakened me, entering with a pitcher of hot water which she placed next to the antique washstand.

"The sun's not up yet, señorita, but Serafin, the head game-keeper, says the wind has subsided and that the day will be perfect for the shoot. Some of the gentlemen are already having breakfast downstairs."

I was the first woman to arrive in the dining room and many places were offered to me. I took one next to Juanito, which pleased him enormously. His bad humor of the day before seemed to have passed. He was enthusiastic about the breakfast of red wine, *migas*—fried breadcrumbs and blood sausage—*chorizo,* fried eggs, fried onions, cakes, and a kind of coffee braced with anise called

Del Mono. I looked in vain for some plain scrambled eggs and fruit. Next to my place at the table was a small bag containing the day's *taco,* picnic, but again I was dismayed to find things that didn't appeal to me—cold fried fish, cold fried breaded veal, a small bottle of red wine, a huge round loaf of bread. I consoled myself with the thought that our soldiers fighting in Germany might do worse.

The spectacle that awaited outside more than made up for the food. An early morning mist hung over a mixed multitude of horses, mules, Jeeps, dogs, and men. Those ready for the day's shoot were gathered in close knots, stamping their feet on the rough ground, excitedly exchanging hearty cheers and salutations. I recognized Enrique Paredes and Hans Lazaar. Their breath and the smoke from their cigarettes made skinny spirals of white steam in the chilly early morning air. Beaters, dog-keepers, and just plain country yokels who had come to gape, were milling about; some were in a group huddled around a small fire warming hands and feet while passing around a pig bladder of red wine.

Luis Quintanilla and his uncle, Eduardo Yebes, were barking out instructions for the day's gigantic operation to groups of workers dressed in rugged outfits which indicated their different occupations. There were over two hundred attendants for the forty-gun shoot. The dog-keepers stood at a slight distance awaiting their orders, and as one group moved away, another approached. The scene and the atmosphere reminded me of the tension and excitement our soldiers might be experiencing someplace in Germany right now, in the trenches before an attack. Again I felt a pang of guilt. Despite the moments of fear and the threats to my life during the past year, it still galled me to think that I was enjoying such adventure and luxury while my brothers and countrymen were in danger.

About an hour later, I was trudging Indian file up a narrow mountain path behind Luis, who, it turned out, had drawn the stand next to mine. In front of us was a procession of loaders, gun carriers, scouters, and guests. Each participant had much equipment— extra jackets or capes, collapsible chairs, water flasks, field glasses, ammunition, and usually at least two rifles.

Top Hat was among them. The night before, instead of picking a number out of the hat, he had said that since he didn't shoot, he would take a spot out of everybody's way where he could photograph the game. Nevertheless, along with the leather collapsible stool strapped to the side of Edmundo's mount, was a rifle which swayed up and down to the pace of his horse as it climbed the steep incline. He had not walked one step and sat slumped lazily on his saddle, a camera slung over one shoulder, bragging to all who passed by that, with his magnifying lenses, he would see their stags better than they.

We laughed at Enrique Paredes as we passed him on the slope at the base of the mountain. He was already sweating and exhausted from the insignificant climb, and with great difficulty his loader and groom were both helping him into the saddle of a rangy-looking hack.

Ahead and above us halfway up the mountain stretched a long line of shaggy mounts. Some carried riders—those who had given up the struggle and decided to make the climb on horseback. I commented to Luis Quintanilla about the tension and the tedious preparations of a shoot being similar to that of a battle.

"Thankfully, it's not," Quintanilla answered. "We've had enough fighting in this country to last through the century. Did you know that the Civil War took the lives of five percent of our population? I lost nineteen close relatives, including all the male cousins my age."

"What about you?" I asked, trying not to let him notice that the stiff climb was making me gulp for breath. "Did you fight as well?"

"I did. I was sixteen when I entered the war."

He paused to rest, and for a long moment we both looked out over the wild expanse of rolling hills filled with thick grayish-green scrub brush and low trees, of deep gorges, and in the distance, stony mountain peaks. The early morning sun cast a golden glow, highlighting the red and orange berries on the holly bushes, making the snow-white blossoms of the rockrose sparkle. I breathed in the sweet-smelling thyme mixed with lavender, sage, and rosemary, and looked up at the deep blue sky, where graceful eagles zigzagged in slow motion across the horizon. Near us, magpies and hoopoe birds made a happy racket.

"Actually," said Luis, turning to look at me, "I was wounded in the war by an explosion of shrapnel in Vitoria and left to die in a field. A nurse, who was a friend of my family, happened to pass by after the battle and recognized me. She managed to find a doctor and to convince him to operate. He saved my life. But I lost part of an arm and a piece of my thigh."

I stared at him in amazement, looking for some remnant of his wounds.

"I would never have guessed that," I said.

"That wasn't all," he said, and I noticed then how affected he was by the memory. His face creased in an expression of sadness. "Even after my operation I contracted an infection, which kept me out of action for a year. I—"

He broke off, staring down at the valley. Then he looked back at me.

"Why am I telling you this?" he asked, smiling.

I was deeply moved by his story. This handsome young man had suddenly taken on a new dimension for me. I wasn't sure exactly what it meant, but I was aware that I respected him in a way I had never experienced with anyone else.

Quintanilla turned and began ascending the path again. I followed. Finally he turned and spoke, but the strain his face had shown before had vanished.

"These aren't topics for such a peaceful day," he said. "Forgive me. You are such a good listener that I forgot myself."

I wanted to say something, but he was again climbing up the mountain. Soon, we came upon Niki Lilienthal, who was getting installed in his butt, and we stopped to talk to him. I found myself distracted by my conversation with Luis. One would never know, watching him laugh and gesture with Niki, that such pain and tragedy lay so recently behind him. The Civil War had ended only four years before. Casilda would know these things about Luis Quintanilla, I thought, and I was reminded of how little one knows of people from their outer facades.

Luis was occupied for some time explaining to the men who were caring for the horses where they were supposed to take them, so as to be out of the way during the shoot. Meanwhile, Niki gave me some advice. "If it's too cold when you reach your post, you can ask your *secretario* to make you a fire. But you must decide that as soon as you get there. It may be windy up there, and any spirals of smoke would frighten the game away and you wouldn't have a chance to get anything."

I told him this was my first big game shoot. "Well, if you down a boar, beware," he warned. "They are apt to be dangerous." I told him I'd already been cautioned about that. "I worry about you, child," he said. "You do take chances now and then." He winked and I knew he was remembering the time I'd rifled his study a year ago.

About this time Luis returned, and the gamekeeper in charge of our line approached the Prince. As he had to every previous shooter, he explained where the other posts were and in which directions the Prince could shoot.

"Above all, *Señor Principe,* I know you are aware that you cannot move from your butt during the drive. The lines are placed so that no one can shoot anyone else if they adhere to the rules."

Niki nodded and then talked with us while his scanner removed the last pieces of equipment from the back of his horse. It seemed that Luis and I were going to be at the top of the mountain, the last two guns on this line.

The other nine men and one woman of our line had already been located in stands below us. Four similar lines of guns were stretched out in other areas of the mountain.

Luis Quintanilla and I wished Niki luck, said good-bye and then, accompanied by the gamekeeper and our loaders, we continued up the mountain.

When we arrived at my post, the young count lingered for a while, giving me instructions on how to shoot. We couldn't actually pull the trigger because a bullet shot before the shoot began was prohibited. But he showed me how to hold the gun and aim and reload. I dared not tell him I'd spent three months in an espionage school learning that and made every effort to appear in need of advice. "Stags are easy to see with their large horns," he explained. "But *jabali,* wild boar, are hidden by the thick underbrush, unless they come across the cropped area, and they're too smart for that. So the only advance notice you'll have is the barking of the dogs chasing them and the noise the boar makes breaking through the dry brush."

Before leaving, he told me not to rush up to a boar if I shot one, that it might be wounded and very dangerous. The *secretario* who accompanied me knew how to kill it with a knife if necessary. He pointed to the gully where the men were now taking the horses and advised me not to shoot in that direction. Then he looked at his watch and, warning me that the drive would soon begin, wished me luck and moved on up the mountain. When Luis got to his butt, he indicated where he was standing by raising his rifle high in the air, so I would not shoot in that direction. When he lowered his gun again, I could see nothing except the mountain peak, several large stone formations, and thick green bushes.

Despite the sun, it was windy, and not being able to move made me chilly. Instead of asking my *secretario* to make a fire, I put on an extra jacket. I was determined not to do anything to scare the game away. The excitement of getting a big stag or boar had gotten to me. Looking down the mountain now, the other posts were as invisible as Luis Quintanilla's. Each had been carefully camouflaged. If the gamekeeper had not pointed the line out to me, I wouldn't know where the guns were located.

Silence reigned, save for the chirping of birds, or the rustle now and then of a hare dashing through the dry leaves. Then one lone shot echoed through the gully and up the mountain. From far away a moment later came the excited barking of several hundred dogs that had just been released. The shoot had begun.

The day passed quickly, I suppose because I was in a constant state of excitement. The barking of the dogs turned to a high-pitched yipping when they were on the scent of an animal. Sometimes I could hear them very close. On the other side of the mountain, a hind with four young ones raced down the slope and then disappeared. I saw the antlers of what must have been a huge male, breaking through the high foliage about four hundred meters away. Six dogs were chasing it and barking frantically. A few moments later, two rifle shots rang out. Somebody had bagged him.

Many females with their offspring came close, but of course, we could not shoot at them. Then suddenly, without the advance notice of the dogs' barking, I saw two stags. Their horns looked impressive. And they were racing directly toward me. My heart beat fast. My *secretario* was as excited as I. "Señorita, one of these will be yours," he whispered. I took the safety off and was ready, trembling with excitement. But at the last moment both animals turned downhill. A few minutes later, I heard the shots from down the line and knew someone else had killed them. Rifle shots echoed from one mountain to another. Stags, hinds, and fawns sprinted across the wide barren slices which had been cut into the mountain, much like ski slopes, so one could see the game better. But nothing came in to my post.

No one was supposed to move from his butt until four in the afternoon when the shoot would be over, but just before that I decided to risk leaving my post for a few minutes. Things had calmed down and no game had been near our area for some time. My loader had absented himself a couple of times and I didn't see why I couldn't also. A bush sufficiently out of view wasn't easy to find, and perhaps I had wandered farther than I should.

Suddenly a noise in the thick underbrush to my left made me freeze. My heart bounced—a stag, maybe a *jabali*—and I didn't have my gun with me! The noise in the underbrush continued steadily, moving slowly, but I couldn't see a thing. Standing ever so still, scanning the surrounding area, I finally discerned down the slope toward Niki Lilienthal's butt, a path of gently swaying branches, indicating something was moving there. Perhaps a dog or a *perrero*. But since whatever it was, was not heading in my direction, I started to wend my way back to my butt. Unexpectedly, one dull rifle shot from that direction pierced the air—a second later, one more. My loader was smiling when I arrived. "The Prince got something, no doubt." His toothless grin revealed his satisfaction. The spirit of the shoot was contagious. We all took part in every shot. "Did the señorita see what it was?"

I shook my head. He added knowingly. "Then it was a *jabali*. They're invisible in these thickets."

A few minutes later, a tremendous racket came from the brush to our right. Niki's loader's sweaty red face burst through the thicket, his eyes bulging and wild.

"Someone shot Prince Lilienthal. He's dead."

We stood for a moment frozen, incredulous with the news. Then my loader pulled a long hollow goat horn from his sack and started to blow with all his might. The strident sound transmitted urgency. Other horns began to answer with the same resonance. In a few minutes Luis and his scanner appeared rushing down from their butt.

Luis Quintanilla's first question was, "Who?"

"It's difficult to tell, Señor Conde. The shot penetrated the Prince's head from the right, but the sound came from the left."

I was the only one on the left. The Count looked at me. "I didn't hear you shoot, Aline." He was still breathing heavily from running down the mountain.

"No," answered my scanner. "There were no shots from here. You didn't shoot either, Señor Conde. We didn't even have any game up our way today."

When we arrived at Niki's post, his loader and two of the men who cared for the horses were already wrapping him in his shooting cape and preparing to carry him down the mountain. There was a discussion about whether to strap the body to a horse or to carry him. Finally it was decided that lashing him to a horse was indecorous. His loader mounted the horse, holding Niki's body in front of him. A man trudged along on either side, one supporting the feet and the other the shoulders. Thus the Prince was transported slowly down the mountain. I was in the group following this sad cortege. Little by little, others joined us, and by the time we reached the house a crowd of the same guests and attendants who had started the day joyously, were standing in gloomy silence. Everyone shied away from the small group of men who were now taking Niki's body from the horse into the back seat of his grand Hispano-Suiza. I noticed the trickle of blood on the saddle and turned away. People seemed to avoid each other's gaze. Were they wondering, as I was, which one had been responsible for the fatal shot?

When we gathered inside, we were all in a state of shock. The fact that Niki was dead seemed impossible. An ominous murmur of whispered comments buzzed throughout the downstairs rooms and hallway. From the distance came the mournful wails of maids in the kitchen. Servants tiptoed about as they handed the luggage to glum-faced chauffeurs who were busy placing weapons and equipment into the cars. Hardly anyone spoke in a normal voice. I went to my room and sat down. Outside, it was obvious that the guests were all anxious to leave as soon as possible.

No one knew who had fired the shot. It had been generally accepted that someone had ambled recklessly too far from his butt. Who? Why? I remembered the swaying bushes just before the shot, which I had mentioned to Luis as soon as he appeared in my post. No *perrero* or scanner admitted to being at that area at that time and no one was in that area at that time except Klaus Fribourg, who had been on the other side of Niki and had not budged from his cover. His scanner vouched for that.

On the way back in Juanito's car that night, I also told him about the path of swaying bushes just before the fatal shot.

"Even if they learn who it was," he explained, "we may never hear about it. Unfortunately, these accidents occur now and then. Sometimes when a particularly large beast is within range, a man loses his calm. Often the stag or the wild boar is only wounded and keeps going. A greedy gunman may track him thoughtlessly through the bush, not realizing he is out of his own terrain. Men, who are otherwise self-controlled, sometimes become irrational when they have the possibility of getting a great trophy. Whoever it was, may not admit it, and if he is discovered—or admits it himself, which is most likely—the Count of Yebes is not apt to mention his name. That's an unwritten law of the shoot, but he will never invite him again, no matter how distinguished the man might be. It was an accident and nothing can bring the poor Prince back to life."

During a few moments he drove in silence. Then he added, "Edmundo could possibly shed some light on what happened. He should have been able to see Niki's butt. Did he say anything?"

I stared into the blackness, my eyes focused on the two paths of the car's headlights. "I don't think he was near enough." My words, I hoped, sounded matter-of-fact. It was true that Edmundo was far from the scene, but again I remembered the rifle sticking out of his saddle and I realized that I was the only one there who knew he was a crack shot. To be suspicious of Top Hat was preposterous, I thought to myself. But in view of Niki's news the night before and of the mysterious way in which Prince Lilienthal had been killed, not to mention the few persons near enough to do the job, the fact that Edmundo had been in range made me think twice. I was also aware that my colleague was not above shady actions. Mozart was also aware of this, I knew. On one of my first visits to the boss's office with Edmundo's report in hand, he had astounded me by saying: "This Mexican's reports are more fantasy than truth, but at least they're always entertaining."

Chapter 7

Instead of another day's shoot, on Sunday we were all in Madrid at the Lilienthals' home attending the wake. In Spain the body is not embalmed, and for that reason it is obligatory to have the burial the next day, usually before lunch. Funeral service would take place from two days to a week later.

I felt frightened and sad. Niki had been a kind fatherly friend and a valuable aid in our work. Carola was inconsolable. I dared not tell the family about the message her father had given me the night before his death or about my qualms that the shot may not have been an accident. Edmundo arrived just as the bier was being taken out of the house, so there was no way I could talk to him. He joined the men who were accompanying the casket to the cemetery. They would walk several blocks behind the open black carriage drawn by four black horses with huge black plumes, and then they would get into their cars to continue on to the cemetery.

Early Monday morning, I went to Mozart's office to give all the details of the tragedy. He was on the phone when I went in and for once did not stand up. His eyes, tiny brown beads, shifted from one side to the other as he spoke. Today the shutters were open and the early morning sun poured into the barren room. Outside on the Castellana, it was quiet. The nurses had not yet brought their broods of children out to play and there were so few cars that no noise could be heard.

When he had finished his call, he asked me to sit down. I told him the events as well as I could remember and gave him a list of all those present. He listened attentively and nodded when I was done.

"It was no accident," he began. "That shooting incident was deliberate. As the Prince warned, someone at the affair knew that Lilienthal was on to him and found this a convenient means of eliminating him. Let it be a warning to you."

He opened a drawer in his desk and searched through a stack of papers, finally extracting one. In the silence, an audible flutter sounded as he wagged it to and fro. "The result of an investigation on Enrique Paredes, who was among the distinguished guests. Evidently, he has many shares in a company we know to be a cover for Nazi espionage activities."

I reached for the report. I remembered the poker games, the German players. My eyes scanned the lines. There was no doubt. Enrique Paredes owned a little less than half the shares of Mercedes-Benz Española, Sociedad Anonima. At first I had disliked the fat man, but lately I'd become fond of him. Quite often I'd been at the same parties with Mitzi and Enrique Paredes and I had discovered that they were both charming, as Edmundo had insisted. But I had to admit this did not mean I trusted him implicitly.

Mozart's voice broke the silence. "Was Paredes placed in a position to enable him to make the fatal shot?"

I tried to imitate the boss's impersonal tone. "Enrique Paredes was on the same line of guns, but too far away, and anyhow there was a hillock between the two butts which would have made that impossible. I saw bushes swaying in a path that indicated some large animal or person was going in Niki's direction just before the shot. But the persons nearest were myself and Fribourg on his other side. And no one in our area that I know of moved that far from his post. Top Hat was farther down, but on a slope with a good view above Prince Lilienthal. He might be able to tell you more."

"Top Hat and I spoke about this last night," said Mozart. "He hopes his photographs, when developed and enlarged, may turn up something. But we're both pessimistic about getting any reliable information. It is impossible to question beaters or others at the Yebes estate without attracting attention. That would risk being recognized as intelligence agents. As you know, we could be put out of the country."

I was surprised that Mozart had already spoken to Edmundo. The chief saw him seldom, not wanting to risk Top Hat being connected too much to Americans. That was why I transmitted their reports to each other.

The chief continued. "Top Hat says that at the time of the shooting, he was unfortunately photographing an area near Lilienthal, but not close enough to include the Prince's butt."

"Fribourg might have some ideas," I suggested.

"Fribourg, I spoke to also. He's as suspicious as I am. You are aware, I believe, that he works for us. In fact, it was Fribourg who informed me that the Mercedes-Benz company was a Nazi cover." Mozart shifted his gigantic weight. The chair groaned.

"And Luis Quintanilla?" He went on. "Tell me more about him."

"He's the fiancé of my best friend," I said. "It's inconceivable that he would do such a thing. He's the most honorable Spaniard I've ever met." Then, appalled by how naive my declaration sounded, I hastened to add, "He was above me and far from Lilienthal."

No sooner had I spoken than I realized I had been too intense in my defense.

"Could you see him throughout the shoot?" the boss asked.

"No. As you know, everyone is concealed behind their butts."

"Then he could have wound his way to an appropriate spot from where he could have taken aim. In other words, he could have killed Niki better than most?"

"No." I felt myself blushing now and was mortified. "He came running down the hill just after the shot. He could not have done that if he was in the bushes that I saw moving below me."

"Miss Griffith." Mozart was smiling now. "Certainly you must realize that if he was invisible to you, he could have come up as well as down and then circled your post to fool you?"

For once the boss was looking directly at me. "I'm not disregarding him as a possible enemy agent, Miss Griffith. The Count of Quintanilla is young and handsome and might impress you too easily. Remember"—and now he shook a fat finger in my direction—"the best agent is the one we least suspect." He coughed. "And he may represent another kind of danger for us as well. Remember the rule? Any agent who gets involved in romantic entanglements risks getting shipped back to Washington. It's still wartime and you have to keep a level head."

As I walked down the hall back to the code room, I recalled my remarks about Luis Quintanilla and felt embarrassed all over again. Mozart was right. Someone had assassinated Niki Lilienthal and we had to locate the assassin before we lost another one of our team. But I knew it wasn't Luis Quintanilla. Even if he did fit the code name of El Guapo. And—the thought hit me like a bullet—even if he was someone Niki Lilienthal might think I'd have difficulty hiding my feelings from.

Needless to say it was with some trepidation that I met Edmundo the next day at the Hotel Palace bar. At first I found myself unable even to approach the subject of Niki's death.

"Edmundo, I've just seen my new agent, Smokey. He's scared to death of the Japanese. Each day, he says, they hide more cables from him and he thinks the head of Safehaven, whoever that may be, has discovered he's working for us and that they're going to kill him. He's a nervous wreck."

We were sitting at our usual table in the far corner—practically our office now—for exchanging clues about the Axis group.

Top Hat leisurely sipped his sherry and looked around the room. "You're not paying any attention to what I'm saying, Edmundo," I complained. "Something is distracting you."

"Now don't get peevish, *Divina.* I have important things to do, too. Didn't you notice the waiter was listening?" He took a sip of his dry sherry. "What did you think about poor Lilienthal's death? Did you notice anything? You were nearer than anyone."

Although I was ready for his question and had decided to face him with my doubts, my voice shook as I spoke.

"You were better situated than I to observe Niki's post." I looked at him meaningfully. "And you had a rifle."

Edmundo started. Then he laughed. "So you think I did the job, *Divina?*" The whites of his eyes gleamed. "Well, I could have easily enough, but why go to all that trouble—for an ally?"

"Well, what about those pictures?" I said. "Surely you must have learned something from them."

"My dear." His thick eyebrows rose incredulously. "Can you imagine, the film was defective and practically nothing—nothing came out." He sighed. "A pity. I might have caught the assassin red-handed or, should I say, rifle-handed."

Again, his laughter rang in my ears. I was annoyed by his reaction, which made me feel foolish and suspicious. "Apparently you're less skilled with a camera than with a gun," I said. "How ironic that you were the only one not shooting."

Edmundo made a face at me and changed the subject. "I'm concentrating on how to catch the big fish, if you really want to know." He lit another cigarette—the first one was still smoldering in the ashtray. "I have a plan. In my opinion the guilty one is someone we know well. My suspicions include quite a few attractive people in this city. Wait till you see how the bad one falls into my net." With a sly chuckle, he said, "Your friend, Luis Quintanilla, is one of the dominoes in my game."

"Good," I said. "With all of the bad apples you know, I'm glad you associate with a few good ones."

"The two are not so easily distinguishable," said Edmundo, giving me an arch look.

I longed to dispel his doubts about Luis, but I was not going to make the same mistake I had made with Mozart. Besides, it seemed strange to defend Luis when only moments ago I had practically accused Top Hat. So I simply smiled and let it pass.

"What does this plan consist of?"

He snickered. "You'll have to wait. But reserve Tuesday night and prepare your best gown for the occasion. I must have a few secrets, my dear."

But Tuesday, Top Hat called to say that his plan was canceled because one of the guests, the Free French ambassador, had just died of a heart attack. It would cast too great a pall on the evening, he said. On reflection, I could not help wondering whether there had ever been a plan, or whether Edmundo had simply wanted to distract my attention from his presence on the mountain behind Prince Lilienthal the day of the tragedy. Again I wondered at my own fondness for this colleague who, despite his charm, had repeatedly given proof of being a fabricator, and now and then something more sinister than that.

For many weeks Mozart hounded me with questions about the shoot. He was indignant that the Spanish police were so ready to accept the explanation that it had been an accident. Top Hat had laughingly admitted that Mozart had ordered him to bribe someone in the police staff to initiate an investigation. Unabashedly, Edmundo confessed he had done no such thing. "This kind of incident happens. It's useless to pursue a matter that has no solution." His words made me more suspicious than before. If Top Hat was innocent, I suspected he had his own idea of who was guilty and had no intention of letting me in on it. Why? I asked myself over and over again.

Chapter 8

During the months of March, April, and May, my progress in uncovering the identity of El Guapo or in finding even one suspect Impressionist painting was disappointing. Despite receptions and dinners in the homes of the great families such as the Suecas and the Infantados—those who were most apt to be interested in valuable artworks and able to afford them—I never saw anything except classic masterworks. Many Goyas, some Velazquezes, only a few Grecos, and a number of Tiepolos: paintings which had been in these families for generations. Nobody had bought anything new since before the Spanish Civil War.

At polo matches in the Puerta de Hierro Country Club, I bumped into most of the friends I had made that year. Ada Fribourg often paraded up and down the path in front of the stands in one of Balenciaga's choice spring suits. Sometimes she had that vague, distracted look which she had borne that day at the Ritz.

Luis Quintanilla's father and his two uncles, Yebes and Villabragima, were the best riders on the team, but I never saw Luis there. He had told me that day going up the mountain that polo had been his favorite sport until the wound in his arm made it impossible to swing a polo mallet. In fact, I hadn't seen Luis Quintanilla around Madrid for some time. When I asked Casilda Avila, she told me he was in Portugal at a golf championship.

Enrique Paredes and his wife invited me to a *zarzuela,* a popular, uniquely Spanish operetta. My initiation into this enchanting old-fashioned musical left me still more enamored with the country. I tried to bring Niki Lilienthal and the fatal shooting party into the conversation, but Enrique repeatedly avoided any discussion of it. Casilda invited me to *El Rocio,* a fair in southern Spain which involved a pilgrimage on horseback and in covered wagons, with flamenco dancing and singing night and day. I had to refuse; there was no way I could maintain my cover at the American Oil Mission and be partying away from Madrid, especially since our pursuit of El Guapo was going so slowly.

Almost every Sunday I went to a bullfight. When Juanito was fighting in or near Madrid and had been successful, he invited me to a flamenco party afterward with the other matadors. When the great star Manolete was in the city, he always joined us. It amazed me that these men who faced death in the ring could stay out late the night before a big fight and seem as carefree and lighthearted as anyone.

But none of this socializing advanced my search. Smokey insisted that the paintings were still locked in the ambassador's closet. He knew this because he had overheard the ambassador ask his secretary twice if any message had been received concerning where the paintings were to be delivered and when. No orders had come in, but Smokey continued on the lookout.

The war news was discouraging, also. The Japanese were slaying our men in the South Pacific. Two of our agents in Italy had been lost or murdered. Our troops were still fighting Germans in Europe. Cables poured in. Mozart was in a black gloom most of the time. My fellow code clerk, Jeff Walters, had problems he didn't want to confide. Bill Mellon, who was the most popular member of the staff, was lost in the French Basque country with no news from him in weeks.

Yet there were two bright spots during those months. The first occurred one night in March when I arrived home from the office. I was preparing to wash my hair when the doorbell rang. My maid, Angustias, opened the door and I heard a woman's voice struggling to make herself understood in Spanish. I ran down the long narrow hallway and gasped when I saw in the open doorway a short slim girl dressed in a shabby gray wool suit and bulky-looking brown shoes. A beat-up suitcase hung from her hand.

No surprise could have been greater or more welcome. It was Magic, my roommate from spy school. I hadn't seen her since December 1943, when we had both left for destinies unknown in Europe.

"Magic," I screamed. Her code name was the only one I knew. During the training program we had been obliged to maintain strict secrecy, not only about our names, but about everything else as well, including our nationalities and the languages we spoke. In fact, anyone giving away the slightest detail about his or her background was eliminated from the school. Magic and I had been the only women among thirty-four students. Every two weeks, several men who couldn't take the strenuous training or the long hours were dropped, but we had made it through the three months' course.

We continued to hug each other and to laugh and cry. I suspected that Magic had been behind enemy lines all this time. I'd never let on, but we had shared a room while in training and she had often had nightmares during which she screamed out in German. It was logical that she would have been sent to Germany to spy.

Magic looked down at her dusty shoes and wrinkled suit. "I've just gotten off the train . . ." She gestured toward her luggage which was now on the floor. "My instructions were to come to this address, but no one told me that the Señorita Griffith would be you!" She took a dirty envelope from under her shirt. "Before I say another word, I want to give you this. It's the German Order of Battle information. I've been worrying the whole time that I wouldn't make it here without being able to give it to someone. It's not even in code! Please give it to Mozart immediately."

I took the dirty paper and pulled her into the hallway. "Of course, I will, but Magic—I'm amazed that no one told me to expect you. Usually Mozart tells me before someone arrives. I don't think even he knew you were coming." I grabbed her suitcase and gave it to Angustias. "But come on in. You'll be comfortable here. Wait till you see how cozy my apartment is."

We walked into my small salon, and Magic collapsed on the sofa. "I'm exhausted, but I don't intend to waste time resting." She smiled. "You don't even know my real name yet, do you?"

"That was the first thing I intended to ask you. That and how long you're staying."

"Only two days. What can you do to show Silke Rosenbaum the town?"

"Silke Rosenbaum!" I repeated her name. "Silke. I won't get accustomed to that. I'm afraid I'll call you Magic—and probably at just the wrong moment."

We laughed.

"Are there any bullfights?"

"Not on Tuesdays and Wednesdays, unless there is a fiesta. But I can call a bullfighter friend and a colleague of mine and we'll get them to take us out for dinner."

When we opened her luggage, I saw she had nothing chic enough for Madrid night life, but I knew we could alter some of my clothes for her. We washed her auburn hair and brushed it till it glistened. I convinced her to take off her glasses, to mascara her thick-lashed blue eyes, to wear my high-heeled custom-made shoes. The result was sensational. I knew she would captivate anyone she wanted.

Three dry martinis in the Palace Bar was the beginning of Magic's two-day vacation. Then Chipén for dinner and La Reboite to dance. About one o'clock I left her with Edmundo, who said he would take her to Villa Rosa for some flamenco. Juanito dropped me at home since I had to be at the office early.

When I left the next morning, my guest was still asleep. When I came back that night, she had already gone out for the evening. Evidently Magic had found a boyfriend. Her note stated only that she'd been all over town that day with a man she'd met the night before and that she was going to dine with him that night. The last words in her backhand scribble said, "The magic of our love for music brought us together. See you before I leave Thursday morning."

It was logical she had made her own plans. She knew I could do nothing to amuse her since I was on duty in the code room Wednesday night, and I was pleased that she had someone to take her around on this short vacation. It was probably the only relaxation she had had since leaving Washington. Thursday morning I saw Magic only for a moment as she rushed to catch the train for the French border. She looked a wreck, and had not removed last night's eye makeup. I smiled, thinking that she'd probably just come back from a great flamenco.

Edmundo called almost as soon as I arrived in the office. "Your houseguest is quite a girl. Not the type I would expect to be a friend of yours. She got herself into a situation that would sizzle the hair on Mozart's head if he knew about it."

Edmundo went on to say that shortly after I had left the flamenco two nights before, he had tried to take Magic home, but she had insisted on staying. Jose, the gypsy, had said he would deliver her safely back to my apartment. Edmundo said he didn't see her again until the following night when they both turned up at La Reboite where she was mano-à-mano with—"You'll never guess who." Edmundo's giggle came through the wire. After a pause sufficient to whet my curiosity, he added, "With an officer of the Gestapo in Spain. Herr Waldner, no less!!!"

I thought he was kidding and was about to hang up when he added, "Take me seriously, my pet. That's not the end of the story. Your friend likes to drink and so does Herr Waldner. Neither knew who the other one was. Evidently they are both amateur violinists and somehow started playing duets at the nightclub and from there went on to a flamenco. They were fascinated with each other and I had a hell of a time separating them to bring her to your apartment. Can you imagine what Mozart would say!"

I was wondering how Magic herself had taken the news when she'd realized who her companion was. It must have been a jolt. Her hatred for the Nazis was something alive and visceral. The afternoon she had arrived, she'd told me, "I have friends and relatives, some of them women, who have been tortured and killed by the Nazis." And then with tears in her eyes, she added, "This past year every time I helped to blow up a trainload of their soldiers, I felt I was avenging my own family and friends."

By now Magic was on her way to the French frontier. There was little I could do to help her except not to tell Mozart about her escapade.

The other bright spot occurred around the tenth of May when Truman declared the war in Europe officially over. Hitler had committed suicide, we were told, shooting his mistress, Eva Braun, and then putting a bullet through his own head. Finally, the monster was dead! Having been a neutral country and not directly involved in the war, however, Spain did not celebrate the occasion. All over the world, there was rejoicing in the streets, but not here. We of the Madrid OSS felt left out, so we arranged our own small party to celebrate in the office. Mozart joined in just long enough to remind us that the war in the South Pacific was still going strong and that it was our obligation to keep fighting, thus putting a damper on the whole affair.

Then he pulled me aside. "As for you, Miss Griffith, you must tell Smokey to work harder. Those paintings are more important than ever. The Nazis are all scurrying away now, like little rats, and if we don't catch them now, we may never have another chance. Keep after him!"

Days passed. Letter drops were uncovered, messages intercepted, and a few Japanese agents taken over. Smokey did not bring me any startling information, just the regular copies of cables. His excuse was that the Japanese were more secretive than ever, especially when any Spaniard was around. Their telephone conversations had become impossible to listen in to now that Japanese officials attended the switchboard.

Top Hat, however, was much more successful than I. He managed to uncover large sums of stolen assets hidden in Mexican bank accounts in Switzerland, which improved his humor and brought rare compliments from Mozart. But the leader of Safehaven in Spain remained a mystery, and Lilienthal's death had passed by with the general belief that it had been a tragic accident. However, Mozart, Top Hat, and myself, although we no longer referred to it, knew that it had been murder and that El Guapo was still nearby.

It wasn't until almost the middle of June that a new scent materialized that looked as if it might produce results.

Chapter 9

I hadn't seen Luis Quintanilla around Madrid for some time. Then I was thrilled to receive an engraved invitation to a party in his apartment on June 21, to celebrate his saint's day. In Spain, instead of birthdays, everyone celebrates the day of his or her name—the 21st was the day of Saint Luis. Top Hat had been invited as well, and we agreed to go together.

He picked me up on a Wednesday afternoon, carrying a strange-looking package wrapped in red silk. "Golf balls," he explained. "The shopkeeper was going to wrap my present in newspapers. Can you imagine!" He flaunted the red bundle. "This country is so removed from the rest of the world that they don't even have wrapping paper. Felisa at Balenciaga, no less, made me a gift of this silk. However, the Spanish custom of celebrating saint's days instead of birthdays is so much more civilized. It eliminates mentioning one's age, although that won't be a problem for you, my dear, for quite some time."

The Calle Conde de Aranda was a small quiet street in the middle of Madrid, near the Plaza de Independencia. On the elevator hung the sign often seen on Madrid's *acensores*—*no funciona*—so we had to walk up two flights of stairs.

The house was filled with people milling about. Our host was standing in an open balcony window talking to the Duke of Lerma and Miguel Primo de Rivera, the pro-Axis minister of Franco's cabinet. When he saw us, he rushed over.

"Have you heard?" He appeared upset. "Ada Fribourg just called. Her best friend committed suicide a few hours ago—jumped out of a window of the Hotel Ritz." Guests collected around Luis to listen to the details. "The woman was connected to the German embassy, nobody of importance but Ada says she was terrified she would be sent back to Germany to face war crimes trials."

While the other guests, some of whom had also known the unfortunate woman, commented on the tragedy, I slipped unnoticed from the room and wandered through the quiet salons which housed Quintanilla's art collection. It had become a habit every time I entered a new home. As a result of frequent visits to the Prado, I could recognize most classic painters. The first paintings I looked at were two small bullfight scenes by Goya. Then I stopped in front of a drawing by Velazquez which was next to a Tiepolo Venetian scene of two ladies in black masks stepping out of a gondola. My eyes roamed the walls and then halted suddenly on something entirely different. It was an Impressionist—the kind of painting I'd been looking for. I went closer and scrutinized it, trying to find a signature. I couldn't find one, but the style could be Cézanne! This was a discovery! The canvas was nothing like the description Mozart had given of the painting with the yellow dog. Yet I couldn't help wondering how it had come to be here, in this house. I looked at it closely, then stood back and looked again. Had this painting once hung on the walls of some Jewish home in Holland before the Nazis stole it? The pale shafts of light which threaded through the dense lace window curtains seemed to come from far away. The room was shady and utterly silent. Then I heard a step and turned to find Luis Quintanilla watching me from the doorway.

I started and moved away from the painting. My host was smiling.

"I was looking for you. Are you bored, roaming through these rooms alone?"

"Not at all. Casilda told me about your collection and I've been admiring your lovely paintings." Somehow, today his presence made me uncomfortable.

"Which do you prefer?" he asked, coming closer to me.

"Goya is marvelous," I bubbled nervously. "Where did you find those lovely bullfight paintings?"

He smiled, and I found to my surprise that I had difficulty meeting his eyes. We had so seldom been alone—just that walk up the mountain the day of the shoot. Now, enclosed by walls and all these paintings, I felt closer. A palpable tension had arisen between us. Luis Quintanilla touched my arm as he pointed to the paintings I had mentioned.

"I didn't find them," he said. "My great-great-grandfather got them directly from Goya. Most of my collection is inherited, except one I bought yesterday in the flea market. You were observing it when I came in. Come, give me your opinion," he said, gently taking my arm.

His touch through my sleeve was making me dizzy, and I was thrown into such confusion that I hardly noticed where he was directing me. I felt each of his strong fingers, and standing so near him I could smell the warm, pleasant odor of leather and cigarettes. It hit me hard: I was falling in love with Luis Quintanilla!

He drew me to the painting I'd believed could be a Cézanne. "This is the one."

His words brought me to my senses.

"You bought that yesterday?" I managed to ask.

My host was engrossed in the painting. He had released my arm and I regained my composure. Now he stood with arms crossed in front of it.

For a moment, I was speechless. The fact that he had just bought it was crucial.

"You can't imagine what luck!" he continued enthusiastically. "I was going through the Rastro and happened to enter one of the small shops at the very moment the owner was unpacking a crate. I talked him into selling the painting before he even looked at it." He waved toward the landscape before us. "I got that for a song. The dealer hadn't the slightest idea of its value. I'm sure it's a Cézanne. You know, Cézanne rarely signed his paintings, only when he was especially requested to do so by a client."

"What luck indeed!" I said. My attraction for Luis combined with my excitement over this discovery made it difficult to keep my voice even. My heart beat wildly. "You say there were others? Also by Cézanne?"

My eyes turned to him. His gaze scrutinized me. Without reason I felt myself blush. The well-tanned face, the light green eyes, crinkled in a large smile. He said nothing for a moment, and when he did his voice was lower, softer.

"There were two paintings I liked particularly." He pointed to the one in front of us. "This and another. I had trouble deciding between them."

My mind reeled. Finally I had discovered something pertinent to Operation Safehaven. "What was the other one like?" I said as casually as possible.

"A young couple picnicking in the country." As he spoke, I shut my eyes. "A woods scene and in the corner—a small dog."

I didn't know Casilda had been standing behind us until she spoke. "Oh, Luis, you're too clever," she said. "You must take me to that *tienda* before the rest of those pictures are bought by someone else. Papa's birthday is tomorrow and a painting would be the perfect gift."

Without waiting for Luis to agree, she turned to me. "Aline, do come with us. A visit to the Rastro with Luis is a treat. He knows all the stalls and shops and bargains better than anyone."

I smiled. Miraculously, she had paved the way for my investigation. "Of course, I'd love to. What fun."

Our host looked from one to the other, obviously not enthralled with the prospect of shepherding us through the Rastro. He stammered something about having to play golf. Casilda insisted that would be impossible because the course was in repair. "What about Ada's friend who died?" His expression brightened. "We should go to her burial tomorrow."

"Certainly not," answered Casi. "You forget that foreigners are embalmed and buried two or three days later. No more excuses, Luis." She grabbed his arm possessively. "You can't escape. Aline and I will be ready around one o'clock." She looked at me. "I'll send the car to your office about one. That's the best hour to go to the Rastro."

The next morning I went to Phillip Harris' office to tell him about the breakthrough on what I hoped would be one of the Nazi shipments of looted paintings. The boss was pleased.

"Good." He repeated the word twice. "Tell the Count you want to buy an Impressionist painting yourself, especially a Cézanne. We'll cover the expenses, of course. You must follow this up. You may be on the track of something."

His powerful fingers tapped the barren desk. "You have not checked with Smokey, have you, about those crates of paintings being removed from the Japanese legation?"

I told him Smokey insisted that they were still in the ambassador's office.

"These paintings Quintanilla saw would have to be another shipment, then. Just proves what quantities of looted effects are in this country." He shook his huge head. "Now, Miss Griffith, what else?"

"I think that's about all." I stood up to leave.

He added, "Let me know immediately what you find after that young count takes you to the Rastro."

A few hours later the gateman of the Montellano palace telephoned upstairs to my office to say that the chauffeur of the Señorita Arteaga was waiting at the entrance. For a moment I was confused. Then I realized that Casilda's last name must be Arteaga, although I had always thought of her as Casilda Avila, because her father was the Count of Avila, and Avila was the name she used. Many people I had met possessed a title or belonged to a titled family, and for some inexplicable reason, the unmarried ones used a variety of names, switching from their own title, if they had one, to that of their parents, and sometimes to their last name instead. In a family with many titles, it was even worse. Each member carried the last name of both parents, which made it necessary for me to remember many long, complicated names.

When I arrived at the street, Sebastian was standing at the door of the Avilas' black Peugeot, an ancient car but as shiny as patent leather shoes. All the automobiles in Madrid were pre-1936, before the Spanish Civil War, but the chauffeurs polished them two and three times a day. To these people, appearance was important—in dress or anything else. There wasn't a dusty or dented vehicle in the city.

"The Señorita Casilda told me to take you to the Duke of Medinaceli's palace, where she and the Count are expecting you."

As he put the old machine in motion, I glanced across the street at the enemy's building, the German Kultural Institut, a cover for the Gestapo. Two tiny *topolinos*—small cars made in Italy years before—beetled down the Castellana, but no other vehicles were in sight. However, both sides of the spacious, tree-lined boulevard were crowded with children in fancy embroidered outfits, playing in the dirt. Their governesses, *amas,* looked like round wooden dolls dressed in bright long-skirted plaids. At this hour there were no empty seats at the street cafes. The deep blue sky, the shafts of golden light piercing the leafy sycamores, the peaceful rhythm of the magical city, the polite handsome people smiling and saluting each other with old-fashioned formality—all of this charmed me, as it did every day of the year.

The flawless June day had an exhilarating effect on Sebastian, too. "Madrid is a beautiful city," he began. "Doesn't the señorita agree?" He indicated either side of the wide avenue. "These palaces! Just look at their massive iron gates and the granite columns!"

By now we were driving around a circular plaza. "That's the Señor Duque's palace." He pointed to the far side of the plaza. "And over there is the Institute of Moneda. That big building down there is the National Library. Now tell me, señorita, are there any finer structures in your country?"

I was, perhaps, more impressed than Sebastian. The entire Castellana from the Museum of the Prado on up for over twenty blocks was lined by classical palaces and ornate public buildings. About every five blocks, there was a lovely circular plaza with trees and fountains, and statues of men on horseback, or mythical figures on stone-carved chariots.

"Madrid is a beautiful city, Sebastian," I agreed, but at the same time, I thought, it is also a city of murder and intrigue. Lilienthal's death came again to mind.

Something else was disturbing me, too, as a doorman swung open the Medinaceli palace gates to let our Peugeot enter. Despite the excitement of finally finding a Cézanne yesterday, when I'd gone to sleep that night, it was Luis Quintanilla I'd found myself thinking of. I was longing to see him again. What had happened to me? He was Casilda's beau and I had no right to find him so devastating. But how could I hide my infatuation from Casi? Not to speak of the embarrassment if Luis, who was in love with her, noticed that he enchanted me. Mozart would send me back if he even suspected such a thing. And I would destroy my friendship with Casi, as well.

At the foot of the wide marble steps stood a liveried footman who led me into a spacious hall, then through two long dark salons whose shutters were closed and thick velvet curtains drawn to keep out the heat of the midday sun. Despite the dimness, I saw that the huge paintings on the walls were Goyas and Velazquezes. Finally we emerged into an immense sunny green garden, where under a group of trees people reclined in antique French armchairs and were sipping drinks. Casi and Luis jumped up at the same moment and hastened toward me.

"Aline, I want you to meet my uncle," Luis said, as we approached an elderly man who was struggling to his feet.

The Duke's pale eyes blinked. "So this is that American girl you've been talking about. Charmed to have you here. My, but you are pretty." He patted a chair. "Do sit down, here, next to me."

Luis Quintanilla was by my side. "Sorry, Tío, that's not possible today. I've promised Casi and Aline to take them to the Rastro, and if we don't leave right now the shops will be closed."

After a round of kissing and handshaking, we left, and several minutes later I found myself squeezed into Luis' Cord, between Casi and the door. I would have liked to have seen more of the incredible garden and the gigantic palace, but there were more important things to do. Today, I hoped, I was going to find the looted paintings and uncover the source. I had made an attempt to prepare myself conscientiously. At eleven, Smokey had met me at a cafe. According to him, the crates were still in the ambassador's office, locked in a closet, and the paintings in the Rastro could not be from the same lot.

"If the Quintanilla painting and those you are going to see are Nazi loot, they may be in crates similar to the two we have. Try to see the boxes themselves and read what's stamped on the outside. You can tell where they came from and through which countries they passed. Those in the legation are marked with exit stamps from Holland and stamps of entry and exit from France."

Luis drove to the Plaza de Cascorro. Here, the buildings were shabby and dilapidated, as were all those on either side of the hill. He parked next to the ragged awning of a street vendor, and jumped out, handing the man a few *pesetas* to keep an eye on the car. Casilda and I were on his heels. We followed him along a narrow passageway lined by stalls whose merchandise was composed of dented pots, old bicycles, bolts of cloth, religious objects, weathered antiques, dishes that didn't match. Now and then a few bad paintings were mixed with the junky paraphernalia. It seemed incongruous that anything worthwhile could be found in the midst of such rubbish.

Now and then, Quintanilla stopped to salute a shopowner—he knew them all. Casi and I trailed behind like speechless idiots. There were more shopkeepers and peddlers than customers. A couple of gypsies followed us—at someone's expense, I suspected. Even the bright midday sun was unable to penetrate our tortuous route. The setting was perfect for cheating and murder—which were probably considered of equal unimportance here.

At the end of a cul-de-sac, Luis sprinted up a spiral iron stairwell which opened into the center of what was undoubtedly the most prosperous shop in the Rastro. It was here, he explained, that he had bought the painting he believed could be a Cézanne. When we entered, the unshaven owner, dressed in dirty rags not very different from his less grand colleagues below, greeted us with an engaging smile and a crafty countenance.

"Señor Conde, good-day to you. How can I be of service?" Luis shook his hand and turned to introduce Casi and myself, in the same manner as, a few moments before, he had introduced me to his uncle, the Duke.

"Don Pedro, we would like to see some of those paintings you received the other day," he said. "I don't think they're worth much, but my friends here may be interested in buying one."

The shopkeeper's attitude changed abruptly. Frowning, he looked at us for a moment. "I'm afraid a dealer from Barcelona bought that whole shipment yesterday."

"Come on, Don Pedro," urged the Count, "don't be lazy. Nobody could have bought all those paintings in such a short time. Why don't you take a look back there?" He pointed to the rear of the shop.

Pedro shook his head. "Sorry, Señor Conde, there's not one left in the shop." He threw his hands into the air, accentuating desperation. He even claimed he was ignorant of the name, address, and description of the Catalan dealer and—equally as important for me—of the person who had delivered the crates in the first place. Although Luis' expression indicated he didn't believe him, there was little we could do.

Later during our luncheon at Chipén, Luis agreed that Don Pedro had been preposterously uncollaborative. "He pretends he doesn't know how to read or write, which gives him an excuse for not keeping references for his merchandise. He has good reason. It's often stolen property."

I didn't want to let the conversation about art drop. "Are many stolen paintings in Madrid?" I asked. "As good as the one I saw in your apartment?"

Instead of answering my question, he said something that made me worry that I had aroused his suspicion. "You seem to take a great interest in art," Luis said, looking at me.

"I'm learning," I said. "Just walking through the Prado is a course in the history of art. I'm in love with that museum. It's breathtaking."

Luis' eyes lit up at the mention of the Prado. Clearly I had hit on a passion of his. "Which painters are your favorites?"

For a few minutes, we exchanged opinions on El Greco, Velazquez, Zurbaran, and others. In his enthusiasm, Luis ignored Casilda and, I suppose, I did also. At any rate, she didn't like being out of our conversation and finally interrupted us. "That's the sort of thing I'd like to do, Luis. Why don't you take me to the Prado sometime?"

He looked surprised. "You've never suggested going there." He shrugged his shoulders. "I had no idea you were interested. In fact, I've never noticed you even looked at paintings."

She pouted. "Now, Luis, how can I be interested in art if no one teaches me?"

It became obvious that these two didn't always get along as well as I had thought. Hastily, I changed the conversation.

Mozart was out when I returned after lunch, so I was able to postpone the discouraging news about not finding the painting. When I told him the next day, his huge fist banged the table, but at first he made no comment. Then his gigantic head turned to the picture frame which was the only object on the table's barren surface. I'd never been able to get a glimpse of the other side and wondered if it was a snapshot of his wife, and what she was like. Top Hat had told me once that there was more to our chief than we imagined.

"He's no hermit, my pet—no, not shy with the ladies at all," he had squealed in his high staccato. "My information comes from a reliable source—a Balenciaga mannequin, who is a rather intimate friend of mine. She presumes to know Mr. Harris quite well." Edmundo's smirk had left no doubt as to his meaning. The gossipy remark only augmented my awe and fascination for the boss. He was becoming more of a mystery for me as time wore on.

Then, speaking softly in the hushed dim room, he admonished me, "Find those paintings, Aline. Time is running out. Just find them."

There was little I could add.

Chapter 10
JULY

Early the next Saturday morning, I tried to find a taxi to take me out to the Puerta de Hierro Country Club, where I had decided to begin golf lessons. Between office hours and the exhausting social routine, I had had little time left for exercise. Of course, the fact that Luis Quintanilla was a golf champion may have had something to do with my decision. To my dismay there was not a taxi on the street, and it was an hour's walk to the club. Well, I needed the exercise anyway, I thought, and set out on foot.

As I reached the end of the Calle Cea Bermudez and began to walk along the empty road that traversed wild open country, one lone car approached and surprised me by pulling up and stopping. I was horrified! The driver was the last person I wanted to see. I knew I would be reprimanded for risking a walk alone in such an isolated area.

"Whatever are you doing? For heaven's sake, jump in."

My embarrassment was total. Mozart glanced at me skeptically as he restarted the motor.

"I'll take you to the club, but be certain you wait for a taxi to bring you back to the city. You don't realize the unnecessary chances you're taking walking alone on this road. You must not become lax in security precautions. The war may be over in Europe, but it's still going strong in the South Pacific, and you must remember you have an agent in the Japanese legation. If anyone finds out, that could make you a target."

The black Packard bounced over the ruts as we neared the outskirts of the city. I sat tongue-tied, and for a while we drove in silence.

"What about Safehaven?" He never took his eyes off the road, despite the fact that there was not a vehicle in sight. Now we were in open country surrounded by retama bushes with yellow blossoms and a sprinkling of umbrella pines. The air was already warm and I could tell the day was going to be a scorcher. "Safehaven's your war right now. If we don't win it, our chances for peace will be endangered even after this war is over."

We turned into the curving drive leading up to the clubhouse. "Of course, Miss Griffith, inside that red handbag you have your Beretta." His tone was slightly sarcastic.

"To be truthful, Mr. Harris, I haven't been carrying a gun for several months."

"That's foolish. What would you do if an enemy agent attacked you to get the names of those on our blacklist? Or the key to our code? That alone would give access to our cables worldwide."

As I descended from his car I realized that he was only being protective, but qualms of embarrassment possessed me. Mozart having caught me in such unprofessional behavior was galling. For the first ten minutes of the golf lesson, I made no progress at all. The way the ball dribbled off the tee was an example of what I felt like. Then a voice paralyzed my swing in midair.

"If you don't keep your eye on the ball, you're never going to hit it."

Before turning around, I knew who it was. Again I felt a surge of humiliation. How long had Luis Quintanilla been watching my disastrous attempts?

During the next half-hour he instructed me on how to address the ball, how to swing, how to follow through—all the things I needed to know. My spirits improved and so did my swing. I basked in his presence, in the bright clear air, in the beauty of the green undulations of the golf course, and the blue mountains in the distance. When my lesson was over, he said he was going out to play on the course and asked his chauffeur to take me back to Madrid. He told me that he came every day at that hour and suggested picking me up himself the next day. It was difficult to refuse, and when I looked at his handsome profile the next morning, I was glad I hadn't. His strong masculine hands gripped the wheel as we drove together under the glorious, sunny, blue-ceilinged Madrid morning.

That same afternoon Casilda called to say she was moving with her family to San Sebastian for the summer and invited me to visit them there whenever I could. San Sebastian was the elegant summer resort in northeastern Spain near the French border where all who could afford to retired for two to three months to enjoy the beaches and the lush countryside. Obviously, Luis had said nothing about seeing me, so I didn't either.

For about ten days, I looked down from my second floor window each morning waiting for the now-familiar Cord to appear. When it did, I felt a ripple of excitement. I grew accustomed to my crush on Luis Quintanilla, and if he was aware of my feelings for him, he was far too polite to let me know. It was a thrill simply to see him each day, and he seemed satisfied to be in my company, too. Yet I realized I was playing with fire. What if he was just luring me on—into some sort of trap. Although I tried to ignore it, in the back of my mind, a faint misgiving gnawed now and then. He could fit the code name El Guapo so well. But one glance at his clear green eyes and honorable countenance dispelled such preposterous notions in a flash.

After the encounter with Mozart, I carried my Beretta in the bottom of my handbag. He was not going to catch me off-guard again. I could still remember the night, a year ago, when a paid assassin had tried to kill me. I'd been returning from this same club, and it was only a miracle I had been able to shoot him first. I had spent months trying to forget that ghastly moment. It was also rumored around the office that one of Mozart's agents had been tortured and killed recently—it had probably been on his mind when he'd mentioned the gun that morning. Besides, we had just received fresh reports on Japanese atrocities in the Philippines and it was known that some of their legation spent a great deal of time playing golf at the club. Sometimes one of them was hitting balls on the practice tee in the stall next to mine, but Luis Quintanilla was there and I felt protected.

Each morning I hoped he would ask me out that evening, but he never did. I refused dates with Juanito and others to be available in case he called at the last minute. Maybe he considered taking me out at night was more unfaithful to Casilda than taking me to the golf club.

And then I received disconcerting news from Top Hat. One of his agents had advised him that the Count of Quintanilla had spent two evenings the previous week playing poker at Enrique Paredes' house, precisely on the nights a man from the German embassy had also been there. Edmundo kept a close watch on these German officials.

With a dismal heart I went to our station chief's office to inform him. This had revived all my worries about Luis. Naturally Mozart would advise me to avoid Quintanilla in the future, which, I glumly supposed, was for the best, from every point of view. But to my surprise, he urged the contrary.

"Stay close to him," he told me, which suggested, to my surprise and shame, that he already knew the Count was taking me to the golf club every day.

"He's valuable for his contacts, whether or not he's a suspect. Get him to talk about those poker games and to take you to his relatives' homes where you may find some of the looted paintings we're looking for."

The next morning, as we rode along the Calle Monte Esquinza, Luis asked the question I had been hoping for.

"Are you free for dinner tonight? Casilda is already in San Sebastian, and my sister and her husband want me to dine with them at Villa Rosa. It's the only place open at this time of year."

I made an attempt to accept as if dining with him held little importance for me. That night I was a nervous wreck. I washed my hair, although it was perfectly clean. Just as I sat down under the ancient dryer, the electricity cut out and my hair was still not dry an hour later when it was time for Luis to pick me up. This always seemed to happen at the most inconvenient times. I changed my mind three times about the dress I would wear. I redid my makeup—I didn't think I looked good enough no matter how hard I tried.

The popular Villa Rosa nightclub on the outskirts of the city was one of the few that stayed open during the three long summer months. It catered principally to husbands who told their wives that their work kept them in town, when actually most of their time was spent playing with their girlfriends. These men were jokingly referred to as "the Rodriguezes," Rodriguez being rather like Smith, a name they often used to pass incognito.

Contrary to general opinion, Madrid was delightful during the summer. While in the North, wives and children fretted in cold and rainy weather, Madrid was dry and sunny in the daytime, cool at night. There was an atmosphere of freedom and abandon, not possible the rest of the year.

That night was the first time I'd been to Villa Rosa. Luis parked the car in front of the huge old palace surrounded by poplar trees and formal gardens. Then he led me along a path bordered by adelpha bushes filled with pink flowers, under trellises covered with white jasmine blossoms wafting their deliciously seductive scent. I had heard the restaurant was famous for its cuisine, but I hadn't expected to find such magnificent gardens. In the pale light of the Japanese lanterns which illuminated our path, I could see massive beds of huge red carnations and blue moonflowers. As we proceeded, another heavy perfume intoxicated me. I looked around and saw that we were surrounded by bushes of tuberoses. When we reached the dance floor, around which the tables were located, the large band of twelve musicians was playing

> *"You've got something,*
> *Something nobody else has . . ."*

There were no microphones so the music was soft, too, the air dry and caressing. And as I followed the maître d' to a table in the corner, I thought I had just stepped into paradise. Luis' sister Isabel and her husband, Kiki, probably among the few socialites still in the city, were being served drinks by a white-jacketed waiter when we arrived. The place was so beautiful and romantic that I regretted we would not be alone, but I was aware that was impossible. The girls I knew did not usually go out alone on dates unless they were engaged.

The icy gazpacho came first and after that grilled crayfish with saffron rice, which was enough for Isabel and for me. But the maître d' insisted that the Señor Duque—Kiki was the Duke of Tamames—and the Señor Conde should also have a third course. He recommended *perdices en escabeche,* partridge in sour sauce. He had already given us an explanation about their excellent fish. "The best *pescado* in Europe," he pointed out. "Loaded into ice trucks before daybreak, just as soon as the fishing boats dock. It must be the finest in all Europe," he went on. "Isn't our country bordered almost entirely by water? The *merluza* we have tonight comes from the Bay of Biscay. And our *chanquetes* straight up from Malaga—from the good old Mediterranean."

Before he had a chance to launch into another speech about Spanish wines, Kiki told him to prepare *sangria* for all of us—a red wine served in a pitcher with lots of ice, soda water, some strawberries, and a drop of cognac.

I liked Luis' sister and her husband from the first moment. When they got up to dance, we did the same. Luis was a good dancer and it was breathtaking to be so close. As we danced a *pasadoble,* he held me tightly, and several times his cheek brushed mine. This was not done in Madrid, and a far cry from my sweaty cheek-to-cheek "hops" at West Point only a year and a half before. I wasn't accustomed to this; his stance was different, as well. When I felt his leg, side to side next to mine, my temperature soared, and I realized I was uncontrollably in love. But I did an admirable job of concealing my emotions.

Later, the four of us walked through the garden path and into the old palace and up the wide marble stairs to the second floor, where there were gypsies and private rooms. Several private flamenco parties were going on already. We selected our gypsies and then went into a five-by-five-meter barren room where we sat on four straight wooden chairs while a guitarist, a *cantaor*— singer, in gypsy parlance—and two women dancers took the four chairs facing us.

For a couple of hours the dancers twisted and gyrated in sensuous movement to the *compas* of the *palmas* (hand-clapping). The intoxicating rhythms drugged me. The eerie contagious wail of the singers became more intense, driving the *artistas* to a greater pitch as the hours flew by. I was spellbound.

Luis leaned close. "I see you've become a real *aficionada,*" he whispered. His breath was warm. His lips brushed my ear.

As I nodded, he took my hand and held it. His touch was caressing. For a moment we looked at each other as his fingers stroked mine. I glanced at his sister and her husband, and I was relieved to find them absorbed in the spectacle. When I looked back at Luis, he had a troubled expression. He pressed my hand once more and then let it go.

The drive to Madrid seemed much too short. At first we rode in silence. For a few moments I mused over my misgivings about Luis being El Guapo, about his possessing that painting, but I soon chased those suspicions from my mind. He was an honorable man and nothing else. I was happy. And I sensed that I was no longer alone in my infatuation.

Then with his attention concentrated on the highway, he destroyed my new-found peace of mind. He told me that the next morning he had to leave for San Sebastian. My heart flipped. I knew he would be seeing Casilda every day. I said nothing. Neither did he, for a few minutes.

Finally he spoke.

"I think," he said, "it's better that we don't see each other for a while."

Crestfallen, I didn't answer. Luis kept his eyes glued on the dark road, which unfurled like a curving ribbon before us.

"Casilda and I . . . it's been settled for so long," he said. "Almost before I realized it. But now . . ." He sighed.

"Casilda's my best friend," I said.

"Exactly."

When we reached my apartment, we were both despondent. Luis walked me to the entrance and we stood awkwardly at my door, neither wanting to say what both of us knew would be our last good-bye. Finally he put a hand on each of my shoulders and kissed me on the lips. When I opened my eyes, he was already getting back into his car.

Chapter 11
AUGUST

When I arrived in the code room on August 10, Jeff greeted me with the sensational news that, a few hours before, an American superfortress had dropped a 9,000-pound atomic bomb from 31,600 feet on Hiroshima, destroying the entire city. The loss of so many lives was awesome and shocked us, but at least it meant the terrors of war were about over. Three days later, we learned that another bomb of the same magnitude had been dropped on Nagasaki. Now the war with Japan was definitely finished. The Spanish press dwelled on the magnitude of the bomb and the tragedies it had caused and, as before, there was no celebration in the streets of Madrid to mark the end of the war. From a Spanish point of view, it was the middle of summer, people were on vacation, and, after all, it had not been their war.

But Jeff and I wanted to celebrate a moment in history we had worked and prayed for. We left the code room and looked for Ronnie, our radio expert, and tried to hear the tumultuous celebration broadcasts from Paris and London. The reception was very bad, though, and we finally gave up.

As we left the radio room, Jeff mumbled. "Be careful, Aline. The war's not over yet."

I looked at him. "What do you mean?"

"You mean, you didn't hear what happened to me last night?"

I'd been out most of the day and shook my head.

"I unlocked my door and walked into my apartment like I always do—and found a man facing me with a .45 automatic in his hand."

"My heavens," I exclaimed. "What did you do?"

As we walked along the hall, he wobbled his head as if still incredulous. "And for once I didn't even have a weapon on me!"

I waited.

"Fortunately, the guy didn't have the guts to shoot. I was able to disarm him before he decided to pull the trigger. But it was just luck."

"But who was he?"

Jeff shrugged his shoulders. "Turns out he was a German from the intelligence department of the embassy. I'd never seen him before, but he thought I knew who he was—that I would place his name on the war crimes list." He looked at me. "So beware, kid. Like I said, the war's not over yet."

Jeff and I went back to the code room, locked the cipher boards and the cables in the safe, and then went home, as on every other day of the week. It seemed incredible to me. What would happen now?

I tried not to think of Luis and was grateful that Juanito Belmonte continued to send me flowers and chocolates while he was fighting bulls in Malaga. Top Hat's Princess Renata was in Mallorca, so I saw him frequently. On the last day in August he called to say that Ada and Klaus Fribourg had just come down from San Sebastian for a few days and asked if I would like to dine with them.

During dinner Klaus and Edmundo discussed the magnitude of the atom bomb and how it would change the direction of the world. Ada chatted with me about what was going on in San Sebastian. She laughed when explaining that the police patrolled the beaches to make certain that women wore skirts over their bathing suits and men wore tops. After dinner we continued on to La Reboite on the Calle Prim for a nightcap.

When our friends got up to dance, Edmundo confessed that he was depressed. "There are rumors circulating. They say President Truman intends to abandon OSS operations abroad." He sighed. "Our jobs are at stake, my pet. What will I do? Spying is the only profession I know." The violin orchestra changed to an Argentine tune. He grabbed my arm and pulled me to the floor. "Come, *Divina,* let's tango while our ship is sinking."

Short, skinny Klaus Fribourg bumped into us as we got to the floor. Watching him as we danced, we couldn't help laughing. His lips, fuller than ever, were thrust out in concentration as he manipulated stately Ada through dips and sliding dance movements. "That's what he thinks is a great tango," squealed Edmundo.

As we were slinking across the floor, just by luck I noticed someone trying to get my eye. It was Smokey, gesticulating from a dim corner. I was amazed. He never went to night clubs, and I hadn't seen him for weeks. He'd taken his wife and children to Alicante to spend August there with his parents. Edmundo and I zigzagged between the dancers to where he was standing. Fortunately, nobody was looking at him, otherwise his agitated manner would have attracted the attention he was trying so hard to avoid.

"Alin-ay," he rasped in his rusty voice when I reached his side. "My news is confidential." Behind the horn-rimmed glasses, the black eyes darted at my dancing partner. Discreetly, Edmundo left us. Still, Smokey was apprehensive.

"Don't worry," I told him. "With the noise of all these violins, nobody can hear."

Drops of spit hit my ear every now and then as he told me that an important Nazi had been in the Japanese legation that very afternoon giving orders to have a defector killed. The German had also said that anyone else found endangering the safety of Nazi effects would have to be eliminated, as well. The bushy black eyebrows twitched.

"Alin-ay," he went on, "things are getting very uncomfortable. I can't keep my family in this dangerous position much longer. What happens with those visas you told me I would get in payment for my work?"

I said I would give the ambassador his news and ask about the visas, and then I thought our conversation was over. But as I turned to look for Edmundo, Smokey touched my sleeve.

"There's something else." His Adam's apple rose up and fell. "The crates from Holland are no longer in the ambassador's office."

"Where are they?" I almost screamed. We'd had Smokey recruit a sub-agent to help him keep constant track of those crates—and now they were gone? I was furious.

"No, no, you don't understand. Listen. The ambassador got in a temper this morning on the telephone. I overheard him tell someone that ever since the war had ended he had repeatedly said he no longer intended to give diplomatic protection to Nazi effects. That the crates had to be removed immediately. That they didn't belong to him to begin with and that he would no longer take the responsibility. It was probably El Guapo. He always calls on the number the ambassador reserves for top secret messages. When the ambassador hung up, he ordered me and Pepe—Pepe's his personal chauffeur—to deliver the crates to another address.''

"Did you manage to get a look at the paintings inside the crates?''

"Well, you see, Pepe was with me all the time and he's very loyal to the ambassador. I don't know if he's afraid of him or if he gets paid extra, but I didn't dare try to bribe him. But Alin-ay, I know where they went! The place they delivered the boxes to is only a small apartment on a street just off the Plaza Santa Barbara. It should be easy to get a peek inside there. No one would suspect that apartment of hiding anything of value. That's why El Guapo picked it, I suppose, when he had to change the hiding spot in a hurry. The owner's probably a relative of a loyal servant, something like that. But she looks tough. She intends to guard those crates as if they held gold, she said. They certainly felt as if they did when we lugged them up those three flights of stairs.''

Smokey became more jittery as we spoke, looking continually from side to side to make sure no one was near enough to hear him. "Are we going to try and break in?'' I could tell he was scared to death. "It'll be dangerous. Those Germans, I hear they're all scared of getting arrested. They're capable of anything. The Japanese, too.''

"Don't worry, Smokey.'' I wanted to calm him. "I'll find out what we can do, and see you tomorrow.''

Looking suspiciously from side to side, all he said was "*Si Dios quiere.*''

Chapter 12
SEPTEMBER

The next day I spoke to Mozart. "That's it. This is our chance," he said. "Now we need a description of each and every one of those paintings. We'll wait for them to hit the market and then we'll trace them back to our man." He slapped his fist into his hand. "We're so close I can taste it. Tell Smokey we'll get him those visas if he gets us a report of what's in those crates." Mozart's answer was firm. "Tell him, 'no work, no visas.' That's final." But when I spoke to Smokey, he was as stubborn as the day before. "I did say we could get into that apartment, but I still think it's too risky, Alin-ay," he said. "Don't you remember, I told you that I overheard the Japanese ambassador saying they would eliminate traitors? If they found me looking inside that crate! No, no, I can't do it. I have my children to think about."

"But we could do it together. And you could finally get those visas."

He was as scared of staying in Madrid as he was of breaking into that woman's apartment. "All right. We'll do it together. But we'll need more information first. Alin-ay, maybe you could find out more about the apartment and where that woman has stored the crates. We just left them at the door—she wouldn't let us inside. But it'll be easy. The woman's a dressmaker, named Doña Angelita, a widow who lives there with her son. I'll bet you could walk right in . . ."

We made a plan. I would go in and order a dress and study what I could of the layout of the apartment and the location of the crates. Smokey and his assistant would keep the apartment under surveillance to learn when its inhabitants were absent, so we could decide when it was safest to do our investigation.

By Tuesday, I had questioned several doormen on the street, asking for a dressmaker. When I got to the address Smokey had given me, as I expected, the *portero* recommended Doña Angelita and gave me her telephone number. Thus I had a credible excuse to contact the woman. I made an appointment by telephone, and the next day, with four meters of red silk and several fashion magazines under my arm, I trudged up the worn wooden steps to *tercero C.*

Doña Angelita didn't seem at all suspicious. Indeed, she was delighted to have a new client and could obviously use the extra *pesetas.* Her apartment had the disagreeable odor of fish fried in unrefined olive oil, however. The stench was particularly intense because the shutters were closed to keep out the hot September sun. I blocked it out and tried to get her to talk. She was pleasant enough, but no matter how I tried, she would only smile and hum to the drone on the battered radio next to her sewing table. All I learned was that her husband had been killed in 1939, the last year of the Spanish war, and that her son worked fourteen hours a day in a *pescaderia,* a fish market nearby. She was so short that she had to stand on a small orange crate to take my measurements.

I went back twice that week for fittings, during which time I discovered that the apartment comprised a kitchen, two small bedrooms, and the salon where she worked. There was only one entrance, no fire escape or back door. The crates from the Japanese legation were in a bedroom piled high with remnants of dresses long since worn out.

The week of investigation finished, Smokey and I met to plot our procedure.

"It's going to be difficult," he said. His constant admonitions were beginning to irritate me. "You'll have to be careful of the son. He's an idiot—literally. A real halfwit. And big. The people who work with him, even the *portero* of the building—they're all afraid of him."

"What do you mean, I'll have to be careful? You're the one who's going in there. I can tell you exactly where the crates are. They'll be easy to open. You'll finish the job in fifteen minutes."

"No, no. It's more logical that you do the inside job. A young girl could never hang around street corners keeping vigil. You know that. I'll keep watch on the old woman outside and Jose— that's the fellow who works for me now—will observe the son, so there'll be no way you can be surprised. I've been keeping track of the widow's comings and goings every day and night this past week. In the morning, she's out of the building about twenty minutes to do the shopping, and then again at night between eight-thirty and ten. That's the hour we should do the job. She goes to the *porteria* of the Villagonzalo Palace on the corner of San Mateo and sits in the doorway chatting with the *portera*. Jose, who's been following the son, says the kid never leaves the shop before ten. Sometimes the mother goes to the Plaza de Santa Barbara and sits on a bench there and talks to friends until her son finishes work. Don't worry, I'll be on the lookout every minute. Nothing can happen to you."

There seemed no way to make Smokey change his mind. And in a way, he was right. It would be easier for me to disguise myself than for him, since I'd been trained in it at the spy school in Washington. In fact, I began to get enthusiastic about the project: this would be exciting, and wait till Mozart found out what I'd accomplished. Smokey was right about the inconvenience of my being the lookout, too. Spaniards took any woman of any age who stood on the street alone for a prostitute.

When I agreed to take the inside job, I insisted on confirming the details personally. Smokey took me to the fish market on the corner of San Mateo and Fuencarral. Through the large open windows, it was easy to observe the activity inside the store. He pointed to a heavyset young fellow behind a wooden chopping block, who was preparing fish and wrapping them for customers.

"That's the guy," said Smokey.

I watched as the fellow took a good-sized *besugo* from the counter, threw it down on the block, grabbed a chopping cleaver, and slashed off the head. Then he picked up a long knife and scraped the scales, slit the fish down the middle and boned it with expert strokes. After that he took a newspaper from the floor and rolled the fish into it. He placed the head back on the counter for sale. There was nothing unusual about him, other than his size and the noise he made chopping, which was audible from where we were standing on the street.

I made one last visit to Doña Angelita for a fitting. When I arrived, the door of the apartment was open and Angelita was pedaling away on the ancient sewing machine. This last visit was to enable me to get one more wax imprint of a door key—to the room where the crates were located. We had no way of knowing if she

locked this door when she was out of the apartment. While Doña
Angelita went to the kitchen to get me a glass of water, I took the
imprint. Others had been taken on previous visits and the keys were
already in the making.

While fitting me, Doña Angelita said the dress would be finished
Friday. That was the day we had planned to carry out the operation.
Wanting to find out if she might change her hours if someone
requested, I asked if I could pick up the dress after ten o'clock
Friday night. She took the pins out of her mouth and put the scissors
on the table.

"There's a problem I haven't told the señorita about." She
sighed. "My son is a good boy, but he is retarded."

"Oh," I said. "I'm so sorry. That must be very difficult for you."

"No. I've become accustomed. And he's good company for me.
Other mothers lose their sons when they marry, and Manolo is all
I have. He's a good protector, too, for me and for our meager
belongings. And he's strong. Do you know, during our war the
military police—they didn't know he was retarded—came here to
find out why he hadn't enlisted. He attacked them with the kitchen
knife. Imagine! Three soldiers were unable to get the better of him.
My Manolo can fight like a bull. No mother could have a more loyal
son."

She picked up the scissors again. "Well," she went on, "it's better
you come at another hour—when Manolo is not here. You see he
wouldn't understand and might harm you. No one can enter this
apartment when he's home and it's better like that. I know I'll
always be safe with my Manolo around."

I asked her what hour was the latest I could come or send someone. "Oh, as long as it's before eight o'clock, I'll still be here and
Manolo will be working."

I felt relieved. Everything she had said confirmed Smokey's findings.

My disguise was ready. It had to be perfect. Doña Angelita was
bound to realize that someone had opened the crates and if anyone
in the building recognized me from my other visits, I could blow
the cover of all our group. I stood in front of my bathroom mirror
to test the effect. I tucked my hair up under the gray wig concocted
for me by the costume designer of the Teatro Maria Guerrero. I
was already changed. Now with a gray eyebrow liner I marked
wrinkles across my forehead. I grimaced and marked two long lines

in the creases down both sides of my face. My hands molded enough wax to make one long big lump and I shoved it under my upper lip. A thick coat of pale powder and little steel-rimmed eyeglasses provided the final touch. I looked at myself, astounded. And delighted. Not even Top Hat would recognize me, of that I was certain.

In normal guise, I met Smokey on the corner of Calle Goya and Serrano and we walked side by side for the space of one block while checking last minute details. When I left him on the corner of Serrano to return to the office, I said, "Everything's going to work out fine."

His sharp black eyes glanced at me, not the least shadow of a smile showing. "*Si Dios quiere,*" was his reply.

But when Friday rolled around, the last key was not yet finished and we were obliged to postpone the operation one day. Picking the lock would have been possible—my training had included such things—but it was always a convenience to have the real thing. Smokey insisted that Saturday would be just as convenient, there would still be an hour and a half—much more time than we needed.

On Saturday, in Angustias' faded black cotton skirt and shabby print shirt, my face transformed, and carrying a beat-up handbag containing keys, knife, pliers, crowbar, hammer, and my Beretta, I sneaked out of my building. Walking to the Calle Almagro, I took a taxi, first directing the driver to the corner of San Mateo and the Plaza Santa Barbara to check that Smokey was at his post. I was relieved to see him seated on a bench reading a newspaper. Then I asked the man to go to the Calle Fuencarral; I wanted to check that Jose was on guard in front of the fish market. When he saw me, he gave a nod. Things were going exactly as planned.

Until I reached Doña Angelita's building. The *portero* and his wife were still sitting in front of the door enjoying the light breeze of the dusk hours. I had a key to the door and had hoped they would be inside. Although I wasn't worried that they would recognize me—when I looked in the mirror, I didn't recognize myself—I was concerned that they might question me, this unknown someone entering the building. So it seemed safer to wait until they left. I ordered the taxi to take a couple of turns around the Plaza and up the Calle Fuencarral again, but each time we passed Doña Angelita's address, the *porteros* were still there. Finally I got out of the taxi a few blocks away and walked slowly back. This time the wife was gone, but the husband remained happily smoking a cigarette, his chair tipped against the side of the brick building. There was no choice. It was almost nine o'clock. Bent and frail, in Angustias' worn black shoes, I plodded up to the door and decided to brave it. The *portero* obviously didn't consider the weak old woman a danger for the building's inhabitants. I entered with no difficulty and started to climb the steps.

So far, except for the delay, things were going pretty well. After all, Mozart only wanted a description of the paintings. The crates had already been opened once and so were probably secured by only a few nails, for which I had adequate implements in Angustias' old shopping bag. Entering someone's home and going through their belongings was a job I hated. But I soothed my conscience with the thought that the whole operation was for a just cause.

As I reached the landing of the second floor, three people emerged from one of the apartments, but they paid scant attention to me. When I arrived at Doña Angelita's door, I looked at my watch. Twenty-three precious minutes had gone by from the time my taxi had first passed by the door. I would have to hurry. Luckily, no one was in the hallway and I was able to insert the key and enter the dark apartment unobserved.

The moment I closed the door, a drawn-out hiss made me cringe. Then, just in front of me, a shadow skittered across the floor of the dark room. I stifled a scream as my hand stumbled along the wall looking for the switch. I had foreseen every detail except my nervousness. More seconds were lost trying to find the switch. When I did, Angelita's gray and white striped cat was perched in a pouncing position on the back of the tattered sofa. I'd thought the shadow was a rat. I breathed more easily.

My seamstress was not a tidy housekeeper; scraps of material were scattered over the floor, two fat *cucarachas* scurried from the cat's plate of milk on the window sill. And, conveniently for me, all the doors were ajar, including that of the bedroom, so I wouldn't have to use the key that had taken an extra day to make, after all.

It was now seven minutes before nine. Without wasting more time, I hastened into the dark bedroom where the crates were located. It was hot and stuffy. Again I had to turn on a light—the closed shutters provided only a silvery gleam. In my haste to find the lamp, I knocked it to the floor. Then when I turned the switch, the bulb did not light. Another five minutes were lost going around the apartment looking for another and swapping bulbs. My neck was damp, my arms, too. Angustias' old clothes were getting warmer by the minute, but I didn't remove the worn shopping bag concealing my working utensils from my shoulder. I wasn't going to take a chance of leaving something there. Smokey and I wanted to be able to return another time, if anything went wrong tonight.

Once the new bulb was working, I could study the first crate. The large knotted cord did not look as if it would present difficulties, but three nails would have to be removed, so I took a screwdriver from my sack and began to loosen one. That did not work, so I took out a hammer to press the top loose. This was going to take more time than we had calculated, especially if I didn't want to leave any telltale signs. I dug into my shoulder bag again for a larger hammer, which I realized would loosen the nail quickly. When I glanced at my watch the next time, I saw to my horror that it was already ten after nine.

Footsteps echoed in the hallway. I waited, my heart racing until the sounds continued past the door and faded away down the hall. Now I began to work on the second nail. This one went faster, but I realized the noise of the hammer blows were resounding through the flimsy walls out into the hallway. Nevertheless, I had no choice. I had to finish the job quickly. In desperation, I banged away.

When I started on the third nail I sighed with relief. Only a minute more and I would be able to undo the cord and lift out the first painting. A pad and pencil was also in my work sack for the descriptions. I looked at my wristwatch again. Eleven minutes left. Recklessly, I struck with the hammer. Just as I was about to pull the last nail out, I became aware of a strong new whiff of . . . fish.

At first I thought a breeze had wafted the odor in from the kitchen. Then I realized the stench was too strong for that. My heart pounded. Before I saw him I knew he was there—in the apartment—a few steps from me.

My eyes flashed to the doorway. Doña Angelita's huge son was standing in the middle of the adjoining room like a statue, frozen and stiff, staring at me with the gaze of an idiot, an expression of malice on the puffed ugly face. My intestines involuntarily cringed into a hard knot.

We observed each other for a moment. Through my mind raced images of the fellow chopping the fish head, the huge powerful hands holding the long blade. Terror numbed me. I knew I was in mortal danger. The only window was closed with heavy wooden shutters. Even if I could have opened them, it was a three-story drop to the ground. There was no other way out of the room. The bag of utensils was hanging from my shoulder, the hammer was still in my hand. But my Beretta automatic was at the bottom of my work sack. To my dismay, I sensed that any gesture would trigger the man to attack me and I realized I would never reach the pistol in time anyway.

Regretfully, I remembered Mozart's unheeded advice—"Keep your gun where you can put a hand on it in a split second."

Where was Smokey? What had happened? I pulled a smile and realized too late that the brute was seeing the grimace of an old witch. The fellow's expression hardened. Without taking his eyes off me, he grabbed the scissors from the sewing machine table.

Then the brute took a step forward. He was blocking the door and glaring at me. The fingers of his right hand slid caressingly over the huge scissors—the blades gleamed in the light of the overhanging bulb.

If I wanted to save my life, I had to do something immediately. Would I still be able to execute those swift kicks to the groin I had been taught in the training school? Remembering Doña Angelita's remark about the military police not being able to control her powerful son helped me make up my mind.

Now his countenance carried a menacing grin, as he clenched the weapon in his hand. I could see he was planning to plunge it into me. I thought of the iron hammer which was still in my own hand, but knew I could neither hit him with it nor throw it effectively enough.

My salvation might be a judo thrust, but it had to work the first time. I knew it would be my only chance.

I crouched and took one step toward him. The brute leaned clumsily toward me with the scissors poised for action. He smirked. It took only a split second to realize why. He was facing a weak old woman. With all my force, I thrust my leg into the air—straight for his groin. Just at that moment he stepped back and I missed my mark, but the scissors fell to the floor. I moved forward and with my other leg lashed out in one elastic motion, my body twisting and gyrating to add power. He was so close that the smell of fish mingling with his heavy sharp sweat would have made me sick if I hadn't been risking my life at that moment. My staccato blow aimed for the mark.

Startled, his face went soft. An expression of amazement, almost fear, crossed his eyes as my leg swung. My gesture surprised him and put him off-balance. With the dogged determination of a fogged brain, he lunged at me, all his body's fierce strength behind the thrust, but his gesture was a hair's breadth too late. Perhaps my assailant was easier to catch than the professionals in the spy school. Whatever—my slicing kick reached its mark. The gigantic fellow fell to his knees, doubled over onto his forehead, slamming into the floor, roaring in pain.

In one second I skirted his agonized body and darted out the door into the hallway. I raced past a man on the second floor landing who must have been amazed to see how fast old women could run these days. On the street level at the big entrance portal, I pulled the lever which released the door and slipped out into the night. Until I saw a taxi, I didn't stop running. Thanks to my spy school training, I was still alive.

Then I wondered about Smokey and Jose. Neither had been outside the building. Obviously, something had happened to them. When my maid, Angustias, opened the door of my apartment, she realized things had not gone well. "Oh, señorita, you look so upset. Don't worry. After you take off that horrible wig and those dirty clothes, things will not look so bad."

Two hours later, Smokey appeared, sweating and harried. He explained that when Jose had seen Manolo preparing to leave the fish market earlier than usual, Jose had rushed to him to ask what they could do. Both decided to block the fellow's return by accosting him in the street. When they did, a terrible fight ensued and two policemen appeared. Instead of taking Manolo to the *comisario,* they had taken Smokey and Jose.

When we had discussed the events in detail, Smokey and I decided that since the boxes were unopened and still tied with the cord, and only a couple of nails had been loosened, we could repeat the process, this time with more hope of success. From what Doña Angelita had told me about her son, I doubted she would believe his story that an old woman had been trying to open the crates. She would probably take for granted that he had done it himself. We settled on the following Tuesday, by which time I could have ordered another dress. A Monday visit with Doña Angelita would enable me to ascertain whether the boxes were still there and whether Doña Angelita had become suspicious. A flashlight would be added to my equipment and I would keep my gun handy in my jacket pocket this time. I suggested Smokey improve protection by hiring two more assistants, fully capable of controlling Manolo if anything went wrong. When we parted, with all plans arranged, he started to open his mouth. Hastily, I stopped him.

"Don't say it, Smokey. This time God will wish it."

It was with a certain feeling of relief and expectation that I went to sleep that night. I knew that Tuesday we'd do the job right.

Chapter 13

All day Sunday I deliberated whether or not to tell Mozart about our foiled plans and finally decided only to tell him that everything was arranged to investigate the crates on Tuesday.

Juanito came back to Madrid and I saw him fight in the Madrid bullring Sunday afternoon. He had a good fight, and that evening we dined together in the garden of the Hotel Ritz, then went across the plaza to El Coto, another garden restaurant, to dance. The September night air was warmer than August, but very dry, not uncomfortable. Domingo, the maître d', brought us a bottle of champagne he had just received from France, in token of his admiration for the great matador's *faena* that afternoon. Juanito had just come from San Sebastian and was pleased to tell me that he had often seen Luis and Casilda there in the Bar Basque. His reference to Luis depressed me. I still thought of him almost every day and hated myself for being such a fool. I knew our romance was just a beautiful dream that could never come true. Fortunately, the excitement of planning to sneak into Doña Angelita's apartment again in two days' time helped me not to dwell on Luis. Just looking forward to presenting Mozart with a description of the paintings cheered me up.

Monday morning, however, when I arrived in the code room, Jeff was waiting at the door. His face was pale. "Mozart wants to see everybody."

As we filed in, we knew a change was about to take place. Mozart didn't beat around the bush.

"I have disagreeable news," he began. Phillip Harris stood facing us, his shoulders slumped. Even his voice sounded disheart-ened.

"Everybody must be out of this country before the end of the week," he went on. "OSS employees' passports are no longer valid for Spain." Although he struggled against showing emotion, we could see he was deeply affected. "The future of the OSS is now being decided in Washington. Articles have appeared in the press criticizing our operations and the money used for espionage. Now that the war is over, President Truman is not convinced that foreign intelligence is necessary."

We were standing, but we had no time to get tired because the discourse lasted only a few minutes. "You've all done great work and maybe one day your country will know of the sacrifices you have made. And I thank each one of you. I, for one, am proud of you. Any problems of a personal nature can be discussed with me individually." With a nod, he indicated the meeting was over. In silence, we filed out.

An atmosphere of gloom descended like a thunderstorm. We knew there was much work still to be done. Not only my Safehaven mission, but other missions some colleagues were already em-barked upon, involving Soviet agents spreading anti-American propaganda and in uncovering Soviet plans to control the middle European countries. All this would now have to be dropped.

I wasn't able to talk to Mozart alone that day. He was taken up with conferences with the ambassador and calls to Washington. But the next morning when I entered the office, I asked if I could see him. He received me immediately.

"Smokey and I have everything ready to investigate those crates tonight at eight-thirty: the men, my equipment, my disguise—ev-erything. We've been working on this for two weeks and we feel certain of success. May we go ahead?"

He shook his head. "Sorry, Aline." He seldom called me by my first name. "It's useless. You must prepare to leave the country. I have received strict orders to terminate all chains, all agents' work, and all espionage."

"But tonight we can get those descriptions which will help un-cover El Guapo—the culmination of all our work for the past eight months."

He shook his head. "I know, it hurts." He raised his huge hands in the air in despair. "But what can I do? I am obliged to order you not to continue. Operation Safehaven is over for us."

I returned to my office, depressed and incredulous. The telephone rang. It was Edmundo. "I have to see you. I'm meeting Agata for lunch and want to talk to you beforehand."

Edmundo was obviously despondent as he walked into my living room an hour later.

"What a day," I said. "I'm in shock. Everybody in the office looks gloomy. And now you, too. And we thought we would be so happy when the war was over."

"I'm desperate." He sat down with his hands on his head, elbows on his knees, in an attitude of total dejection. "I want to marry Renata and I cannot do so while working for the U.S. government, because she has not been cleared of my accusations that she was a German agent. That's ironical, no?"

"Your stories were too good, Edmundo. You made her out to be such a valuable enemy agent—controlled by you."

"Well, I've decided to resign tomorrow. I cannot leave here without her, or I may never see her again."

"But you lose so much, your extra pay, your return expenses," I answered.

"My mind is made up. Will you come to the wedding?"

"Of course, but this all sounds so hasty. I didn't know you were in love with Renata. You certainly hide your feelings well."

"I don't know that I am. But I want to marry her and so I will, despite the U.S. government."

Edmundo was still an enigma to me. He was delighted to have a German princess as his bride, despite the fact that her family had lost their enormous fortune in the war. Their properties were in East Germany, now occupied by the Russians. He had pretended to be interested only in getting himself a title and in wealthy women, but he was not the frivolous snobbish man he feigned to be.

I, too, was despondent about leaving Spain—the warm people, my fascinating work—and Luis. And even more, my aborted mission made me feel I had failed.

Chapter 14

The following Friday was one of those typical September scorchers, like sitting in a dry airless oven. The cafes on the Castellana had been busy all day and on into the evening. But as I hurried toward my house, it was getting dark and a sudden refreshing breeze wafted down over the city from the Guadarrama mountains. When I turned into the Calle Monte Esquinza, the *serreno* was already on his rounds and rushed to accompany me to unlock the door of my building. Others down the street were clapping their hands for his attention, but he hastened to find my key from the mass hanging on a string at his waist, although we both knew I was skinny enough to slide through the iron grating which served as a door. I waited for him to turn the lock, gave him his tip, and then ran up the marble steps to my second floor apartment.

When I opened the door, I was surprised to find Angustias standing there. Her worried expression warned me that something was up. "Señorita, a man has been waiting for quite a while." She pointed a finger toward the salon. "He refused to give his name."

Instinctively, my hand gripped the bag where my Beretta rested and I entered the small room with caution, remembering Jeff's experience. The man in front of me was the last person I expected to see. For almost a year, the only news I had had was his code name at the beginning or end of a top secret cable. I remembered the year before, in Washington, when he had told me I had passed my spy training with flying colors and that my destination would be Spain. That had been a disappointment. I'd been hoping to be dropped in a parachute behind enemy lines in France. Spain was not what I had wanted at all—a neutral country far removed from the real excitement. How wrong I had been!

Now the Washington chief of secret intelligence for the Iberian Peninsula was standing in the middle of my small living room, grinning broadly, probably at my expression of astonishment.

John Derby, code-named Jupiter, looked the same, impeccably dressed in a classic gray herringbone suit, white shirt and muted tie, thinning gray hair, rosy complexion, confident blue eyes. I was relieved. "I can't believe that you're really here," I said. "What are you doing in Madrid?"

"My main purpose is to see you. Come, let's sit down and talk. I don't have much time."

Although I offered him a drink, he refused and we sat down facing each other on the green chintz sofa. Casually he leaned over and took a red carnation from the bowl on the table, but instead of placing it in my hair as Pierre had done one unforgettable night over a year ago, he slowly peeled off the green petals underneath, broke the stem and placed it in his lapel. Pierre had been a colleague at the spy school in Washington, handsome, European in birth and manners, and an important OSS agent in southern France during 1944. He had made several visits to Madrid during that time, and my infatuation for him had almost led to my getting killed. Derby continued to pat the carnation flat against his lapel, and only when it was properly in place did he begin to talk in his slow deliberate manner.

"Everyone in Washington sends their regards, as well as some friends in France, where I've just been. Whiskey and Magic are hoping to meet you in Paris soon." That was good news. Magic had been such a short time in Madrid. And I'd had no news whatsoever of Whiskey, the head instructor when I'd been at "The Farm," our training school. Jupiter stood up, and went to the window which looked out onto the Calle Monte Esquinza, now in blackness except for the pale gaslight from the streetlamps.

When he turned around, his expression was more serious. "It's important I speak to you before you are shipped back to the U.S. with the others."

Angustias appeared at that moment. I asked her to bring us some water. I was thirsty, more from the emotional shock of John Derby's unexpected appearance than from the heat of the day.

"Are you pleased to have received word of returning to Washington?" John Derby asked as he lit a cigarette.

"Not at all," I answered, as matter-of-factly as possible.

"That's fortunate, because the purpose of my visit is to tell you that you are the only member of the secret intelligence section of OSS in Madrid to be kept on."

My relief was so great that we both began to laugh. The prospect of leaving Spain and having to look for another job—anything would seem humdrum in comparison to what I'd been doing—had chilled me every time I thought about it. Which was most of the time. Until now I hadn't dwelled upon the enormous differences that had been wrought in my life. It had been a considerable leap from a typical small-town existence and four years in a Catholic college to the luxurious life I had been leading in Madrid, not to mention the danger, the excitement, and an expense account which included dresses from Balenciaga.

Derby was still grinning as he continued to explain. "OSS is being disbanded, but a small organization for the collection of intelligence is being created to preserve a nucleus of trained espionage professionals." He flicked his ashes into a bowl. "Intrepid and Bill Donovan himself are the driving forces behind this endeavor and . . ." The pale blue eyes stared. "You're one of the lucky ones to be included."

His news was too good to be true. I tried to figure out why I'd been chosen. I wondered if Whitney Shepardson, chief of secret intelligence worldwide, was among the new group, too. He'd sent a cable only yesterday, which I had decoded, thanking the entire OSS staff for our good work. But the only cable of congratulations to an individual in Spain was the one he had sent to me. That, I felt, would remain my own private medal, registered in the archives in Washington, if anyone ever looked that far. Or, maybe Mozart, despite his severe attitude, had recommended me. Perhaps for getting out of jail on my own in Malaga. Or for breaking into Prince Lilienthal's safe that weekend to search for German documents. To me it seemed that my worthiest achievement had been contributing to the Allied deception of the invasion in southern France. But even then I had been unaware, really, of what I had been doing. What had I done to deserve this?

But John Derby continued to talk and I dared not ask him questions. What if he changed his mind? "You will have to convince Mr. Culbertson, who is acting ambassador at present, to allow you to remain in Spain," he was saying. "You will have to prove that you have a bona fide job in this country. And you must convince him that you won't be doing espionage in the future. You may or may not be able to do this. But your job with us depends upon your ability to be persuasive."

I chuckled. "You mean, my ability to lie."

Jupiter winked. "Well, after working in this business for almost two years, I take it for granted that you've mastered that." His voice became more serious. "We now have a good group of professionals and General Donovan doesn't intend to lose them. At the moment, the State Department wants to control us, but Donovan and the rest of our group believes that intelligence should be a separate entity, so it can operate with total secrecy."

He proceeded to give me an address in New York where I was to cable for a job; a reply would arrive promptly, providing valid proof that I had one. Jupiter added that if I was able to get permission from the embassy to stay, I would then receive explanations of how to proceed. We settled upon a private code for use in the future—one which could be sent by letter or cable using normal prose.

"If everything turns out as we hope, you will be in an elite group, Tiger. Congratulations." He stood up, and before either of us had touched the water on the table, said he regretted his time was short, wished me luck, and left.

Forty-eight hours later, I received the telegram and experienced my first surprise when I saw that it was signed John J. Derby & Sons. So Jupiter was still my boss! It was just like him to keep even that a secret. Immediately, I requested an interview with our acting ambassador.

Mr. Culbertson was charming but suspicious and asked if I would swear on a Bible that I would not be doing espionage. I heard myself swear serenely, as I prayed I would be forgiven for such deceit.

Chapter 15
OCTOBER

Everything went as planned. Within four days, I became an employee of Derby & Sons and opened a branch office to renew sales of cotton fiber, which had been paralyzed since before the Spanish Civil War. I located an office at number eleven Calle Marqués de Riscal and began contacts with Segarra & Company and other manufacturers of cotton cloth in Barcelona.

As was customary in my work, no one informed me of extraneous information. I didn't know which part of the government my espionage activities were listed under nor what our organization was now called. My salary started to come in from John J. Derby & Sons instead of the American Oil Mission. To all appearances, I was now the employee of a private firm with no connection to intelligence.

These activities took place while my colleagues were preparing to leave for Washington. Chains were dismantled, agents paid off. The Germans were also scattering. Hans Lazaar had left on a boat for Rio, disguised as a Franciscan monk. Gestapo agents paid huge sums for passage on merchant ships leaving Malaga and Lisbon for Buenos Aires and Colombia. Inside of a few weeks, practically all the intelligence agents from both sides of the war had abandoned the country.

Top Hat and Renata's wedding was small, and I was one of the witnesses. To my amazement, they behaved like young newlyweds and left for Mexico in a state of elation. Edmundo's apparent indifference about having been obliged to resign from OSS made me wonder if he had been kept on to spy in some other part of the world. If that was the case, he didn't give me an inkling. It was sad, also, saying good-bye to Jeff Walters and to the others, especially

Mozart, strangely enough. Within weeks, I was the only member of the Secret Intelligence Department of the OSS left in Spain.

Now I had to make my new cover appear realistic to the Spaniards and American embassy officials. Having been obliged to abandon the plans to investigate the crates in Doña Angelita's apartment was a big disappointment, and unfortunately for Smokey, his visa had never been issued, due to the haste of disbanding Spain's OSS. Although I had cabled Jupiter about this, he replied that approaching the consulate now would endanger the new cover and would not produce positive results for Smokey anyway. Authorities in Washington were refusing to fulfill commitments made by OSS. But he promised to look into it for me.

I missed Top Hat. I missed the danger and suspense of those last months of the war. I was still frustrated about leaving Operation Safehaven, but I knew the work I was now doing would provide security for me and for other agents in the future. I hired the head of my women's chain as my secretary, opened bank accounts, and traveled to the beautiful port city of Barcelona to obtain orders for cotton fiber from textile manufacturers. Two months passed, uneventfully, although I had never worked harder in my life.

Then, just when I was becoming accustomed not to think about him, Luis Quintanilla called to invite me to dine. Casilda was in Portugal. There seemed no reason not to accept his invitation.

That first evening we were alone at Jockey, a new restaurant, cozy and elegant, with thick green carpeting, wood paneling, and a more modern atmosphere than other restaurants in Madrid. During dinner, Luis' cool green gaze flickering in the candlelight worked its magic all over again. Afterward we went to our favorite night club, La Reboite. The night was loaded with enchantment. And when we danced, the touch of his arm around me, his body next to mine put me in a spell like before. Just being with him was an intense pleasure. When he left me at my door at three in the morning, I climbed the steps to my apartment in a daze. The next day, I was jittery each time the phone rang and absolutely desolate when night arrived and I had not heard from him. He didn't call until two long days later. Then he asked me to go to the golf club and the agony ended. Suddenly, it seemed that no one could be so happy, so lucky as I.

It was a clear, cool day, one that reminded me of our first trips to the golf course so many months before. I watched the rolling hills of green retama bushes, the clumps of umbrella pines glide by

my window, and realized that I had never expected to find myself
again in this car, tracing this familiar path.

"You seem lost in thought," Luis said.

"I was thinking of how much has happened since we last rode to
Puerta de Hierro together," I said. "The war's ended . . ." Of
course there were many changes I couldn't mention to Luis: the
dissolving of OSS, which had scattered my colleagues in all directions. And I would have liked to ask him how he felt about Casilda
these days. Instead, I said, "I feel older now."

Luis looked at me with amusement. "And what does feeling
older feel like?" he asked.

"I realize that things can change," I went on. "So much of the
time one spends planning and worrying about the future turns out
to be useless. I'm not going to do that anymore."

Luis was driving more slowly now, glancing at me with interest.
"You're perfectly right. I've gone through some changes too." His
expression became less carefree. He didn't speak for a moment, and
then said in a lighter tone, "So from now on you'll live for the
moment?"

I laughed. "Who knows? Yes, on second thought, perhaps I will.
This moment, for example, is a nice one."

Luis smiled at me and turned back to the road. "We agree on
that. I'm ready to live for many more moments like this."

We embarked on two wild weeks of joy—meeting each morning
for golf, then dinner every evening. Casilda remained out of the
country and neither of us spoke about her. We no longer disguised
our feelings. He never asked anyone else to dine with us and the
hours alone flew by. Often when I went to play golf in the morning,
I had slept no more than five hours, yet I felt wonderful. I had lost
my head over a man who, of course, would not marry an unknown
foreigner, but I was too enraptured to care.

A few days later, seated in a cozy corner of the Pulpito restaurant
in the Plaza Mayor, he took my hand and told me he had broken
up with Casilda.

"One day I'll tell you why I did that." His voice was caressing.

"You don't have to tell me." I wanted to tell him that nothing
could make me stop seeing him now, not even Casilda, who I still
considered my best friend. I wanted to tell him he was the only
thing I thought of night and day.

"First," he answered, "I want you to meet my father and my

stepmother. Next week I'd like you to go to a dinner they are giving." When he left me at my door that night, he kissed me. But we jumped apart when we heard the *serreno*'s stick banging the cement sidewalk.

"I hope we won't have to put up with this much longer," he said. "I'll be in Toledo for two days, so we can't have dinner until Thursday night. I must speak to my grandfather who is spending this week at his *finca* there."

As I fell asleep, I wondered exactly what he had meant. I dared not let myself think he might be referring to marriage.

The next morning, as I walked in the door, my secretary handed me a cable. I could tell by her expression that something significant had happened. It was from the New York office of Derby & Sons. As I read it, I felt I was receiving my death sentence.

CLOSE MADRID OFFICE IMMEDIATELY STOP PROCEED TO PARIS STOP ROOM RESERVED AT HOTEL ST. REGIS STOP NEW OFFICE IS IN THE HOTEL PLAZA ATHÉNÉE STOP OUR PARIS REPRESENTATIVE IS AWAITING YOU WITH INSTRUCTIONS THERE. REGARDS JOHN DERBY.

I sat down without saying a word. How could I leave immediately? What would I say to Luis? How would he understand that I had to follow orders? That espionage was not like other jobs. But I knew I could never explain. Rule number one: never blow your cover!

By the time Luis returned, I had done the necessary—advising clients and agents that we were terminating our work in Spain, dismantling chains, paying off sub-agents. I decided to keep my apartment and my two maids, since those expenses were minimal and keeping a home in Madrid gave me the feeling that I would return . . . somehow . . . sometime. I wired Derby that I would be in Paris the following week.

I knew the minute Luis arrived in Madrid, because what appeared to be a truckful of flowers was delivered to my apartment. Angustias was already packing my things when they arrived. A short time later, he called.

"When can I see you? How about lunch?"

I was obliged to tell him that dinner was the soonest I could make it. I couldn't explain that I still had a few agents to pay off. His voice became formal and I found it difficult to explain further. I dared not tell him on the phone that I would be leaving in only two days, so I put the disagreeable task off until the evening.

When he picked me up that night, as usual, he grabbed my hand and pressed it as soon as I got into his car. I was uncomfortable and he noticed.

"Look, Aline, tell me, what's up? Even your voice on the phone was different this morning."

"I have to go to Paris two days from now. It's a new job—opening another office there for my company."

His glance was distraught. "For how long?"

"I have no idea." Although I felt like crying, I tried to make my voice sound normal.

"That's impossible," he said. "I thought you liked Madrid—Spain."

"I love Madrid, Luis. But I'm a working girl and there's no way I can avoid fulfilling my obligations to the company I work for." Then I told him that I was keeping my apartment and asked him not to make things more difficult for me, because I was absolutely miserable.

"If you were so miserable, you wouldn't leave," he said, his voice now cold. I realized that he could not understand what it was like to be part of a world where people were not free to live according to their whims. What could I say, I wondered? There was still nothing binding between us and there was no way I could ask him to marry me—that was his role.

Luis said he would try to go to Paris to see me, but explained that it would be difficult. Spaniards had problems getting exit permits. Officially, they were not allowed to have money outside the country, and an exit permit necessitated an explanation of how their expenses would be paid. Yet something made me feel that he would find a way. It was a sad evening. I was aware that my leaving made him think that I didn't care, and I was clumsy about telling him that I did. Not only was I heartbroken to leave Luis and his beautiful country, but I hated to leave without having uncovered the yellow dog painting and the man who controlled the looted Nazi assets. The new intelligence group might have decided to abandon Operation Safehaven. But I had not!

Chapter 16
MADRID, APRIL 1947

Although I consistently tried to return, I didn't get back to Madrid until over a year later. The first two months were miserable. Despite the beauty of Paris, which I was seeing for the first time, I was homesick for Luis and for Spain. Telephone calls were difficult. Luis called me every few days, but the static was so great we couldn't understand each other. At least his calls made me aware that he missed me and was trying to get an exit permit to come to Paris to see me. When I called him, I sometimes had to wait for hours to get through, only to have the communication cut just as we began to speak. Finally, we resorted to letters, which, although slow, made it possible for us to communicate. Luis' letters were not long, nor did he say he was in love with me, but he explained the difficulties he was having trying to get an exit visa. I realized he was as desperate to see me as I was him.

Then one day, exactly three months after I had arrived, a telegram came, in which he asked me to dine with him in Paris the following Tuesday. After waiting all day, I finally got him on the phone in Madrid and told him I was delirious with joy and looking forward to Tuesday. Before the static became too loud, he managed to tell me that his father would be with him and would have dinner with us that night as well. Although I would have liked to have dinner with him alone, I realized that having dinner with Luis and his father was a good sign. Things were going to be all right, after all.

Meanwhile my work in Paris was time-consuming—consisting of helping to set up a cover organization for our new espionage group, under the name of Worldwide Trade, Inc., an international import-export company. I also had to meet authentic French business people, as well as influential social figures. The latter had been made easier through the many letters Luis and other friends in Madrid had given me. As Tuesday drew near, I became more excited. I rushed the completion of an expensive new dress I had ordered at Balenciaga and thought of little else except seeing Luis again. He and his father would pick me up at the Hotel St. Regis, where I lived, and we were dining at Le Grand Vefour that night.

Tuesday morning, however, when I arrived at our offices in the newly restored Hotel Plaza Athénée, I found that Jupiter had done it to me again. My colleague handed me a ticket on the night express to Zurich for that same night, explaining that urgent orders had come from the States. A meeting had already been set up for me with an agent from Eastern Europe on his way through Zurich the following day. Jupiter had said I should take all my luggage. I would probably have to stay there to open a branch office.

The shock was devastating and became more so during the day, as I realized that Luis and his father were already on a train halfway to Paris, and I had no way of letting him know of the change in my plans. Since I had no idea where they were staying, I left a letter at my hotel explaining the situation as best I could. Luis, I knew, would have a hard time understanding why I could not put off a trip to Zurich for at least one day. And I worried that he had convinced his father to come mainly to dine with me.

As my train puffed out of the station at seven-thirty that evening, I realized that Luis was already someplace in Paris, and I had no way of knowing if he would get my letter. After a sleepless night, I arrived in Zurich and went to the Hotel Baur-au-lac where Jupiter had made my reservation. In my letter, I had asked Luis to leave a message for me where I could call him, and I hoped that I would find a telegram on arrival. There was nothing. Nor was there any word from him until several weeks later, when I reached him on the phone in Madrid.

His voice was cold, his words formal. "It's obvious to me now, Aline, that I will never understand you," he said. "And I would like to add that it was most embarrassing for me to have you stand up my father as well. He'd made a great effort to accompany me on the trip."

Nothing I could say changed his attitude. He'd never received the letter I left, and he was bitter. When he hung up, I knew I would not hear from him again. I wrote long letters, but had no reply.

Fortunately, in Switzerland, my work kept me very busy, and I consoled myself with the thought that one day soon I would get a vacation and be able to return to Madrid. Jupiter was encouraging about that, but the replacement agent that would make a vacation possible did not arrive for a long time—not until April of the next year. I had not seen Luis in many months.

An ancient war-torn train took me from Zurich to Paris, where I changed for another to the Spanish frontier. Because of the difference in the width of railroad tracks, French trains could not enter Spain, a precaution to make invasion more difficult. Everyone plodded over the bridge, tired from the journey and eager to reach Irún, where I would catch the night express to Madrid. Halfway across, I stopped and leaned over the railing, gazing down into the water. For a few moments I thought about all the critical meetings which had been held in this spot over the centuries between French and Spanish kings and representatives, of the meeting only a few years ago between Hitler and Franco, when, fortunately for the Allies, Franco had managed to avoid joining the Axis forces.

It was nearly dusk. Below, a small motorboat chugged by; several fishermen were busy casting their lines at different points along the banks. I wondered what awaited me in Madrid. I only knew I had to go, like a homing pigeon. What would it seem like to be in Spain on vacation? No paintings to look for, no need for a revolver, no secrets to be unraveled. I laughed to myself. Secrets! Just to find out where Luis was and who he spent his time with would be work enough in the beginning. Maybe he wouldn't want to see me after so much time and our failed meeting in Paris. And how would I feel when I saw him again? Was I really as in love with him as I'd been imagining myself to be? I remembered my mother's last letter, telling me about two more friends' weddings and reminding me that I would soon be twenty-four, an age when a girl should be thinking about marriage instead of a career. I wondered about Smokey, I wondered if there would be a good bullfight in the Madrid arena on Sunday. But most of all I wondered about Luis. And I was happier than I had been in a long time.

When I awoke in my old-fashioned *wagon-lit* sleeping compartment the next morning, I knew the luxuriant green of the Basque country would be far behind. Quickly I rose to my knees on top of the bed, separated the wine-colored plush drapes and the lace window curtains, and raised the shade. We were just pulling into the small station of El Escorial. Passengers were descending and others were boarding. Packages were being lifted onto the train, mail sacks thrown up to the conductor. The whistle blew forlornly two or three times and we slowly crept out of the station. I stayed glued to the window. The four towers of the monastery Phillip the Second had built rose over the little village like an upside-down parasol. My heart beat faster. Madrid was now only one hour away.

The train clicked along, swaying pleasantly through a world of rugged gigantic rock formations, pine forests, and multicolored open fields. I took a deep breath as I looked out at the austere beauty of sun-drenched Castile. Everything I saw reminded me of Luis. Never had the Spanish countryside looked more appealing, the little whitewashed houses with their worn rust-colored tile roofs, the austere lemon-toned stone walls of the ancient buildings. Sometimes a barren field was broken by stretches of undulating fields of waving green wheat. Under clumps of live oak trees, cows and donkeys shared the meager shade. Earth, red as brick, moved by my window, to give way to pearl-gray expanses, then dark brown turf with stripes of bright orange. The view from a distance looked like a mosaic whose design and color had been invented to please my eye alone.

The magical country seduced me. I was in love with Spain. Would I still be in love with Luis when I saw him? One fear gnawed at my happiness. Would he be engaged to Casilda or to someone else? I knew he hadn't married, because friends' letters would have mentioned that. Would he still be too annoyed with me to want to see me? He had never answered my letters and the last time I'd heard his voice was when I'd called him from Zurich months ago.

When the train pulled into the Estacion del Norte in Madrid, Angustias and Cecilia were there waiting. They ran along the *anden*, following the train as it slowed down, waving and shouting. I leaned out the window and called to them. I was home and I never wanted to leave again.

When I arrived in my apartment, huge red roses, forsythia, calla lilies, narcissis, and tuberoses—all the flowers of Madrid's month of April—filled my small salon, the little room I'd fixed up as a bar, and my bedroom. Angustias didn't have to tell me. Luis had sent

them. She admitted to having telephoned the Count about my
arrival because he had called repeatedly asking for news of me. If
I'd only known! Unfortunately, Angustias couldn't write.

Before I'd even opened my suitcase, Luis telephoned. His voice,
although matter-of-fact, made me gulp. When he invited me to dine
that night, I had difficulty sounding normal. Excitement raced up
my spine like an electric current. All those months had numbed my
longing, but now it was as if I'd never gone away.

He was due to pick me up at nine-thirty. The late Spanish dinner
hour, so different from the Swiss, seemed almost unbearably far
away. I had to wait so long to see him. When I heard the bell ring,
I was ready and ran to the door myself. Before, when Luis had come
to take me out, he would wait in the car below to protect my
reputation, and his driver would knock on my door and inform me
that the Count was waiting. But this time he was standing there
himself, in the belted beige trenchcoat I remembered so well, his
face tanned, his eyes scrutinizing. Then he smiled.

"Well, I was wondering all day if you were going to stand me
up again." He raised my hand to his lips.

I stood there looking at him like a fool, completely entranced.

"Are you going to invite me in?" he asked.

With a wave of my arm, I took a step backward. He brushed by
me in the narrow hallway and nonchalantly went to my bar, poured
himself a whiskey and soda. Then he raised his glass in a toast. "In
the future, my beauty, you're not going to fool me so easily."

That night with his sisters and their husbands, we went to the
Palace Bar and then had dinner at Chipén, followed by Villa Rosa
for flamenco. Nothing had changed, except that Luis was more
formal than he used to be. Nevertheless, we dined together three
times that week, but never alone.

Luis didn't mention Casilda and neither did I. I had called her
the day after I arrived, but the butler said she was not in Madrid
and he didn't know when she would return. I left a message that
I had called, wondering if she was in but didn't want to speak with
me. Had she heard about my going out with Luis a year and a half
ago? As the week progressed, I realized that, with Spanish society
so intimately related, she must know. Had they broken up? Did she
consider the fault mine? She was my best Spanish friend. I was very
upset and would have liked to talk to her about it. But since there
was no news from her, I finally sent an affectionate note with a

bottle of Chanel Number Five perfume, her favorite, which I had bought for her in Paris a year before.

During my second week back, Luis took me to El Pulpito in the Plaza Mayor, a restaurant which we both enjoyed. I looked around to see who was joining us.

"Think you can bear to be alone with me tonight?" He smiled. I was thrilled—the first time alone. We went dancing at a new *boite* called La Barca on the Calle Castillo. Although his sisters were there, he escorted me to a small intimate corner table where nobody could join us. For the rest of the night, we were alone. When we danced, his arms held me tight.

He murmured in my ear. "This time, you're not going to escape, *guapa.*"

I froze. His using the word *guapa* reminded me of El Guapo and my old misgivings. I turned to look at him. No, it was impossible. I put the thought out of my mind. Nothing was going to spoil my vacation.

I told him I only had a month in Spain. He squeezed his arm around my waist. "That's what you think."

Each morning at nine-thirty, Luis would call for me in his super-charged Cord, and we would head for the golf course, Puerta de Hierro. In 1947 this car was the personification of power and style—a total reflection of his personality. It was low and long and I had to stretch my legs out straight in front of me. On days when I wore silk stockings, the heat of the engine was such that when I got out of the car, the stockings would be in shreds. We laughed at that, because Luis' car had been imported into Spain before the Civil War and, like all the other cars in the country, was over twelve years old.

We saw each other daily and I tried not to think that I would have to leave in a few weeks. I did my best to prolong my vacation, sending cables to Jupiter to request more time. I called Smokey and his wife, who invited me to lunch. When we talked, Smokey suggested trying to enter Doña Angelita's apartment again to see if the crates were still there—he hadn't given up hope that something might activate his visas. It seemed unlikely, but I wired Jupiter, who telephoned me almost immediately to say that Safehaven no longer entered into our activities. He noted that he was still working on Smokey's visas.

One day Luis took me to a *tienta,* a "testing" of the young bulls being mated for the bullring, that was being held at the ranch of his uncle, the Count of Mayalde. Several matadors were invited to these fiestas, and an invitation was considered a great treat. The ranch, near Avila, was typical of the great breeding farms, complete with a picturesque whitewashed miniature bullring. A hearty country feast had been prepared for the festive occasion and about eighty people milled around the buffet table, drinking red wine and enjoying the paella.

Juanito was not there, but my good friends, matadors Manolete and Gitanillo de Triana were. Instead of *trajes de luces,* suits of lights, they were dressed in short brown wool jackets, tight, high-waisted gray pants, wide Cordobes hats, and beautifully embroidered leather chaps—the typical costume for country riding in southern Spain.

I'd been to a *tienta* with Juanito a year ago and knew that although it would be similar to the big *corridas* fights, the bulls were never killed and there were no *picadors.* I also knew that the bulls were only two years old, while those in the ring were usually four years old. But they had sharp short horns and attacked the cape ferociously, like their fathers, and could wound painfully and kill, too. When I went with Juanito, he had actually encouraged me to try bullfighting myself, and he held one side of the cape and I the other. This was called *al alimon.* The bull had passed between us like a toy. It was exciting and I had enjoyed it. I'd always wanted to try it again—alone.

Today the bulls came and went. We laughed and drank red wine from a pigskin that was passed from row to row. Finally, both matadors retired to great applause, and our host offered his guests a chance to try their skills. Two men entered the ring, one after the other, and were relieved to escape uninjured. It was amusing to watch their scared and somewhat clumsy passes.

Then the great matador Manolete turned to me and asked jokingly, "Would you like to try this one, Aline? I think he's a good bull. He seems to follow the cape well."

I think Manolete never expected me to accept, but I couldn't resist the opportunity. As I stepped down the cement rows to the *barrera,* my heart was throbbing. The young bull was being kept busy on on the other side of the arena by a peon who was tossing a cape in front of it. Manolete asked me if I would like him to take the other half of my *capote.* This would, of course, protect me and he would make certain the bull never gored me. But I wanted the excitement of trying it alone and told him so. With a wry smile on his long thin face, he handed me the bright pink *capote.* I stepped behind the *burladero,* the wooden protection. The bull was still on the other side of the arena. Manolete motioned to the peon controlling him, and the man turned from the bull and jumped over the *barrandilla,* leaving me alone with the bull in the arena.

I'd seen so many fights. I'd listened to Juanito and his friends discuss bulls for hours. I was quite certain I knew what to do. With my heart pounding faster and faster, my whole being stimulated by wine, to which I was unaccustomed, and by Manolete's encouragement, I stepped from behind the *burladero* into the ring. I knew Luis was in that crowd watching, and I wanted to make a good impression. I could imagine my American mother in Pearl River, New York, saying, "Don't be a show-off, Aline."

The bull turned my way and, imitating the great matadors, I swung my cape back and forth as I'd seen them do in the big rings. But, in a flash everything changed. That young bull, though small, was the son of a courageous father. Lowering his head, he charged. His speed shocked me; those horns quickly became bigger, longer, sharper. My brain screamed, "Aline, what are you doing?" The beast seemed to be rushing at me as fast as a locomotive, but it was too late to change my mind. I lifted the cape, then lowered it for the classic first pass. The bull swished by, flinging my thick heavy cape high into the air, as if it were a piece of chiffon. He spun around so quickly that I was hardly ready for him when he came at me again from the other direction. He stormed through the red cloth, tossing his sharp horns. I suddenly experienced the incredibly dangerous exhilaration of the matador. I loved it. I heard a rumble of admiration and looked up. That was my big mistake. In that split second, the bull spun around and raced at me, straight for me. I wasn't quite ready when he hit my cape. He tossed the cape and me, and I flew into the air like a rag doll. Astonished by his strength, I hit the ground with a hard jolt which rolled me over on my face and filled my mouth with sand. Semiconscious, I heard a lot of noise and felt someone pulling me to the side of the ring by one leg. I had a vague impression of men shouting and the sound of flurrying capes.

It was total confusion and flying sand; I couldn't see a thing. Then I heard a beloved voice. "What a silly thing to do." And then the voice said, firmly, and I'm sure of the words, "You'd better stop these wild American pranks and marry me."

I opened my eyes wide. Luis was lifting me. "Are you all right?" he went on. His expression was worried, but I could not have cared less. He had proposed! I stood up and tested my bruised legs. My head ached, too. By a miracle, that was the extent of my injuries. The bull's horn had ripped right through my leather jacket, something I'd often seen happen in the ring. But I was only thinking of Luis' words. Being tossed by a bull was worth it, if that had convinced Luis to marry me.

But as we drove back to Madrid that night, he never mentioned another word about marriage. He talked about the bulls, scolded me again for being so foolish, and recounted stories about famous matadors who had been killed in these *tientas*. Had he been simply playing with the idea or did he intend to ask me to marry him? Afraid of finding myself in an embarrassing position, I said nothing about his remark. When he dropped me at my building, he was still bantering me about my dangerous escape. And I climbed the stairs to my apartment very sore and very confused.

Chapter 17
MAY 1947

In May of 1947, Eva Peron arrived in Madrid on an official visit to Spain. Her husband, Juan Peron of Argentina, had provided Spain with much-needed wheat during those war years, and as a result she had to be royally received. Luis took me to several parties in her honor. The striking Eva was everywhere: the country club, the races, even the bullfights. Eva shocked government officials, however, by arriving late at state functions in her honor, and their wives disapproved of her pompous manner and flashy, revealing clothes. Rumors about her dubious profession before she met Juan Peron, and the fact that she had been his mistress prior to their marriage, did not endear her to the very proper Spanish people either.

At first, Eva paid no attention to anyone, but after we'd been repeatedly introduced at social affairs, and finding me at her side one day, she began to chat. From then on, we usually exchanged a few words whenever we met. She was egotistic and arrogant, and had a raucous, bawdy sense of humor. I wasn't surprised that strait-laced Madrid society did not admire her, and she in turn made no effort to win them over.

One late afternoon at a reception in her honor in the small garden behind the Argentine embassy, she singled me out. "I'm aware that you're not Spanish, although when we met you had me fooled. Therefore, I know these stuffy señoras"—her arm raised in an arc indicated all those present—"must bore you as much as they do me."

I didn't know how to tell her that I liked and admired Spanish women. Their reserved manners clashed with Eva's blatant contempt for anyone else's opinion. I longed to tell her to tone down her makeup, lift her necklines, and be courteous to the women, but I realized that she considered herself more important, more beautiful than any other woman, and was not apt to accept advice from anyone, much less me.

The Argentine embassy was crowded that afternoon and when Eva and I began to speak, people interrupted almost constantly. Finally I went to look for Luis and found him admiring a lovely blue and white vase.

"That's an unusually good piece of Ming china," he said. "I wonder where the ambassador got it? I have a small collection, but I've never found anything to compare to that in Madrid."

As I looked at the vase, I remembered Ada Fribourg's hysterical tale about the Ming vase. Could it be this one? Here at the Argentine embassy? Many of the Nazis' looted objects had been sent to Argentina, and I knew that Juan Peron not only had been a friend of Hitler's, but had received Nazi funds which, it was said, had helped finance his rise to power. I wondered if some of the very objects I had been looking for had been sent here to the Argentine embassy for safekeeping. Unfortunately Ada and Klaus had already left for Switzerland for the summer, I thought, or they might have been at this reception, as well. I could have asked them about the vase.

At that moment Eva came into the house from the garden and stopped to say good-bye. Luis turned to her and complimented the ambassador, who was with her, on the Ming vase.

Eva glanced at it and looked at me. "Do you like it, too?" she asked.

"I think it's lovely, but I would love to know where the embassy got it. Luis tells me that those ancient blue and white pieces of china are difficult to find."

"I have a small collection," Luis went on to say, "but my pieces have all come from abroad."

The ambassador looked surprised. He said that it had been there when he'd arrived in Spain and he had no idea where his predecessor had found it—most of their paintings and furnishings of value had been sent to the embassy residence from Buenos Aires.

After they moved on, Luis said, "I don't believe the ambassador even knows that it's a Ming vase."

I told him about Ada Fribourg's story of several years ago, of how she discovered a Ming vase in an antique store that had been stolen from her husband's collection. I wondered if this could be the same one. Luis thought the connection far-fetched, and I had to agree. Nevertheless, the episode served as a reminder that if Safehaven stolen objects were still in Spain, then so might be the man who had run that business. The current ambassador might be unaware of the details, but something told me Eva was not. She probably did not know a Ming vase when she saw one, but I'd bet she was aware of the funds which Hitler had sent to Peron only a few years before.

The next day I revisited the antique shops on the little streets off the Calle del Prado, but I found no Impressionist paintings, nor important pieces of blue and white china. My heart was heavy. I was leaving Luis and Spain. And now I finally had to admit to myself, once and for all, that I had failed—not only with Luis, but with my Safehaven mission. I would never find that painting of the yellow dog.

A cable arrived from Jupiter stating that my next post would be Czechoslovakia; I was to proceed to Washington for a briefing without delay. The time allotted was twenty days.

When Luis picked me up a few hours later, I told him, "Luis, I have to go back to the United States. This time my work is going to take me far away and I don't think I'll be able to return for years."

He was impatient with the idea. "You know we're going to get married one day. You should give up your job and stay in Spain with me."

"Luis, I cannot quit my job."

"Why not?"

"Because I work for a living." I realized too late that it sounded like a bad excuse. None of the girls Luis knew worked for a living. I made another attempt. "If we're going to get married, you will have to name a date now. Otherwise I have to be in Washington no later than two weeks from today. Even if I could afford to," I continued, "I wouldn't want to stay on here without a purpose, without a job. And my parents would be scandalized."

"Well, we'll get married," he said vaguely, and that was it.

Since he said nothing further, I decided not to mention the subject again and to try to enjoy my last few weeks in Spain. I ordered a train ticket to Paris and to Le Havre, and from there I reserved space on a ship back to the U.S.A. I wired Washington that I would be there on the 10th of June. On the 18th of May I went through the painful business of telling Angustias and Cecilia that this time I would have to close down the apartment. Together, we began packing my many belongings in large trunks. My maids carried on as if we were having a Spanish funeral every single day.

Sometimes, when Luis came by to pick me up, I wondered why he did not notice the change in Angustias when she greeted him at the door. By now, she considered him responsible for her misery and was taking a definite dislike to him. At two o'clock on the 23rd of May, Angustias opened the door and let him in.

"Why is Angustias crying?" questioned Luis in surprise.

"Because I am leaving tonight. I'm sorry, Luis, but I will not be able to lunch with you today. And, since I'm leaving for good, I am having my last lunch in Madrid with a friend."

"What?"

"All this time I haven't seen anyone but you. None of my other friends. And I'm sorry, Luis, but I have a luncheon engagement at Jockey." This was true, but I was miserable about it. I just felt too hurt and upset to be able to lunch with Luis again like every other day, as if it meant nothing to me to be leaving him forever. And anyhow this was my last chance to see if he really cared for me or not.

"How can you have a luncheon engagement at Jockey? You always have lunch with me."

"Luis, I've explained it over and over and apparently you did not believe me, but I am—*leaving—tonight*—on the sleeper to Paris and from there on to Le Havre to catch the ship to America. This time it's permanent, irrevocable."

"You're really leaving Spain?"

"Tonight. Here are my tickets."

He stared at the tickets I had handy in my pocket. I gestured broadly around the room. "And as you can see, I have packed all of my things—this is not spring housecleaning that you see here— this is my last day in Spain."

Angustias, God bless her, burst forth in loud and miserable tears. He was looking from me to her, to the trunks, the barren apartment: finally believing, yet disbelieving. He was flabbergasted.

I went on blithely, "Now if you will excuse me, I don't want to be late." I was amazed at my own calmness. I was trying so hard to hide my misery that I was actually succeeding.

"But I thought we were going to get married?"

I stopped. "What an incredible coincidence. So did I."

"Aline, be reasonable. You never told me you had made these preparations. Only once did you mention that you should be in Washington sometime in the future, but you didn't give any importance to it. Until right now I've been unaware that you really intended to leave. Do you think you have been fair to me?"

"But the man is supposed to ask the girl to marry, not vice versa. It embarrasses me to keep mentioning the subject."

"Keep mentioning! You have imagined all of this. I've been asking you to marry me since I first met you. I will talk to my father right now."

"No, Luis, I think you would like to marry me, but I also believe, if you were decided to do so, you would have made it definite before now. I understand, your family would not be pleased to have you marry an unknown American working girl. Forget it. I don't want to put you through any disagreeable situations for my sake. And I really have to go. Good-bye." I grabbed my bag and gloves and started down the steps so Luis wouldn't see the tears I felt welling up in my eyes. He followed behind me.

"Wait. At least let me take you there."

"No. I prefer to go alone." I dared not even look at him.

A taxi passed by just then. I ran to stop it. *"El restaurante Jockey, por favor."* I left a very confused Luis standing on the street.

Raimundo Lanza was waiting for me. "Aline! This is my lucky day. You didn't break our date."

I tried hard to smile, and I fear my conversation was not very entertaining. Raimundo was a good-looking Italian prince with whom I had broken many dates that past month. I could barely eat anything.

We were having dessert when Luis appeared at our table. He looked pale under his customary tan. "Aline," he said, "I would like to speak with you. Alone."

I asked Raimundo to excuse me for a few minutes and we crossed the room to a corner table.

He began immediately. "My father is at my apartment waiting for you right now, and our family priest is there too. Everything is set."

"Luis, what do you mean, everything is set?"

"Naturally, my father has to talk to you. And since you didn't believe that I was going to marry you, how else could I prove to you that I'm serious?"

"Are you telling me that you asked your father if you could marry me?"

"No. I *told* him that I was going to marry you."

"Look, Luis, no more of your stories. I don't want to play games with my government . . . I mean my company." My nerves were such that I slipped, but he was more upset than I and seemed not to notice. I continued. "I waited for you to make something definite for weeks and weeks and now they're expecting me for a briefing at home and I have to go."

"Aline, my father and the priest are waiting. Come and see for yourself. We'll be married one month from today, that's the quickest we can arrange the papers, I'm told. You can send a cable saying that you will not be returning. Ever."

He grabbed my arm, escorted me quickly through the restaurant as I gave a feeble wave to a perplexed Raimundo. Luis opened the door of his car, slammed it shut behind me, and vaulted into the driver's seat. In one quick motion he flicked on the ignition and the powerful engine snarled to life. Luis slammed the stick shift into first and we screamed away from Jockey. It was similar to the traditional Le Mans racing start. To say the least, we were quickly in front of his apartment building.

Luis' father was distinguished and handsome. I had met him several times before. On Sundays, Luis had twice taken me to the hippodrome instead of the bullfights—his father was the president of all horseracing in Spain, and Luis owned racehorses as well. I would sit in his father's box in my best outfit with a large brimmed hat, looking more often at the rolling green hills surrounding the city than at the races. The box was usually filled with generals, their uniforms resplendent with colorful war decorations, and with their wives, in large pastel hats, many as uninterested as I in horseracing.

Today, Luis' father was polite as always, but not warm. He shook my hand. His English, like Luis', was flawless.

"My son says he wants to marry you. For us, in Spain, this is a serious decision. As you may be aware, we cannot dissolve a marriage in this country. It is for better or for worse and for always. I suggest you think this matter over for a while."

I wanted to make a good impression, but I did not intend to let Luis down, now that he had finally spoken to his father.

"I have already thought it over, and I am aware of your customs and laws, and I am also a Catholic. Even if I were not, please don't think that everyone in the United States gets divorced!" The Count began to smile and I sensed that he regretted his first words, yet I knew it was a disappointment for him that his only son would marry an unknown foreigner.

"But is it necessary that the wedding take place within a month?" he went on. "Why do you set this ultimatum?"

"I cannot afford to live in Madrid without working, and my parents would not approve. I would like to get married to Luis in the United States, but since foreign exchange is restricted, he says it is difficult to get visas and to leave the country."

"In that, Luis is correct. It would be disappointing to have him married outside the country, since none of us could go to the wedding." The Count of Velayos turned to the priest: "One month is not much time to prepare a proper wedding, but I suppose it can be done."

The priest, who had remained silent most of the time, nodded to me to sit down and began to explain the necessary papers which I would have to request urgently from the United States.

"Luis," said his father, "you had better take Aline to meet your grandfather. You need not telephone. He is expecting you."

We were in Luis' car again, heading toward the Plaza de Colon and then along the Castellana, finally turning into the entrance of number 36, the Romanones palace. For one whole year of the war, I remembered looking out from the OSS offices on the top floor of the Montellano palace and admiring this turn-of-the-century mansion which had been the center for Spain's political and cultural life before the Spanish Civil War. We swept up the curved drive, walked up the marble steps, and stood at the columned entrance. I glanced quickly at the small garden, the two sycamores on either side of the stairs. I had never expected to enter this home.

I noticed that Luis was a bit tense as we stood there. A footman opened the door, and we went in.

"Look, Aline, do not be frightened by *El Abuelo,* my grandfather. He is overpowering, but if he does not like you at first, he will eventually. Everyone in the family is afraid of him, but he's really very affectionate, and his sense of humor is famous."

By this time we were in a large entrance hall with a ceiling three stories high and a wide curving stairway which led to a floor above.

At the foot of the stairs on either side were suits of armor. Like a child I longed to raise the visors on their metal helmets and take a peep inside, but I continued to walk sedately up the stairs. The walls were covered with tapestries. The enormous house was so silent, it almost gave the feeling of being uninhabited. Upstairs, thick carpets suppressed the sound of our steps as Luis led me through one room after another.

He explained, "My grandfather is accustomed to getting his own way. Everyone in the family is careful to be on his good side."

I whispered, "But Luis, are you afraid of your own grandfather?"

"Absolutely. I wasn't when I was small. He used to take us children out shooting. Sometimes there would be as many as ten of us, between eight and twelve years old. He had the courage to place us in butts on either side of him. He would take, say, butt number six, right in the middle, a dangerous position because children with shotguns are apt to make mistakes." Luis smiled. "We obviously didn't kill my grandfather, but he has lots of buckshot in his body as reminders of our wildness. He did teach us all how to shoot and handle firearms safely. But more important," he added, "he taught us a love and appreciation of Spanish country life. But when we grew up, his attitude toward us changed. He has written a book of his own proverbs. One goes like this: 'Children are like asparagus. When they are young, they are tender and you want to eat them, but when they grow up, they become tough and you can't even swallow them.' He certainly acts that way with all of us. But don't worry. I am going to marry you, no matter what he says."

The Count of Romanones, former Prime Minister of Spain, friend of the exiled King, author, businessman, the most famous and respected man in the country, was sitting in an armchair with a plaid blanket over his legs, staring at me with piercing bright blue eyes. He had a prominent chin, a big nose, and an unhandsome face. He rubbed his hands, one inside the other, as he continued to observe me in silence. He was eighty-four years old, and although he could barely walk, his expression was alert and there was an air of vitality about him. Unabashedly, as if he were inspecting a mare, starting at my feet, like any good horseman, his eyes traveled slowly up my body to my blushing face. He then peered into my eyes and I stared back unblinking. Those eyes, as blue as his Spanish sky, became warm and inviting. His mouth crinkled into a half smile. I liked him immediately.

"Quien es? Who is it?" he said in a rasping voice.

Luis pushed me in front of him. *"Abuelo,* this is my *novia."*

"Quien es?" he repeated. He was hard of hearing and had a penetrating voice as if he were already annoyed but somehow I realized that he was not at all.

Luis repeated, *"Abuelo,* it's my *novia.* I would like to present my *novia."*

With that statement, the Count of Romanones asked me to move closer while continuing to look me over carefully. Finally, the old man said, *"Bueno,* so you want to marry my *nieto,* my *primogenito?* Tell me, what do you see in him?" And he chuckled as he indicated a chair.

I turned around to see if Luis was going to sit down too, but there was no Luis! He had slipped out the door, closed it, and left me alone with the old lion. I couldn't believe it. But I had no time to dwell on that because *El Abuelo* was speaking to me.

"I'm sorry that I do not know your country, although I have traveled to many other places. Tell me, what is it like? Did you know that until 1898 as many people spoke German as English in your country—and that the fact that you speak English today was decided by only one vote in favor?" *El Abuelo* was looking at me with those glinting blue eyes. "Sit down," he said, and gratefully I sat on the edge of the chair in front of him.

"Bring the chair closer."

Still looking into his eyes, gaining confidence from them, I inched the chair forward.

"Closer."

I pulled the chair in front of his. We were sitting knee to knee.

"That's better," he said. "Now give me your hand."

I gave him my hand and he took it in his and held it on the arm of his chair. He said, "Whenever I have the good fortune to be with a beautiful woman, it has always been my custom to hold her hand. I can think better this way. It relaxes me. Now, tell me, what sort of fellow is the President of your country? They tell me that Truman is doing very well and I can bet that you're going to have him for another term." We talked for over an hour, never about Luis, but just about America and politics. He did much of the talking, but his questions came so fast that he kept me busy, too. He told me some amusing anecdotes about a certain American Ambassador Moore, whom he had known well years ago when he'd been Prime

Minister, and the great admiration he had always felt for the United States. After a while, Luis returned, approaching us as if he was making his way toward an unexploded bomb. He stared at us holding hands and came closer.

El Abuelo smiled. *"Bueno,* Luis, your marriage has my blessings. What this family needs is some new blood, and Aline is just the one."

I could tell Luis was pleased, the way he took my arm and squeezed it as we descended the wide curved staircase. Probably relieved, too, just as I was. But more than that, I was happy. I'd actually had fun with that famous old man. And I'd just made a new friend.

It took a whole day to get a call through to my parents in Pearl River. "I'm getting married, Mother."

"Oh, Aline, I'm so happy. To whom, dear? Some boy in your office?"

"No, Mother. He's a Spanish boy who lives right here in Madrid."

"Spanish? Oh, no . . . Aline, you're not thinking about marrying a Spaniard?"

"Well, I'm more than thinking about it. I'm going to marry him."

"Oh, Aline, I hope you're not doing anything rash. Can he speak any English?"

"Better than I can. He also speaks French and German and Italian and . . . look, Mother, have faith in me. You're going to adore Luis."

"What's his name?"

"Luis. Looo-eees . . ."

"Aline, I don't understand what kind of name that is. You must get married here in Pearl River. When are you coming back?"

"No, Mother, you will have to come here. It's difficult for Spaniards to leave the country and I'm afraid he might change his mind if I go away."

"But you will live here in America, won't you?"

"Oh, no. We will live in Spain, Mother."

"Oh, Aline, why on earth would you want to live in Spain?"

"I love Spain and Luis was born here."

"But what kind of living can he make over there?"

"Don't worry about that, Mother."

"I have to worry about you, dear. Now what does Luis do?"

"Well . . . I don't know exactly, but it's not important. He's the champion golfer of Spain."

"Oh, no, Aline. A golf bum. Don't tell me, please . . ."

"Mother, he's no kind of a bum. I fact, he's a count."

"A count? You mean a bookkeeper? I think you had better give this a lot of thought. You should come right home. In a little while, you'll forget all about it."

Feeling like a coward, I cabled rather than telephoned Jupiter that I was resigning and getting married. He surprised me by appearing in Madrid two days later.

"You should think this over, Tiger," he advised. "Do you realize you are giving up a great career? An exciting career? No other young woman today holds such a unique opportunity. And you are still so young."

I did have misgivings about leaving espionage. It had become the salt and pepper of my life. It was second nature to me, always looking under the surface of things, but I was in love and nothing could stop me. However, the way it seemed to be starting, nobody was really crazy about our marriage except us and *El Abuelo* Romanones.

Chapter 18

JUNE 1947

With his personal ordeal behind him, Luis completely devoted himself to arranging our wedding, which was a maze of pomp and tradition.

"According to the Spanish custom," he said, "the groom selects and pays for the bride's gown." That was a pleasant surprise. "And since I have that right," he went on, "I'd like for you to have one exactly like my mother's . . ." He showed me a photograph of his mother in her wedding dress. She had been killed in an automobile accident when he was eight. Her dress was done in a simple princess line, with a chain of orange blossoms at the waist reaching to the floor and an enormous skirt ending in a long train of white satin damask. On her head was a tiara covered by a lace mantilla which reached the full length of the train. "That," said Luis, pointing to the tiara and veil, "you will have to wear. Every bride in my mother's family has worn it for two hundred years!" I looked at it and couldn't imagine anything more delightful than to walk down an aisle wearing such a magnificent heirloom.

He drove me to Balenciaga to have my measurements taken, so that they could begin copying it. Later, driving home, he said, "It is also the custom that the groom give the bride a diamond bracelet."

"But Luis, I'd like a ring. In America, the custom is a ring."

"Well, maybe I'll give you a ring, too, but you must have a diamond bracelet because that is the custom."

The next day, he handed me a small box. "This was a present from my grandfather to my grandmother, then from my father to my mother." I opened the box and saw the largest ruby ring in Spain. As I stared at it, I remembered that around age ten I had been fascinated by a red-stoned glass ring in Pearl River's five-and-ten-cent store. And now here was this one, so much bigger and more real than that toy!

A few days later, he gave me his mother's pearl earrings and necklace. And several days later, still another ring made from a brooch of his mother's, with two gigantic canary diamonds. So I had my diamond ring, too. Then the diamond engagement bracelet arrived. That was breathtaking! I was becoming accustomed to receiving an incredible new jewel almost every day. I, who had never wished for or even dreamed of such things. It worried me that I did not appreciate Luis' gifts enough.

"Luis, what about women in Spain? Isn't there some custom that we're expected to follow?"

"Yes. You must buy me a gold cigarette case. I've already chosen the one that I want at my family's jeweler, Paco Sanz on the Gran Via. When you go there, he will show it to you."

Sanz is the most expensive jeweler in Madrid. I went there the next afternoon. "I'm the *novia* of the Conde de Quintanilla . . ."

"Ahhhh, si, señorita, el Señor Conde has selected the loveliest cigarette case that we have."

It was also the most expensive. The cost made me dizzy. I thought of the jewels he'd given me, and I smiled at the salesman. "It's perfect."

I had planned on buying a few dresses at Balenciaga and getting myself some nice lingerie, but with so little money left, I had to find an inexpensive way of getting a trousseau. Luis had already rented a house in Capri and intended to take me on an extensive honeymoon. I needed a large wardrobe.

Then I remembered Doña Angelita. During the past weeks, I had almost forgotten the yellow dog painting and all that was related to it. But now I recalled what a really good seamstress Doña Angelita had been. And, more important, how inexpensive! I telephoned and she was still in the same place and would be delighted to see me whenever I wished. I worried for a moment about the idiot son, Manolo. But even if he saw me, I figured, he would never connect me with the old lady who had knocked him down.

I went shopping in Zorrilla, Madrid's leading store for material, bought the latest French fashion magazines, and the next afternoon was climbing the familiar steps to Doña Angelita's apartment on the third floor. Despite the time that had passed and the changes in my life, I was curious to see if the crates were still there. I laughed to myself as I knocked on the door. What if, at this late date, just as I had left espionage forever and was about to become a Spanish countess, I uncovered the Nazi spy, El Guapo!

Doña Angelita's face lit up when she saw me. "Oh, señorita. I read in the *ABC*"—Madrid's leading daily newspaper—"that you are going to marry the *primogenito* of the Conde de Romanones." Her head bounced up and down. "That's quite something! A little American girl, a stranger in our country, to marry into such a famous Spanish family!"

While she continued her exclamations, I glanced around. The small abode had not changed. Threads, bits of material were scattered over the floor. The cat's bowl of milk was still on the window sill. And the radio next to her Singer sewing machine was droning on, as usual. I maneuvered my steps so I could see through the open door into the bedroom. The crates were not there. Maybe it was just as well. If I had seen them there, how could I have resisted trying to find out what was inside!

It was only after we had spent a long time discussing my new wardrobe and prices, that I asked her about her son. Doña Angelita was standing on a box taking my measurements. For a moment she said nothing. Then she took the pins out of her mouth and stepped down.

"They've taken him away. My poor Manolo! He's in one of those hospitals where they tie people up."

I was sincerely upset for her and asked what had happened.

She shook her head from side to side. "It's a long story, señorita," She sighed deeply. "The señorita did not know this, but I was guarding two very valuable crates. A good job, it was. Paid me five hundred *pesetas* a month. For nothing. Just to keep them here. That's the easiest money I ever made."

"Whoever would pay so much for so little a favor?" I asked.

"Oh, I never knew the man. But you can be sure he was a rich one."

She pulled up a chair for me from the table where I had been writing down the descriptions of each dress. "My Manolo opened those crates one night. There was no way I could stop him. He was a good boy, but very stubborn." She looked at me in a glance of astonishment. "Do you know, those boxes were filled with paintings? Manolo took them out and put them all over the room. He loved them and spent hours just looking at them." She lifted her shoulders. "There was no way I could get him to put them back into those boxes. And after all, what damage could he do? Just looking?"

"But what happened to Manolo?" I asked.

She sighed. "Well, one day I got a call that two men were coming to pick up the crates. I was holding half of a five *peseta* bill and they had to give me the other half, so I would know they had the right to take those boxes." She looked at me. "Smart people, eh? Those boxes must have been very very valuable! Well, the men came, and were shocked to find the paintings on the walls where Manolo had placed them, but said little. They very carefully packed each one and took the crates away." She sighed. Doña Angelita had never been as talkative as this before. I wondered if the new status I was about to attain had loosened her tongue. At any rate, she rambled on. "Very upset, I was," she said. "I was going to miss that money! But there was something worse. I never expected that when Manolo saw that the paintings were gone, he would go crazy. Absolutely crazy! Do you know, señorita, he screamed and banged on the walls? He even broke this very chair that I'm sitting on." Doña Angelita pressed her lips, holding back a sob. "It was *espantoso,* horrible." She sobbed. "A neighbor called the police; two came, but Manolo is so strong, he threw them down the stairs. It finally took six police and four strong guards from the crazy hospital to put him in the ambulance and take him to the hospital." Tears came into Doña Angelita's eyes. "The terrible scene was the talk of the neighborhood and nobody speaks to me."

I was not really listening, but speculating: if that old lady's kick to Manolo's groin had not been right on target, there would be no Luis, no wedding, nothing.

I didn't find out anything new about the yellow dog painting, nor was I able to wheedle any more information from Doña Angelita about where the paintings had gone when they had been taken from her house. But I did get a beautiful trousseau at an average of twenty dollars a dress. I never even missed the outfits I had intended to buy from Balenciaga.

Wedding gifts started to pour in, most of them to Luis' apartment. One day he called. "What do you think! Eva Peron has sent us a wedding gift! The blue and white Ming vase. I'm sure she has no idea of its value."

I was astonished and even wondered if she imagined she was bribing me—to win my silence. Or was it merely that having seen both Luis and me admiring the vase at the Argentine embassy, she had ordered her ambassador to send it to us? Again, I thought, what a pity the Fribourgs were in Switzerland and I couldn't ask Ada if this was the vase she had mentioned to me two years before!

The wedding was rapidly approaching. Other gifts continued to pour in and my wedding dress was ready, but there was one thing I had not yet done. I had not told Luis of my former occupation. How would he react when he learned that I was a trained U.S. espionage agent who had been spying on his country? Like all Spaniards, no matter what side they had fought on during their frightful Civil War, he was extremely patriotic. He might be shocked enough to call off the wedding!

I kept telling myself that the proper moment for my confession would occur, but of course, it never did. Finally, one evening, while dining alone in a restaurant on the Calle Jorge Juan, I pulled together all of my courage and told him.

"Preposterous," was his comment. "You, a spy! Really, Aline, you do have a great imagination. And you'd better not tell your fantasies to anyone else. It wouldn't improve their opinion of you."

Ignoring his remark, I continued to confess. "I even suspected you of being a Nazi agent."

He looked at me for a few seconds and then threw back his head and roared with laughter, startling the couple at the next table. Trying to control himself, he pointed a finger at me and gasped. "You a spy!" And he started laughing again. Gaining some control and rubbing his eyes, he said, "That just proves it. If you'd been a spy, you would have been the world's worst. Why, everyone in Spain knows that I and my family were always pro-Allies. Even in World War One, when *El Abuelo* was Prime Minister, he wanted us to fight against Germany. Bah!" He shook his head. "Obviously, you could never have been a spy."

A few days before my parents were due to leave Pearl River for the wedding, my brother Tom had a serious automobile accident, so they sent my brother Bill in their place. He arrived a day before the wedding. Bill was nineteen and had never been to Europe before. The wedding, arranged by Luis at the home of his sister, the Duchess of Tamames, was to be at eight o'clock at night and followed by a dinner and a dance. The church of San Fermin de los Navarros was the same church in which his parents had been married, and most of his family for that matter. It was also very close to the American ambassador's residence, where our OSS offices had been hidden during the last year of the war. This was going to be the social affair of the season.

Bill and I stood side by side in the back of the church while the bells chimed, waiting for the signal to enter; I, in a replica of Luis' mother's wedding dress with a damask satin train a mile long, and Billy in a rented morning coat, striped pants, and gray stock, which Luis' valet had knotted for him. As we stood there, Bill was calm, but I knew he was in shock. He didn't know anyone, nor did he speak a word of Spanish. As I placed my arm in his, I noticed, to my surprise and for the first time in my life, that my arm was trembling. In front of us were Luis' many relatives, all the grandees of Spain and *El Abuelo* Romanones in the front pew. The church was packed with hundreds of people, most of whom I did not know at all. The only ones I felt I had on my team were Luis, my brother, and *El Abuelo.*

"Bill," I whispered, "we must walk very, very, slowly. Just keep in step with me."

There are no wedding rehearsals in Spain, so this was it, our only chance, and it had to be perfect. The organ sounded the first chords, a strange sort of Arabic music, and we started down that long, long aisle. I'd been the bride in many fashion shows, so I had actually rehearsed this moment often. As I walked through the huge church nave, I looked up at the distant altar and prayed that I looked like the wife Luis wanted his family to see.

The ceremony was different from any in America. Ten men, dressed in morning coat or military uniform, formed a semicircle near us on either side of the altar. These were witnesses, friends, and distinguished members of the family. Then Luis' sister and my brother, taking the place of his mother and my father, stood at our side. At one point Luis dropped, piece by piece, twenty-five glittering gold coins into the priest's hands. I wondered if this was a holdover from medieval times, when dowries were paid, or when wives were bought. The ring went on the right hand instead of the left. As the ceremony proceeded, I passed from one surprise to another.

When it was over, after signing many documents and before we joined the wedding party, Luis said, "Let's slip out and go to *El Abuelo*'s house to say good-bye. We'll never have time before we leave for Rome tomorrow morning."

Luis' grandfather had not been strong enough to withstand a dinner for 350 people and looked up in surprise when he saw us walk in. I was still in my wedding dress and the Count of Romanones took both my hands, smiling at me.

"Aline, I have seen many weddings in my life. I have seen many people of different station joined in matrimony, but I want you to know that today I was very proud of you. You walked down the aisle like . . . a queen."

I looked up at Luis and saw that he was as moved as I was.

The next day as we began our honeymoon, who should be seated across from us in the almost empty first class cabin of the Iberia plane to Rome but Eva Peron. Her dyed blond hair was pulled back in a huge chignon, her eyes outlined in thick black mascara. But her skin, despite the dollops of red on the cheeks, was luminous. A mink stole, which had become famous in Madrid because she flaunted it at all the official receptions despite the hot June weather, was draped over the arm of her seat. A pink straw hat adorned with feathers crowned the bulging blond hairdo, and a black veil floated over the brown eyes.

When Luis got up to talk to someone in the back of the plane, Eva moved across the aisle to the seat he had left. In her hand she held the *ABC* newspaper, which carried a picture of Luis and myself on the front page. Pointing to it, she asked who had made my wedding dress. Then she chatted for a while about the difference between Balenciaga in Madrid and dress houses in Rome. She explained that she was obliged to give much importance to her attire and coiffure because she was expected to create a sensation each time she appeared in public. "My *descamisados* would be let down if any woman outdid me." She paused and, with an arrogant toss of her head which set the feathers on her hat aflutter, added: "But no woman ever does."

Although I knew Luis did not like me to get involved in espionage, and although I had told Jupiter that I was *cortando la coleta,* a bullfighting expression meaning giving up the fight, temptation beckoned as she continued to talk. Her bodyguards were now in conversation with my new husband and, it appeared, would be for some time.

Deftly, I thought, I thanked her for the lovely Ming vase and directed the conversation gently around to the unfound art works looted by the Nazis during the war. Then I referred to the Nazi money sent to Argentina. Eva looked at me severely. I had obviously hit upon a delicate topic. Her silence was ominous. A tension arose between us. When finally she spoke, the words came out with such venom that I feared Luis would hear.

"Querida," she said with that Argentine intonation, "take my advice. If you want to live long enough to enjoy your honeymoon and the life of a grandee countess, do not ever talk about such things. It can be very dangerous. *Comprende?"*

And she moved back across the aisle to her seat.

PART TWO

Chapter 19
MADRID, 1966

Nineteen years rolled by. I was so engrossed in fulfilling the role of Spanish wife that I had little time to think about the yellow dog painting, or El Guapo. There was so much to learn and to do, so much to get used to, even the little things.

For instance, I was in the habit of waking up earlier than Luis. I would ring for my maid and quietly have my breakfast tray brought to me in bed while he was still sleeping. One morning, I was enjoying my usual orange juice, pancakes with maple syrup and butter, bacon, and hot chocolate, when I heard, "But this is impossible."

I hadn't realized that he was awake. I kissed him good morning. "What's that, Luis?"

He was raising himself on one elbow, groggily. "That's what I want to know. What is that?"

He was staring at my breakfast tray and at the same time touching his cheek where I'd kissed him good morning. Apparently a small amount of maple syrup had transferred itself from my lips to his face.

"Aline, I really can't stand this. You must change your breakfast habits or I'll have to move into another room."

"I'll change anything. Anything you say. Just tell me what's wrong . . ."

"These smells, those repulsive things you Americans eat at this hour!" He looked at the clock and moaned. "Eight-thirty! No Spanish lady is awake at this time. It's not fair to the servants. They can't be up until midnight and then breakfast at eight. You should sleep until eleven o'clock." He rolled his eyes. "And this food! Aline, you don't have to fortify yourself to work in a field all day."

"But what does a Spanish lady eat?"

"For breakfast, a cup of tea and a small piece of toast, or a croissant with a bit of marmalade, but that's all."

I wasn't going to risk my husband for any breakfast in the world. In some ways, I could see that this life might be more difficult than espionage, but I accustomed myself quite easily to sleeping later. However, after my Spanish lady's breakfast, I died of hunger waiting for lunch until two-thirty.

There seemed no end to the habits I had to change. "Aline, I really wish you'd try a glass of wine with your meals, or water, and give up that milk. It looks so revolting on the table. But, most important, you must eat faster."

He explained that in Europe, especially in Spain where table seating goes according to the strictest protocol, a guest is, more often than not, seated next to someone he would prefer not to be obliged to chat with for very long.

"The trick is," he said, "not to dawdle over your food, so the hostess can move the group to the salon quickly, where people can enjoy coffee leisurely and sit with whoever amuses them."

The next day during lunch, another problem surfaced. He was shaking his head.

"Luis," I choked. "I can't eat any faster."

"It's not that. It's your left hand under the table. That's not attractive. In fact, it's very bad manners."

"But I was taught to eat like that. You're supposed to have your left hand on your lap when you're not using it."

"Well, perhaps in America, but that's not the way it's done here. Also, you need both hands to eat properly. That American custom of cutting your meat, then putting the knife down, then changing the fork over into your right hand, then putting your left hand in your lap! Aline, I get dizzy watching you. Why go to all that trouble? Try it our way. The fork in your left hand, the knife in your right and keep them that way."

As he spoke, I remembered that one of our American agents had been caught by the enemy despite speaking French like a Frenchman. He had been recognized as American precisely because he ate with his fork in the right hand.

"And," Luis continued, "I wouldn't want anyone to suspect that you had your hand on the man's leg next to you at a dinner party."

I looked at him, horrified.

"Oh, yes. That's just what they might think. So no more hand in your lap, please."

My Spanish conversion was still taking place a year later when my first son was born one February morning at seven-thirty. I think he was only about ten minutes old when I asked Luis what we would call him. He told me that the child's first name could be his own or his grandfather's, but that the other five names should be those of his ancestors on both sides for the past several generations.

"Of course, I want the first son to have your name, Luis," I said.

"It's quite simple then," he said. "He will be called Luis, Enrique, Alvaro, Alfonso, Baltasar, Manuel—those are the first names of my ancestors. And then my last name—Figueroa—and yours—Griffith."

"Well, what about my father's and my grandfather's names?"

"Of course. He should have those names also. Let's see, your father is William. That's Guillermo in Spanish and your grandfather . . ." I was astounded. The result was about eight or nine first names alone. But it wasn't going to be as easy as that. Only a half-hour later, before eight-thirty, early for anyone in Madrid, I heard a commotion in the hall outside and a nurse burst into the room.

"We are all so excited. The Conde de Romanones is here. We just cannot believe it. To have that famous man here in our little British-American hospital."

A moment later *El Abuelo,* eighty-five years old, came limping into the room. He always limped. He'd broken his ankle at the age of nine when he'd been thrown from his father's carriage. In those days, they didn't set bones very well, and he had been left with a limp.

"Congratulations, *nieta,*" he said, kissing me on the cheek. "I knew you'd do it right and have a boy." He sat down in a chair the nurse drew up for him next to my bed. "I've come to see my *primogenito.*"

The nurse ran out and brought the baby in. *El Abuelo* looked at him for quite a while and then smiled broadly. "What good luck! He has my nose."

I stared at my child. I glanced at the *Abuelo*'s nose. My heavens, all the suffering I just went through . . . to bring another nose like that into the world! But I smiled. The last thing I wanted was for him to sense my displeasure. I changed the subject. "We've just decided on his name, *Abuelo.* We're going to call him Luis."

"Luis?" He growled, wrinkling his brow. "Luis? But that's not possible. Not possible at all. He is my primogeniture and he must be called Alvaro. He will inherit my titles and he must have my name."

Although the *Abuelo* had numerous great-grandchildren, he was charmed by Alvaro and came to the hospital every day, staying on and on. We held hands and talked for hours. On one visit the nurse came in with the baby crying loudly.

"What's the matter with that child?" asked *El Abuelo.*

"Nothing, *Abuelo.* It's just that he's hungry."

"Then let him eat." He glared at the nurse. "What's wrong with you? Feed him, nurse. And hurry."

"Well, *Abuelo . . .* you see, it's that I have to feed Alvaro. Uh— personally."

"You?" He turned to the nurse, confused. "But aren't you the *ama mojada,* the wet nurse?"

"No, Señor Conde. The Señora Condesa feeds him herself."

He turned to me. "But he should have a wet nurse. Your husband must be mad. I will send for one immediately. From the Basque country." He nodded. "The Basque women have the best milk."

"But *Abuelo,* I want to feed my own baby."

"A skinny thing like you? How can you nourish Alvaro properly? Besides, when you leave here you'll have things to do and you won't be available all the time to feed the child. Leave it to me. I'll get you a good strong Basque woman . . ."

This time, at least, I did not give in.

Over two more years came two more sons. After Alvaro came Luis, and then Miguel. This dispelled my father-in-law's worries that American women were more apt to divorce than to produce children. I was also kept busy restoring an old palace that had been in Luis' family since 1231, through twenty-three generations. Nobody had set foot in it since the French had invaded Spain in 1808. On the surrounding property, we improved the farming and ranching methods, and set up schools for our shepherds' and cowherds' children. Then, right away, I had to learn how to shoot partridge, one of Luis' favorite pastimes. Although I'd been taught how to shoot men in the spy school, I discovered it was a lot more difficult to shoot red-legged partridge. I also learned Spanish paleography, script from the Middle Ages through the seventeenth century, so

I could read family archives which dated back to the year 800 A.D. To me it was a fascinating world of mystery and excitement.

Then came that night of the Windsors' dinner party, and the past came storming back to remind me of the even greater mysteries I had left behind.

In a way, I should have been warned. Only a week before, I had had another reminder, one I had quickly dismissed, but now it took on greater significance in my mind. I was getting ready for what Luis considered a much too-early dinner—nine-thirty—at the American embassy. Spanish afternoons begin when when lunch ends, at four, and last until nine. Dinner invitations are normally for ten, not before.

My hairdresser was late, but just when I was beginning to despair, I heard footsteps and my maid ushered Carmen into the room. The *peluquera,* hairdresser, approached in tense quick steps, dropping her bag as she reached out to take my hand. I presumed her flustered manner and hectic appearance had to do with being late. "Oh, Señora Condesa, please forgive me for not getting here on time." Even her voice was unusually tense. Nervously, she began to place her utensils on the dressing table helter-skelter and I wondered if it wouldn't be better if I did my hair myself.

"Such a terrifying afternoon, Countess." By now she had started to brush my hair. "Two hours attending to the hair of the Señora de Peron and refreshing her makeup, too. It was *espantoso,* horrible." Her shudder added emphasis to her words.

Carmen was certainly not her normal self and I was surprised that attending to Peron's pretty young second wife, Isabel, would be disagreeable, and I told her so.

The hairdresser's voice hit a high pitch. "But Countess, it wasn't Isabel Peron, it was his first wife, Eva."

I thought the woman had lost her mind. "What are you talking about?" I asked. "Eva Peron has been dead almost fifteen years."

"That's what made it so frightful, Countess," Carmen's voice was shrill. "Just the memory of that dusty yellow hair sticking to my hands makes me ill." She put the brush down. "Señor Peron stood behind me all the time, watching and giving orders. That hair coming out really upset him. He said the Señora had thick black hair when he met her and even when she dyed it blond, it remained thick. He said she had to look like she always did, and he made me go to Madrid to find a hairpiece to match her color."

Everybody in Madrid knew that Juan Peron had had Eva's body embalmed in Buenos Aires by a famous specialist and that he had brought the coffin containing her body to Spain when he came there to live in exile. I had never liked the man—so big and pomp-ous and such a friend of the Nazis during the war. Nothing he did would surprise me. I asked Carmen how often she had taken care of this peculiar client.

"For me, the first time, Countess. And the last." She picked up the brush again, and the energy she expended backcombing my hair reduced her answers to breathless phrases. "Señor Peron says that he is planning to return to Buenos Aires. That's why he wants her to be in good condition. He says Doña Eva must go too, that her *descamisados* will want to see her."

Carmen delved into her satchel searching for her comb. I hoped it wouldn't be the same one she had used on Eva. She went on explaining in a high-pitched nervous voice.

"I suppose the Condesa knows that the Señor Peron keeps the body in the garage of his house in Puerta de Hierro. Well," she went on, "when they opened the casket, through the glass cover she looked quite well. I don't mean looking at her didn't make me feel queasy. I must admit it was a shock, but I didn't shake like a jelly. Not yet. But when the chauffeur raised that glass I wanted to run away. The smell was like the powder they spray on the fields when there is a plague of locusts. The light was shining right on her face. Her skin looked like a dry lemon peel." Carmen sighed dramati-cally. "Señor Peron got very agitated when he saw the tiny flecks roll off her face as I put on the makeup base. He said I was rubbing too hard and, Countess, believe me, I was barely touching her."

While the hairdresser finished my hair, I thought about that last time I had seen Eva Peron in the plane going to Rome. That night, I told the hairdresser's story to Luis, and we marveled about it, and then I put the story, and the past, out of my mind. Until a weekend after, when Jupiter called and got all of my thoughts to tumbling. I twisted and turned that night, dreaming of people who had been part of my life twenty years before: Jupiter, Magic, Top Hat. I woke, surprised to find that it was 1966, that I was in my own house, and that those happenings were far behind.

As I sipped my breakfast tea, however, I mused about Magic's appalling assassination and flirted with the idea of accepting Jupi-ter's proposal. But how would I get around Luis' insistence that I never again involve myself in these endeavors? Years ago John Derby had complimented me on my war work in front of Luis, thinking he was doing me a favor. Luis had finally realized that it was true, that his wife had been an American undercover agent. He had been astounded and not pleased, especially when I did a few things for the CIA later on. I knew I would have to be careful if I ever went back to that work again.

The Duke and Duchess were leaving that morning for the express train to Irún, a city on the northern frontier, and from there would change trains to catch the night express to Paris. The Duchess refused to travel by air, and they both hated long motor trips. Martin, their Spanish chauffeur, had brought their car by road and already left to return with the Duchess' thirty-seven pieces of matched Louis Vuitton luggage, engorged by her shopping sprees, much of which were Christmas presents for their servants. Although it was February, she started her shopping early. After all, they had twenty-four servants including gardeners and those at the gate house, and many of them had families. Since the Windsors had no family of their own, they derived an enormous amount of pleasure from a big Christmas celebration for their servants. The car could have gone by rail, but the Duchess was thrifty and frowned upon unnecessary expense.

Anxious to inquire about the painting before she left, I picked up the phone and called the Hotel Ritz.

Her voice was rushed and nervous. "Precisely what I was going to telephone you about, Aline." Her sharp staccato words jumped through the receiver. "Would it be a terrible imposition to ask you and Luis to bring that painting when you come to visit us next week? It's already paid for, but the frame had to be fixed. They said it could not be delivered until noon today, which of course will be too late."

She gave me the address, which I jotted down. Before I could ask more details, she had hung up. The night before, I had never had a chance to ask her about the painting. The guests had kept the two of us busy every minute. Only when the Windsors were leaving did I manage to get near her, but then everyone was lined up waiting to curtsy to say good-bye, and it had become awkward. I thought of telling Luis to ask her about the painting, but he was too far away, already at the top of the steps, waiting to accompany them to the car.

Not having been able to obtain a description of the painting from her tantalized me, so I decided to go to the shop myself and pick it up before meeting John Derby for lunch. Wouldn't it be fun, to show Jupiter the long-lost yellow dog painting! I knew that it was a long shot, but I was already envisioning myself marching into the restaurant with the Cézanne under my arm.

Since Luis and I were not leaving for Paris for a week, I could have postponed my visit to the antique dealer. In fact, I could have sent the chauffeur or asked the dealer to deliver it, but I wanted to see what the shop looked like. When I asked Luis if he recognized the name of the place, he said he'd never heard of it, despite the fact that he knew most of the dealers in town.

We were having our breakfast in his study on the third floor. He had just finished coffee and was lighting a cigarette. "Of course," he said, "the chances are slim that it's the same painting you were looking for twenty years ago."

"I know that."

"Then why are you so excited?" He asked, his pale green eyes smiling at me. "You do have a tendency to exaggerate, you know. Do you realize how many paintings have dogs in them? And anyhow, the Windsors just don't have an eye for good paintings. They'd be the last people to uncover a gem like that."

He was right, as usual, and so observant. I fidgeted and looked at my watch, waiting for the moment I could leave. I had several things to do that morning and I wanted to be sure to arrive at the antique shop before lunch.

"The point is," said Luis, "if it does turn out to be the missing painting, what then?"

"Well, I'll try to find out where it came from. Naturally, I'd still like to uncover the fellow who ran that Nazi loot business. I've always suspected he could still be around."

"You know I don't like you getting involved in that again. In Spain, you're Spanish like I am. You shouldn't be doing espionage for the Americans." He flicked his cigarette into the ashtray. "I know John Derby's visit here yesterday was just social, but don't let him talk you into anything. Remember our agreement."

So far, my conscience was clear. I had kept my promise to him, but I had also omitted telling him that Derby had already asked me to do another mission.

When I stood to leave, I went over to give Luis a peck on the

Madrid, 1945: Wearing Belmonte's pink satin vest from his "suit of lights."

Juanito Belmonte.

With Smokey's daughter, both of us in flamenco costume.

Edmundo Lassalle, "Top Hat," with his typical brand of humor. The sign on the man's derrière reads, "Gone with the Wind."

October 1945: At Top Hat wedding—Renata is on the right.

My maids, Cecelia and
Angustias.

August 1947: My marriage to
Luis. I was now the Countess
de Quintanilla, later to be
Romanones.

With Luis, his father, and his three sisters, 1947.

Dressed in formal mantilla, 1947.

A grand soirée at my home in Madrid, 1966.

The Duke and Duchess of Windsor, 1966.

With Jupiter and Ambassador Angier Biddle Duke, 1966.

The Duchess watching flamenco at my house in Madrid. She is talking to the famous flamenco dancer Antonio. I am directly behind her, in white, and Luis is to my right.

t the Rothschilds' ball, me with my headdress, Audrey Hepburn in her birdcage.

Richard Burton, Elizabeth
Taylor, and Audrey Hepburn
at the ball.

The Duchess of Alba, Jacqueline Kennedy, and me in our mantillas at the Seville bullfights, 1966.

Jackie and me riding with bullfighter Fermin Bohorquez at the Seville Fair.

cheek. He pulled me down and gave me a proper kiss. That sealed it. I wouldn't be tempted by Jupiter's proposal, no matter what. Who would take a chance of losing such a husband!

A couple of hours later, as I directed my little white Seat 600 up to the Calle del Prado and into the narrow Calle Leon to the address the Duchess had given me, I wondered how she had heard of a shop in this part of Madrid—a strange place indeed for anyone to know about, much less the Duchess of Windsor. As I suspected, the shop was modest and small—only a pair of splintered chairs and a cracked seventeenth-century table in the window. When I opened the door, I saw paintings of saints and madonnas hanging on the walls, helter-skelter at crooked angles. On the floor were broken candelabra, stacks of porcelain, old leather-bound books. Everything was dusty. At first I could see no one and wandered through the jumble of shabby objects until a plump middle-aged man appeared from a back room and stared at me over silver-rimmed glasses. It was already about a quarter to two, and the man had a huge key in hand ready to lock up for the long lunch hour.

When I told him that I had come to pick up the painting for the Duke and Duchess of Windsor and pulled out the receipt they had left with the Hotel Ritz concierge, he gave a deep sigh. Instantly, I realized there was a problem.

"Perhaps the señora could return after five. We're closed from two to five," he said, as he continued to stare.

When I insisted that it was still not two o'clock, he didn't seem to know what to say at first. Then he shuffled toward an old desk in the back corner and picked up a gilt frame, stretching it out to me.

"This is the frame Their Royal Highnesses chose, but unfortunately the painting has already been sold to someone else. It was picked up this morning." He bent down and took a few sheets of newspaper from a stack on the floor, piled there for wrapping packages, and began to wrap the empty frame.

I shook my head vehemently. "Why would Their Highnesses want an empty frame?" I was indignant and disappointed. "And why would you take their money if the painting was already promised to someone else?"

He opened a drawer and pulled out a check. "I didn't take their money, señora," he said. "Here's their check, and if you will give me a receipt for it, that will save me the trouble of mailing it to them." He shook his head. "How was I to know when Their Royal Highnesses appeared here unexpectedly yesterday that the painting belonged to someone else? It had no sold sign on it. I am sorry. Their Royal Highnesses are very pleasant, but when I arrived here today, Doña Carmen, she's the lady who owns this store, had removed the painting. I thought she was going to be pleased to learn that such distinguished people wanted it, but Doña Carmen said the painting was reserved for a previous buyer."

When I tried to pry more details out of him, he shook his head. He knew nothing about the painting. Doña Carmen had recently inherited the shop from her uncle. The salesman was not able to give me a description, and I left in a state of frustration, with the Duke's check instead of the painting.

Chapter 20

J ockey was only half full when I entered at two-fifteen, it being still a bit early for its prestigious clientele to have lunch. But Jupiter was sitting at the banquette on the left and jumped to his feet when he saw me. Again, I was surprised at how little he had changed over the years—the same stocky, athletic build, the sparse hair now completely white. His face was rosy and young and the pale blue eyes had the same golden specks. Despite having dated many glamorous women, he had remained single, probably because his work was incompatible with marriage, until a short time ago, when he had married a beautiful French divorcée. I knew his business continued to take him all over the world, the perfect cover for his work, about which he was always secretive, unless it included something with which I could help. Even then, he never told me any detail I needn't know. Secrecy and John Derby had become synonymous.

As soon as Gerardo, the maître d', had taken our order, I hastened to tell Jupiter about my fruitless visit to the antique shop—and about my naive hope that I might have found the yellow dog painting after all these years.

"Not so naive," he said. "There are still hundreds of paintings like that which have never been recovered. It is certainly possible that some of this stolen art is still in Spain." Then he changed the subject and addressed the topic that was on his mind.

"When are you going to see the Duchess again?"

I explained that Luis and I would be spending the following week at their house in Paris.

"Good," he said.

I frowned and shook my head that I did not understand.

"Just an idea I had. What if you persuaded the Duchess to help you? Think of it! Two of you making the rounds instead of just one. The chances of success would be so much greater."

I shook my head again, too astonished to speak.

He ignored me. "On the night she was killed, Magic told our Paris station chief that she expected to be able to prove the identity of the NATO mole. The assassination occurred near the Pavillon Albert, a restaurant where Magic thought there was some kind of dead drop that would be used that night. She left no specific instructions for us to follow up on, except to mention the names of a few outstanding figures in Paris who sometimes invited the mole to their affairs. Your friends, the Windsors, were among the names she alluded to. We're at a complete dead end. We believe Magic's assassin is the mole in the American European Command and that he was in Paris that night of February first, the night she was killed. You're the only one I can call upon who frequents those social circles in Paris."

I shook my head. "The answer is still no. Luis would be furious. And as for the Duchess, it would be unfair to get her involved in an espionage affair, even if she were willing to, which I doubt."

Actually, the latter was not exactly the truth. The Duchess liked intrigue and was also a wildly patriotic American. The more I thought about it, the more I suspected she might be enthralled with the idea of catching an enemy spy. But I wasn't about to tell that to Derby.

Jupiter ignored my excuses. "Let me emphasize again the drastically serious nature of the leakage we are facing."

I nodded reluctantly.

"Just consider again what it means to have a mole providing the Soviet General Staff with America's response plan to a nuclear attack. To learn about our nuclear defense, our submarines and air power, the secret situation of missiles, the exact location and numbers of every weapon in our arsenal for security. The disclosures provided to the enemy leave the entire Western world vulnerable to an attack by the Soviets, at whatever moment they might initiate it." John Derby's voice was so low I had difficulty hearing him.

He stopped speaking and sipped his red wine. I waited.

"The French agent killed with Magic, the one with whom she developed an intimate relationship, worked for the KGB. He was the cutout, the go-between. His messages were in code, probably giving the location of the dead drop where the film could be picked up. This transaction usually took place during some social event— we don't know how—sometimes in a restaurant or public hall, or even in a private home.

"The cutout never told Magic who the mole was," he went on. "He was too frightened of what the Soviets might do to him. As you know, they're all covered by Soviet surveillance teams. The most she could do was trail him, then wait until he emerged from the party or reception, and follow him to wherever he delivered the coded message. That's probably how they caught on to her. She refused to use our own surveillance teams. It was very foolish. If she had, she might be alive today. Our teams are very good, very trustworthy—retired French cops whose pensions would be diminished if the French learned they were working for us. We're sure they're reliable."

"John," I said, "tell me how Magic was murdered."

For all his manipulations of me, I could tell this was one thing Jupiter genuinely didn't want to talk about. He hemmed and hawed a bit, and lifted his napkin to his mouth before finally speaking. "She was found at the entrance of the Metro of the Porte Dauphine, impaled on the spikes of the iron grating."

Involuntarily, my stomach muscles clenched. Taking a deep breath, I asked who had found her.

"An anonymous telephone call to the Police de Sécurité gave the alarm."

"When did someone from the Company see the body?"

"An agent in the police department advised our station chief, who went to the hospital immediately. She was not yet dead."

"My heavens, then she was able to tell him who had done it?"

"Not really. What she said was unintelligible. She was delirious and could hardly breathe."

"But what did she say? If you don't tell me all the story, I'm not going to consider doing this mission."

He sighed. "Really, I can't tell you any more because I didn't see her myself. I was away in Morocco. Anyway, she confided in no one. You know she trusted few people."

I felt disloyal saying this, but had to ask. "John, what about her drinking? What if her death was simply caused by some thug with whom she might have gotten drunk?"

"No, they tested her blood. It contained no sign of alcohol. She was particularly cautious in her last days."

I shuddered. "The mole must have been strong enough to be able to throw her up on the grating."

"Not necessarily. Magic was small and light. And it didn't have to be the mole himself, it could have been a professional. Those fellows are monsters. She was a terrible mess when they found her."

"Oh, what else had the monster done to her?"

Jupiter reddened. "I'd rather not go into that."

If he didn't want to give the details, it must have been ghastly. I felt weak. I remembered that first time I had seen Magic, when Sphinx had delivered me to the room I was going to share with her in the spy school outside Washington. She was sitting on one of the simple white beds studying a book on ciphers—a young and fragile girl. I didn't know then she had already lost most of her family in Europe and had been through situations I had no idea existed on this planet.

Jupiter and I continued our lunch, discussing other things, and it was not until later, as we were saying good-bye in the street outside the restaurant, that Jupiter put the pressure on me again.

"You must consider this mission seriously, Aline." His voice was pleading. "The next dead drop in Paris will be serviced sometime in March, we believe during some kind of fancy ball." I immediately thought of the Rothschilds' ball, which was one of the reasons we were going to Paris.

"We think the mole has advised his KGB agent where to pick up the top secret data at that affair," he went on, "or at least pass on some kind of information."

He placed his hand on my arm as I turned to walk toward my car. "The information would be in a roll of film. It'd be very small, no bigger than a matchbox. You know the Minox? The tiny German camera? It's about the size of a cigarette lighter, and extremely clear and precise. I'm sure they're using that to photograph the documents."

At that moment, a friend came out of the restaurant, and, unaware he was interrupting a private conversation, stopped to chat with us for what seemed an interminable length of time. When he finally went on his way, Jupiter continued.

"Streets are always safer to transmit critical information, anyway.

Those banquettes in that restaurant were much too close together. Pay attention. It's important that you understand exactly how this operation works. If the location of the dead drop is passed on at this ball, it'll most likely be by hand, by means of a coded message."

Now I was standing still in the middle of the sidewalk, listening to his every word. He knew this kind of intrigue could animate me to do this mission. "Of course, you know, a dead drop is never used more than once," he went on. "And in this case, since it is improbable that more than one person in the American European Command is involved, the mole will have to load the drop each time himself. That's when he is clearly exposed. If you go to Paris, you would probably be going to that ball, Tiger."

I hadn't heard my code name in ages. That also had its effect.

He was still talking. "Magic didn't believe she could even get near this ball, she simply didn't have the right contacts, and that's why she risked everything on covering the dead drop near the restaurant. We must find the next dead drop, Tiger, and we must find the man who uses it."

I started to walk slowly down the street toward my car and Jupiter kept talking as we walked. "I can give you the names of the specific officials we are investigating, men who have legitimate access to this kind of top secret material but who would normally be above suspicion. Maybe they're as guiltless as they seem, but it's a beginning. The Duchess' help would be invaluable. Think about it, Tiger."

Again the code name—as far as he was concerned, I was already working on the case.

"If you change your mind, I'm here for two more days. I can't believe that you're not itching to get back into the game. And don't forget, if it had been the other way around, Magic would have tried to avenge you."

He was right. But I gave a shrug and said nothing, kissed him on the cheek, and got into my car.

Chapter 21

As soon as the Duchess reached her house in Paris the following day, she called to thank me for the dinner. I told her that the shopkeeper had returned their check for the painting. She was disappointed, but when I asked her to describe it, she only mentioned that it was a scene of a couple having a picnic in the woods and that what she most remembered was a little dog, just like the one she'd had years ago.

"Which corner?" A tingle of excitement raced up my spine.

"I think it was the left."

"Was it yellow?"

"Was what yellow?"

"The dog."

"Yellow?" She paused. "I suppose you could call it that."

I was sure of it now. I burned with the desire to find it, as if all those years had not passed by. But the Duchess was still talking.

"Aline, I telephoned you mainly so you could choose which dinners you and Luis will want to go to next week when you come here. The one at Lady Wortham's will be a bore for young people like yourselves. David and I must go. We have no choice. Maybe you'd like to arrange something else for that evening. We'll be giving a dinner for you and Luis the night before you leave for the Rothschilds. Their ball is the talk of Paris. I suppose you're having sensational costumes made in Madrid. Here all the theatrical designers are in a frenzy concocting marvelous things for our friends."

The Duchess went on. She was not one to waste time on a long distance call. "Since the dinner is for you both, is there anyone special you'd like me to invite?"

My adrenaline rate shot up. I just couldn't resist the temptation. Her question suddenly made Jupiter's request so easy. "As a matter of fact, there is. Someone from NATO I want to meet."

"NATO? Really? Well, of course. What's the name?"

"I'll have to call you back about that. I've . . . I've lost the address."

"But who is he?"

"Oh, just an American friend of a friend. I'll get back to you as soon as possible."

That same afternoon I called Jupiter to tell him the Duchess had offered to invite anyone I wanted to her house for dinner with us. I said that I would study the possibilities of doing the mission when I went to Paris, and I made it clear that I had decided nothing, that everything would depend on her reaction.

He was enthusiastic and came right over. "This is fantastic news. If the Duchess helps, our chances are immeasurably better." He searched in his pocket for a small pad he always carried. His notations were in a scribble only he could understand. "Here's the name of two men who may not, I repeat, may not be guilty, but we want to know who their friends are, who they talk to when they go out—everything you can find out. If the Duchess could invite one or both, then we'll have a start." He wrote down the names, and handed me the paper, which I knew I was supposed to destroy as soon as I had memorized its contents. "Begin with the one she considers most socially popular. Then we'll go on from there."

As he was speaking I realized that if I was foolish enough to accept this mission, from then on my life would be obsessed by the case until it was resolved. Espionage was like that. It took over and became the only thing one thought about—a dangerous but exciting addiction. I told him that I would think about it and call him from Paris. He gave me a number where I could reach him the following week, and as soon as he left, I called the Duchess. I didn't know exactly how I could explain what I wanted.

"I'm calling to give you the names of two Americans from NATO. Frankly, if you knew either, it would be a great favor to me if you would include one couple in your dinner."

"Are these friends of yours, Aline?"

"No, but I am anxious to meet them, whichever couple of the two is the most social, that's the one I want." As a thought struck me, I added, "And please . . . don't mention this to Luis."

"Aline, this sounds so mysterious."

I laughed. "Well, in a way, it is." I gave her the names. "Colonel and Mrs. Michael Chandler, and Colonel and Mrs. Paul Ferguson."

"Well, this isn't an easy order. Let me see." There was a pause. "Can you repeat those names?"

When I did, she responded unenthusiastically. "Neither are close friends. Ferguson sounds familiar, but I doubt that he and his wife are what I would call socially prominent. On the other hand, I know a French general who has some very important post in NATO and who is most charming. I could ask him what American . . ."

"No, please, don't mention this to anyone until I speak with you. Not even to your husband. Please. Just invite either of those Americans. It's a trial, I know, but I'll explain when I see you."

"Oh, my! You can be sure I'll do what I can. I can't wait for you to get here."

Chapter 22
PARIS

As usual, Martin was waiting at the airport and drove us in the Duchess' old Packard along his customary route across Paris through the Bois de Boulogne to the Rue de Champs d'Entrainement. At the gate, he stopped the car and got out to ring the bell for Germaine, who appeared a few moments later, a short navy cape clasped tightly over her shoulders to protect her from the cold gusts of wind. She opened the huge black iron gilt-spiked gates and the car followed the slightly curving driveway past the barren sycamores and the low dahlia bushes the Duke had planted years before, up to the classic, small, turn-of-the-century palace.

Georges, the butler, in gray pants and blue black tails, stood waiting at the bottom of the steps to open the car door. Just behind him was Olegario, a young footman we had sent from our ranch a few months before, proud and self-conscious in his grand uniform—a far cry from the worn cap and corduroy pants he had worn when taking care of our sheep.

"Madame la Comtesse"—Georges bowed —"Monsieur le Comte." Georges was smiling as usual. "Their Royal Highnesses are waiting in the boudoir."

When we entered the large hall, the Duke and Duchess were standing at the top of the curved marble stairway looking over the railing. "Aline, Luis . . . come up . . ." the Duchess called out. "Oh, how good to see you."

The dogs were barking, as always. Those noisy pugs.

"Oooh, these dogs, David . . . ohhh, what a racket . . . I can't stand it," complained the Duchess.

"Diamante, shut up . . . Ginseng . . ." The Duke sounded exasperated. "Shut up, I said . . ."

There was an elevator, but we ran up the stairs and, as always, they waited for us on the landing. His Royal Highness wore a blue checked suit and she a Chanel suit, also blue, with just the right jewelry for daytime, what they called their "sentimental jewelry"— small things they designed together, often in remembrance of trips or special shared occasions, and made by Cartier or Van Cleef.

I curtsied to the Duke and then kissed him hello. I didn't curtsy to the Duchess. Since we were both American, it seemed a silly thing to do.

From the early days of our marriage Luis had informed me that the rules about treatment of members of a royal family are unwavering. A lady always curtsies to members of a royal family, be they man, woman, or child, even though she may be so close a friend as to follow the curtsy with a kiss. The kiss is for the friend and the curtsy is for the ancestry, for the royal blood. So, I always curtsied to the Duke when first seeing him in the morning and when kissing him good-night.

We had arrived at tea time and they led us into the room between their bedrooms, "the boudoir," they called it, a cozy room with a fireplace and French windows overlooking the garden, and with comfortable upholstered armchairs, a sofa, a large table against the wall chock-full of photographs of friends, and the Duchess' desk in the corner.

Tea was brought in by Georges and a footman, who set up individual tables for each of us. The Duchess went to her chair while the Duke sat in his, next to which the men placed a silver tray with tea things. The Duchess never took tea nor did she make a gesture to serve it, so I stood up to help until the Duke waved me down.

"Aline, Aline, let me do the tea."

"Sir," I said, "the Duchess told me your hip was bothering you again."

"Don't be silly, Aline." He was busy pouring the tea. "I remember you like it with a wee bit of milk, as I do." He then strained to get to his feet to hand me the cup.

"Sir, that's hurting you."

"Bah," he said. "I never pay attention to that." Then he did the same for Luis.

The Duke didn't eat much with his tea and the Duchess took nothing, as usual, but he knew I was always hungry and passed me the plate with tiny circles of cheese and cucumbers on bread. For a while we chatted about the partridge shoot the week before in Spain; then we discussed the painting. The Duchess was really upset when I told her the description sounded very much like a Cézanne that had been lost in Spain during the war. Missing a good bargain bothered both of them.

The Duke looked at my cup. "That tea must be cold." Taking it from my hand, he studied the tea service. "Where's the slop bowl?" he called out, "Georges, you've forgotten the slop bowl . . . ah, no, sorry, here it is right here on the tray . . . in front of my eyes."

Then he emptied the remains of my cold tea into an antique silver bowl and poured me a fresh cup. "Iced tea is all right, but if there's anything I hate, it's cold hot tea." He sat back in his chair and lit a cigarette.

"Oh, David. Not another. That's the beginning of a new pack and it's only six o'clock." The Duchess shook her head in despair.

When the two men began to discuss racehorses, the Duchess gave me a knowing glance. "Aline, while our beaus talk, I want to show you what I'm wearing for the Rothschilds' ball on Saturday. Givenchy made the dress. The headdress was an idea of Raimundo Larrain, who is a genius. The whole thing cost a fortune and I'm not sure I should have spent so much."

We walked into the cozy blue bedroom, her pug following, jumping up on the chaise longue next to her when she sat down. I knew she was anxious to learn why I wanted to meet someone from NATO.

"Now, Aline dear," she began. "For the dinner we're giving for you and Luis, I've invited the Fergusons. I finally discovered that they were the American couple we met at a dinner in the British embassy. I hardly spoke to either, so I wasn't sure about them. But I don't think I know those Chandlers, so that makes it difficult to invite them. I hear the Fergusons are very social. He must have a large personal fortune, because they live in a pompous apartment on the Avenue Kleber where they entertain a lot. Most military officials live outside Paris near the Camp des Loges base since few have enough money to live in town, and I suppose, too, it's nearer their work. Wait till you see Ferguson's wife!" She threw her hands in the air. "What clothes! And she has social aspirations. You know the type. But he is good-looking and they know everyone. David will find the wife a bore. I took care to invite the Cabrols to have someone who outranks them so there'll be no danger of the wife having to sit next to David at dinner.''

I was seated facing her on the dressing-room chair, from where I could watch the Duke and Luis in the next room. I didn't want either to appear unexpectedly. Her elbow leaned on one skinny knee as her red-lacquered fingers reached out to tap my hand.

"Aline, what is this all about?"

For a moment, I pondered whether I should tell her about Magic's terrible end, but decided to restrict myself to the story of the mission. The Duchess' unique sapphire blue gaze was focused on me.

"To give you a hasty idea: There's a person connected with the American European Command and NATO here in Paris who is delivering critical information affecting American security to the KGB. He is suspected to be a high-ranking official, possibly one of the names I gave you. The man we're looking for frequents top social affairs in Paris—the kind of places you go to. We want to know who his friends are, who he speaks to, what people he makes an effort over—that sort of thing. This Colonel Ferguson is a good beginning."

Her eyes opened wide. "Then you're still a spy!"

Instead of answering, I smiled. She had suspected my espionage work years ago at a dinner in 1948 in New York, when Luis and I were on our honeymoon. General Wild Bill Donovan, founder and director of OSS, had been seated next to me at the Duchess' table and had spoken about my work in the war, which let the cat out of the bag for the sharp-eyed Duchess, who was always more observant than others.

"You could contribute, too," I said. "Do you realize what a useful spy you could be? Apart from knowing everyone, you have another advantage—no one would suspect you."

She was thoughtful. "It's true that I know everyone in Paris' social world and then some." She wrinkled her rather large nose. "Unfortunately, as you know, they're not always the most amusing."

Through the open door into the boudoir, I could see Luis and the Duke engrossed in conversation. Briefly, I told her that I did intelligence now and then for the U.S., but that this time even my husband did not know about it. I went on to explain that my boss,

Jupiter, had learned that this mole would be attending an important ball in Paris during the month of March, and that a vital bit of information would be transferred during the ball. That he wanted me to discover how this transmission took place and, of course, who did it.

"That has to be the Rothschilds' ball at Ferrieres next week," interrupted the Duchess.

"Yes, that's what I thought, too," I answered. "It would be great if we could ask Marie-Hélène"—that was the Baroness Guy de Rothschild—"if these Chandlers or Fergusons have been invited, but that would make her curious."

"She's too smart; we might arouse her suspicions. She wouldn't know what was particularly interesting about either, but she'd take care to find out," said the Duchess. "But I'll look around at the ball and I'll do my best to discover what NATO officials are there. Because of David's eye—it's never stopped bothering him since the operation—Marie-Hélène has thoughtfully asked us to spend that night at Ferrieres, so we don't have to drive back to Paris late. He will go to bed early. But I'll stay up, and if there's any high-ranking Americans there from NATO, I'll find out."

"Just knowing their names would be useful," I answered. "That's something I couldn't do. I don't know anyone from NATO."

"I hate to disappoint you, Aline, but I don't see many NATO officials in this city myself. Oh, I do hope Colonel Ferguson turns out to be useful. As I remember, he is a West Pointer and all that—not the kind to be a traitor. But, as you said, it's a beginning."

"Who knows, you may have a knack for this sort of thing. And one thing I can assure you—looking for traitors certainly spices up dinner parties."

Rather than shying from collaborating, the Duchess was eager to help. Her only reservations were that her husband not know about it and that her name not appear on any CIA document or list. She also said that the French government had been extremely considerate in renting them the house in the Bois for their lifetimes, and for that reason she did not want to do anything that would be detrimental to France. I assured her that the operation had no anti-French elements.

"I'm very American, Aline, despite my years abroad. I like to do things, to feel I have a job or a cause to work for. There's no challenge in running two homes and tending to household problems. Spying might break the monotony." She giggled. "You might not realize it, but I'm a good worker. First of all I've always been an early riser. Now in old age more than ever." She grimaced. "It's awful to realize that I'm already sixty-nine. Just the thought gives me the shivers." She paused. "Well, as I was saying, David and I are usually here in my room in bed chatting until three every morning and I'm awake at seven. Did you know I had a job at *Vogue* before I married Ernest Simpson? And the first year of the war here in Paris I really worked hard at the Red Cross."

"Before we go any further, I should tell you there's an element of danger involved." I observed her as I spoke. "The man we're looking for is vicious and cold-blooded."

She shook her head. "I must admit," she sighed, "I'm not brave at all. I'm afraid of so many things—flying, skiing. The only airplane I ever took was for David's operation on his aneurysm in Houston. And that was because it was a matter of his life. I'm always afraid someone will break into the house at night. That's why we have a night watchman. I'm not at all like David, who's afraid of nothing. But I'm good at getting people to talk, finding things out. If you think I can be helpful despite my being such a fraidy-cat, I'm willing to try."

As she looked at me, I noticed that the color of her eyes matched the sapphire ring on her finger. Then my glance passed to the blue and gray Portuguese rug which had been designed by the Duchess with the Windsor feathers. Every table in the room had terra-cotta pots of orchids straight out of her hothouse. Nothing in the house or their lives had changed in years. I didn't feel guilty. Espionage would bring in some needed excitement.

Their marriage, so famous worldwide, had always seemed a bit sterile and sad to me—all those problems created by her being American, and having been divorced, and then married at the time she met the Duke, which had obliged him to abdicate in order to marry her! Then no children of their own, and to be ostracized by his own family and by many friends, too! The Duchess had no family at all, only Aunt Bessy, whom she loved dearly and who was still alive, although completely senile. The two royals were innate homemakers. He loved gardening. She loved cooking and prided herself on being a good housekeeper. She had confessed to me that long ago they had both become fed up with parties and travel.

"But," she had said then, "we continue our meaningless life and try not to complain. With the English, you must keep a stiff upper lip and never show your feelings."

At the foot of the bed, on a bench upholstered in the pale blue now commonly referred to as "Windsor blue," was a pillow. It was hand-embroidered with the words, "You can never be too thin or too rich." I mused that the quip, which had been invented by the Duchess years ago and had become famous, might then have seemed amusing. But today, sadly enough, it was far from true. Looking at her, I thought, her excessive thinness was probably one of the reasons she never had energy to exercise. And the many servants—a sign of wealth despite her complaints that they were poor and that all their friends had more money than they—obliged her to spend the greater part of her days solving their quarrels and personal problems. She was both too thin and too rich for her own good.

My attention moved to the Duchess, who was still talking. "With a few more clues, we might uncover the man in no time," she was saying. "Really, this does sound fascinating, but almost too easy."

I laughed. "Don't worry. This sort of thing is never easy. You'll see."

She looked at her watch. "We have to dress for dinner, Aline."

In the other room, our husbands were still talking. I stood up and started toward the door. The Duchess detained me, placing her hand on my arm. I glanced down at the thick blunt fingers, the reason she hated her hands and wore gloves as much as possible.

"Aline," she giggled, "I'd say you have a case of the spy bug. And I'm very much afraid you have contaminated me with the disease."

I smiled.

She whispered. "You don't have to incriminate yourself, nor tell me anything I shouldn't know. Just let me know how I can help. The only intrigue I usually hear is whose husband has an affair with whose wife. Espionage is a role I might find to my taste."

Ophelia appeared at the door to announce that the hairdresser was downstairs.

The Duchess squinted again at her wristwatch. "My heavens. Edouard is late and so am I. When he's finished with me, I'll send him up to you, Aline. And, by the way, tonight is small black tie.

Save something grander for tomorrow at Jacqueline de Ribes's dinner."

When I left the room, she was sitting at the dressing table and letting down her thick beautifully dyed russet-brown hair. I knew the makeup artist would come later and do her maquillage and place the absolutely perfect false eyelashes so no one could tell.

As I walked through the boudoir, from the open door into the Duke's bedroom came the sound of someone plunking away with one finger on a typewriter. Luis was standing there looking out the window and turned around when he heard my steps.

With a questioning glance, I pointed wordlessly to the Duke's room.

"He's giving me the address of a friend in America who can recommend the best golf clubs," explained Luis in a low voice, "and he's typing it out himself."

"Darn," came the Duke's voice as he hit the wrong key. Luis and I tried to smother our giggles, as the plunk, plink, plank sounds continued.

"Go on up," Luis said. "I'll be with you as soon as the Duke finishes."

I'd never known that the Duke used a typewriter, and it was a surprise. I laughed out loud as I climbed the narrow stairs to what the Duchess called the attic rooms—our two bedrooms with a small hall and bath in between. At the Windsors it was always a sensuous experience to go from one part of the house to another. Each room had a different scent. As I entered, a new fragrance was wafting throughout our rooms from the Guerlain perfume burner. Luis came up behind me and went into the red, white, and blue men's bedroom, where the walls were lined with shelves of miniature soldiers of the Duke's regiment. Sydney, the Duke's valet, had just finished unpacking Luis' suitcases and was on his way out carrying clothes to be pressed over his arm.

As soon as Sydney was out of earshot, Luis asked. "What were you and the Duchess talking about for so long?"

"Our costumes for Saturday's ball, what else?"

Nonchalantly, I picked up the blue cardboard folder on the desk and took out the sheet with the plan for the week, which listed the lunches and dinners, including the names of the guests at each, with an explanation, such as banker or man of leisure. This was one of the advantages of visiting a Royal Highness—a guest list of every person attending the dinners they accepted was provided them. These details made it easier to know what to discuss at table later on.

"Luis, do look at this schedule. The president of the French Jockey Club will be at the dinner tonight, and tomorrow also. You can talk horses as long as you want. Also, I see the Duke has arranged a golf game for you both at St.-Cloud."

Instead of taking the paper, he pointed to my closets. "Really, Aline, couldn't you travel with a few less clothes? I was embarrassed when I saw the stack Marie took to iron after unpacking you. I don't know where they'll fit. Look at the armoires—they're both already full."

He was right. Each outfit was neatly placed in one of the two built-in wall closets, the hats on a shelf above and the shoes on a rack below. Furthermore, my makeup had been neatly arranged on the dressing table next to a lovely white and lavender Cateleya orchid from the Duchess' hothouse.

From the table bar in between our rooms, I grabbed a ginger cookie.

"Haven't had one of these since the last time I was here."

Luis put down the blue paper with the schedule for the week and poured himself a whiskey.

"I had quite a conversation with the Duke. He never lets on that he's unhappy but, of course, he is. After abdicating, he said, he had always expected to be given some kind of useful work to do for his country, perhaps as an ambassador or a job that would enable him to take advantage of his contacts around the world, to open up new markets for British products. Not only was he not given anything to do, but he's been prohibited from engaging in any business venture or commercial activity of any kind—it's all considered inappropriate for an ex-king, detrimental to the reigning family. He's allowed to be as frivolous as possible, but not permitted to engage in anything serious. He said that he'd been brought up to be industrious, that when he was Prince of Wales he had made an effort to know the workmen in his country and to help solve their problems. He enjoyed that. But that Baldwin—Stanley Baldwin, the Prime Minister then, do you remember him?—considered him too liberal, too modern. He used his desire to marry the Duchess simply as an excuse to get rid of him. Leading the life of a dolt, he said—that was the word he used—would be unbearable if it weren't for the Duchess."

"I think she feels pretty much the same. They're two wasted people. No one is more aware of that than themselves, but do you notice? They try to fool each other, to make each other think he or she is perfectly happy?"

"I've noticed, though in my opinion the Duke makes more of an effort at that than she does."

Luis went into his room to dress when Edouard, the hairdresser, appeared. After my hair was done, he returned while I put on my makeup. "I can't stop feeling sorry for the Duke," he said. "You know he rarely talks about his own feelings and I'm flattered that he did so with me. What got him talking about all this was the ball on Saturday. He hates to wear costumes and those silly headdresses. Says he usually avoids all that by wearing his kilt. I hate it, too. We're both going to look like fools. Anyway, I can see that he's very homesick for England. He was in London for that eye operation and perhaps that trip made him more nostalgic." Luis sighed. "He confessed that he never felt close to his parents because he didn't see them enough. I understand him. My sisters and I were never close to our parents either."

While Luis was talking, I wondered when I could contact Jupiter. My mind was made up. With the Duchess so willing to help, I suspected we had a fighting chance of uncovering anyone we needed in this city.

When I reached Jupiter by phone the next day, he was enthusiastic about the Duchess being willing to help. He code-named her Willy and dubbed our particular mission Operation Magic in honor of my old friend.

Chapter 23

That same afternoon, I went to the CIA offices in the American embassy in the Place de la Concorde, where Jupiter had suggested I might pick up a few additional details related to the case. When I reached the station chief's office on the top floor, it turned out he was out of town, but an assistant urged me to follow him into another building to meet the case officer who had been in contact with Magic. I was astounded as the fellow led me through a double French window onto a catwalk which spanned several buildings joining the embassy to the other offices which occupied what used to be the Rothschild palace in the Faubourg-St.-Honoré. "If you don't mind heights, this route saves going down to the street and walking a block and then climbing back up to the third floor."

As I followed him Indian file across the narrow bridge, I looked down on the backyards of the mansions of the Faubourg-St.-Honoré, and then up, over the rooftops of the Hotel Crillon, where the wide Champs-Elysées stretched out. At this hour it was jammed with an endless line of cars and buses emerging from the Place de la Concorde.

We entered a small room filled with file cabinets, two huge desks, and a string of telephones. Through the only window I could see the rosy-tiled rooftops of Paris' ancient buildings. My colleague pulled out a chair for me and sat down behind one of the tables.

"Magic was a secretive operator and a loner. I hope you'll be more cooperative." He leaned back in his chair. "I hear she was a friend of yours?"

I nodded.

"Two other agents in the office were working on the case," he went on, "but she was convinced she could catch the mole single-handed. I hope you realize it rarely works that way."

It occurred to me that I would have to remember to be more cautious about keeping the Duchess' identity secret.

He picked up a stack of papers from his tabletop. "Let's go over the process Magic had uncovered. She may have known more, which she did not divulge."

During the next hour, my colleague repeated much of the information Jupiter had already given me. "We believe the documents are being removed from the file in the American European Command and photographed by a Minox camera. At first, Magic believed the mole was using a 'roll-over camera.' You know what that is, don't you?"

I had to admit that I did not.

"Well, it's a small device that rolls over whatever has to be copied and takes an instantaneous picture. The Soviets invented it, and we copied it, but the quality of this material is far too precise to have been done with a 'roll-over.' " He went on. "These documents are numbered. Anyone taking one out at night, probably on the way home, would have to replace it the following morning."

The case officer said that the material could be photographed inside the office, but that the Minox, although small, might show up on the detector, through which everyone had to pass on their way out of the building. So they were inclined to believe the man did the work at home. "To do it that way would mean that the official was definitely high-ranking, because even getting out of the building with top secret papers is difficult.

"And, of course, he's also managed to keep the location of each dead drop hidden from us. No doubt about it, the fellow's a slick professional."

"But didn't Magic give you any clues? According to Jupiter she believed she was close to uncovering the mole," I said.

"Frankly, we don't know how Magic tracked this mole. She hung out with several shady characters, one of whom was a cutout for the KGB. You've been told that, haven't you? Right. We believe she developed a close relationship with him in order to find out how he knew where the dead drops were, and this fellow advertently or inadvertently led Magic to the drop. We don't have any real proof of that, just the fact that she was murdered. Nowadays, these guys don't bother to go to such extremes unless the matter is of prime importance.

"We're working closely with the French DST, the *Directoire de Service Territorial,* on this. That's their CIA. When we run into any French nationals, the DST is very helpful and provides us with a report as soon as we request it. Other than that, you know about as much as I do now. Just stay close. Don't go wandering off on your own the way Magic did. And good luck. You'll need it. I don't want to discourage you, but you might think about going to take a look at the NATO building on the Porte Dauphine near the Etoile at the end of Avenue Foch. Look at all the people coming in and out of there. There are thousands of them. And only one of them's our traitor."

Chapter 24

The afternoon of the Windsors' dinner, Luis and I attended an art exhibit in the Rue Royale and arrived late at the house in the Bois. I rushed into the bathroom where my tub had been drawn; the water was the perfect temperature and the maid had placed bath oils and perfumes ready for use. Marie had also removed the toilet paper from the roll, cut it with scissors in two-square lengths, and piled it on a small table near the toilet. Dinner guests had been invited for eight o'clock.

We hurried, since the Duke and Duchess were always punctual and would expect us there before the others. Being accustomed to the ten o'clock Madrid dinner hour, it wasn't easy.

As I got to the bottom of the narrow wooden stairway leading from our third floor rooms to the second floor landing which circled above the spacious square entrance hall below, four maids emerged from the ironing room on the far side, each supporting a corner of a bedsheet. When I asked what they were doing, Marie explained.

"Señora Condesa, we're taking this sheet into Her Royal Highness's room to prepare her bed for the night. We don't make it up until evening, because the spread would cause wrinkles. Her Royal Highness does not like wrinkled bedsheets. The sheets have just come off the ironing table and we will now remove the spread and place the sheets."

Since I knew that the Duchess covered her bed at night with a plastic sheet so her pugs could sleep there, this excess of care was hard to understand. I waited while they passed by and looked down over the ancient tattered royal banner of the Kings of England which was suspended over the hall from a pole attached to the ornate wrought-iron railing. The Duke and Duchess were waiting below. A candle winked on a table next to the guest book and a chart with the evening's seating arrangement. Both were placed in front of the red box which, during the eleven months he had been King of England, the Duke had used for correspondence between him and his Prime Minister. The red box had belonged to his father, George V, and it was one of the few things he had taken with him when he abdicated. Our ex-shepherd and another footman, both in scarlet jackets, were standing at the door, and outside, two more men servants waited to open car doors on both sides, so that no one would have to slide across a seat getting out.

When Luis and I joined our hosts, the Duchess gave me an approving smile. "That Balenciaga dress," she said, "was my favorite in the last collection, but in Paris the price is too exorbitant for me." The dress was a green strapless silk crepe empire line with a small train. She often made that kind of remark in front of the Duke, to impress him with the fact that she did worry about how much she spent on clothes despite his belief that she was extravagant. The Duke was always careful about money. She was, too, but not when it came to clothes or jewels.

"Señora"—Luis used the Spanish manner of addressing a royal highness— "I have always admired the necklace you are wearing." It was a beauty—emeralds set in diamonds. She was wearing it over a magnificently well-cut, blue satin, long-sleeved Givenchy sheath.

"What a coincidence," said the Duke, "that you like this particular necklace. That large emerald pendant belonged to your last king, Alfonso XIII . . ."

The arrival of the first guests interrupted him. The minute I saw them I knew this was the Fergusons. The man was taller than most Frenchmen and distinguished-looking. The woman, a bit too plump, wore a print summer dress which was not right for a dinner at the Windsors, nor flattering for her figure. Just behind them were the Duke and Duchess de la Rochefoucauld, entering with an attractive young couple from the Brazilian embassy, Gloria and Paolo Parangua, and then Enrique Paredes, and a second later, Princess Ghislaine de Polignac. Enrique had come to Paris unexpectedly and since the Duchess needed an extra man, she was delighted to have a rich Spaniard who spoke many languages. Mitzi Paredes had died two years before in an automobile accident, but neither sorrow nor age had affected Enrique's massive build. Since the war, he had become one of Europe's most successful business-men—and long ago had given up poker for horseracing. Georges was taking the guests' wraps and then directed each to the guest book. After signing and saluting the hosts, the newcomers moved into the flickering candlelit blue and silver salon beyond.

Quickly, the room filled up. The magnificent flower arrange-ments, the Duke's collection of jeweled Fabergé boxes, the lovely Louis XVI furniture, the Guerlain Extrait de Pot Pourri house perfume, and the guests themselves, created an atmosphere of cozy luxuriousness. There was little opportunity for me to speak to Colo-nel Ferguson before dinner, because he went into the orange and yellow library with Enrique Paredes, where they exchanged a few words in front of the dancing flames of the fireplace. Languidly, Ferguson stood with one arm draped on the mantel, looking up at the Duchess' portrait. Even if my mission had not concerned him, I would have been curious to know more about him. He was definitely someone who stuck out in a crowd, mostly because of his lean good looks and the way his tuxedo hung from the fine-boned frame, despite his pointed chin and long thin nose. The eyes were blue slants in a tanned face adorned by vigorous gray-white hair. Altogether, he possessed a gracefulness and harmony that gave him an air of distinction.

Dinner was a trial for the Duchess, who struggled throughout to get the American colonel to talk, though no one but myself was aware of it. Although she had placed me on one side of Paul Ferguson, I had to be attentive to my other neighbor as well. He was the head of a French hunt, and the Duchess knew he would interest me, since riding was my favorite sport. Halfway through the dinner, I turned away from him and made a valiant effort to involve Paul Ferguson in a discussion. Although courteous, his answers were monosyllabic and his tone did not invite conversa-tion. Nevertheless, his manner transmitted a mystery that intrigued me. There was something unusual about Paul Ferguson.

Soon, he turned to our hostess again, while I, hopeful that the Duchess would get more out of him than I had been able to, listened to my other neighbor explain how the French hunt stags on horseback. Next to the Frenchman was an exotic Parisian woman who appeared to be in her late thirties and whom someone referred to as Claudine. She had thick dark hair, wide-set eyes and a décolletage that not only attracted the men guests but also my ex-shepherd, who was serving table for the first time after two months' apprenticeship in the Windsors' servant's quarters. I was terrified he would tip the serving dish or pour the water on the table instead of in the glass. At the other table, the glamorous Jacqueline de Ribes and the Duke were both laughing heartily at something that had been said by the French diplomat, Gaston Palewski.

After the raspberry pudding dessert, which was the Duke's favorite and his Danish grandmother's recipe, tiny cups of a peculiar cheese soufflé were served, along with strong jellied ginger candy which stung one's palate. Then the doors were opened and we moved into the blue salon again for coffee and liqueurs. The graceful ivory candles in the brass wall sconces had been put out with long snuffers, like those used in churches, when we had entered the dining room. Now they'd been relit, the cushions puffed up, and a man at a grand piano was playing "I Can't Give You Anything But Love."

Not until the others were surrounding the piano singing "Give My Regards to Broadway" did the Duchess have the opportunity to speak to me.

"Lockjaw, that's what I'll call Paul Ferguson from now on. He may be good-looking, but did you see how he sat there throughout the entire dinner without pronouncing a word! How dare he? No one has the right to come to a dinner and sit like a piece of furniture. One is supposed to contribute to the party. I wanted to tell him the Sphinxes are in Egypt, not in the Bois. If it hadn't been for my new secret job, I'd have given up. But at least I was able to find out one thing: he was *not* absent from Paris during the month of January, though I couldn't discover for sure if he was definitely here on February first. I've a feeling he's not our man."

With a quick glance, she scanned the room and looked into the library. Most of the guests were still around the piano, but a few were seated on the sofa in the library.

"It's 'change-partners-time.' I must break up those tête-à-têtes. To keep a party going, a hostess has to move people around—never let them get stuck." She tapped my arm and giggled. "I'm off, these are my working hours, my dear."

I went to the corner and leaned on the piano watching the Duke do a few steps of the Charleston. He was very good at it and appeared to be having a wonderful time. The Duke de la Rochefoucauld slid onto the piano bench next to the pianist, who smiled and beckoned to the striking Frenchwoman called Claudine, to take his place. Then François de la Rochefoucauld and Claudine proceeded to bang out a duet of the Duke of Windsor's old favorite, "Alexander's Ragtime Band." Paul Ferguson was leaning on the piano next to me, and I took advantage of it to ask if he knew the attractive woman at the piano.

"I met the lady once at a dinner NATO gave for the French press." His tone was so quiet, it was almost seductive. "Her husband, Edouard de Jorans, is a prominent writer, but I can't say I know him well either." Ferguson seemed to be more absorbed in the music than in my presence. Yet when the duet at the piano changed to "You're The Top," without uttering another word, he put his arm on mine and drew me to the floor.

His every movement was a delight and I drew myself back to look at him. "Where did you learn to dance so well?"

"I danced a bit before the war. On Broadway," he answered unenthusiastically.

"No one I know in Europe dances like this," I said. This was really fascinating. "How in the world did you become a military officer?" Finally, I thought, Colonel Ferguson is going to chat. But I was wrong. He kept moving in marked rhythm to the beat of the music without answering my question. For a minute, it seemed he was going to ignore it. Then abruptly, he said, "The war ruined my life."

And there was no way to get him to pronounce another word. The professional pianist took over again and went into "Let's Do It." The Duchess grabbed Luis and beckoned the others to join in. Colonel Ferguson and I continued to dance for a while and when the next change of tune occurred, he led me back to the piano, without making the slightest effort to answer my questions about the war.

His mentioning a NATO dinner for the French press had renewed my interest in Claudine de Jorans, who at that moment approached me.

"I've heard a lot about you," she began. "From a close mutual friend."

"Who is that?"

We stood watching the others dance. Paul Ferguson was at a distance, leaning on the piano as before. She smiled coyly. "This friend is quite unusual. The kind one is either fascinated by or . . ."

At that moment, Edouard de Jorans joined us. Glibly, Claudine changed the subject. She obviously didn't want to speak about our mutual friend in front of her husband. Since there was no other opportunity to talk to her alone that night, for the time being I put the remark aside.

Before the evening ended, Edouard de Jorans and I danced a tango, to the amusement of our friends, and then he led me into the cozy, orange-walled library. "I'm always attracted to Americans," he began, as we sat down on the long yellow banquette along the far wall.

I studied the handsome man. He must have been in his early forties. His thick graying hair was attractive, but the eyes were his most striking feature—incredibly black and large and round. Or maybe it seemed so to me because he was focusing them on me in an intense gaze. "I'm anxious to talk to you." His smile revealed wonderfully white teeth. "Not only because you're a beautiful woman," he said with the usual French courtesy, "but because I hear you were born American. It happens I have a special fondness for your country of birth. I have an American mentor, you see." His English was flavored with an alluring French accent.

Before I asked, he explained. "We met in a most unusual way." He took the glass of champagne Georges was handing him. "I was nineteen and it was in Biarritz. I'm sure you go there sometime during the summer—all you Spaniards do. So you must be familiar with the famous beach, the Chambre d'Amour, no?"

I nodded.

"Well, it was one of those rough days. The surf was extremely dangerous, and this man was in trouble." Another dazzling glance. "To make a long story short, I saved his life."

He went on to tell me that the drowning American turned out to be a philanthropist from Chicago, who was so grateful to Edouard that a few months later he had sent him a first-class ticket on the best ship going to America. He had also offered him a year at the university of his choice, with all expenses paid. In those days, according to my new friend, for a young student like himself, this gesture was extremely impressive.

"That was in 1936. I was at the Sorbonne," he recalled. "I intended to accept his generous offer after I finished studying there, but by then it was 1939, the war broke out in Europe, and I couldn't go."

From the other room came the Duchess' strident laughter, while on the opposite side of the library from us, the Duke reclined on a small Louis Seize sofa, smoking and chatting softly with Ghislaine de Polignac and François de la Rochefoucauld.

Edouard went on. "For one reason or another, I was never able to accept his offer, and I never saw him again. But he has kept in touch with me throughout all these years, encouraged my efforts, and helped create my reputation as an art critic in France and in America. So you can appreciate why I have good reason to admire Americans."

Edouard put the champagne glass down. "In fact, I'm quite excited these days. For the first time in all these thirty years, my benefactor is coming to Paris—to study the possibilities of financing a foundation to benefit French artists. If it goes through, he intends to name me the director. President De Gaulle has asked the Minister of Culture to assist me in organizing a series of affairs in his honor."

I told Edouard that I knew the coast of Biarritz well and that he must have been a remarkable swimmer to have saved anyone in that dangerous surf.

His smile evaporated. "Not good enough, I'm afraid," he answered. "The following summer, my younger brother and I were swimming in the same place. It was a bad day. We should never have gone in. I wasn't able to save him. He drowned. I've always felt guilty about that." Edouard de Jorans squirmed uncomfortably, took two yellow pillows from the many stretched out around the wall sofa and placed them behind his back. I sensed he wanted to tell me more and remained silent. "That turned out to be the worst summer of my life. Other tragedies occurred then, too." He searched in his pocket for his cigarette case and, after offering me one, lit one for himself. "Why am I telling you this? Let's change the subject. I don't want to make you gloomy, too."

During the next ten minutes, however, his mood improved, and we found several topics of mutual interest. In that short time, I felt we had become friends. Yet he was a nervous man, with a tic of stretching his neck and pulling on his collar. His fingers tapped his chair incessantly, and sentences were punctuated by a staccato cough. If he had not been so attractive and charming, he would have made me uncomfortable.

The party lasted later than usual, but by eleven-forty-five everyone had gone. The Duchess waited, as she did after every dinner party, until the servants had placed the transparent plastic slipcover on the antique sofa in the entrance hall, and then the four of us went upstairs to the boudoir for a nightcap. As soon as we entered the room, the Duke shuffled happily over to the small table bar in the corner next to the window. He picked up a crystal decanter and poured a whiskey for Luis and then one for himself. The Duchess shook her head.

"Now, David, no more whiskey tonight."

"This is my compensation, darling, for those Fergusons. They may be worthy Americans, I don't want to criticize your compatriots, but that woman . . . I can't understand a word she says. One of those Southern accents. I still don't know why you invited them."

When we went to our rooms upstairs, Luis, too, commented on Maureen Ferguson. "That Ferguson woman was sitting next to me at the table. The Duke's right about her accent, but I thought she was quite fun and not at all pompous. Listen to this. At one point, she made a remark about the servants wearing white gloves to serve and told me that Americans found that especially elegant. When I explained that we didn't consider that elegant at all, and that it was done only so we knew their hands were clean, she roared with laughter. Really, quite witty. A good dinner partner."

The next day, the Duchess and I had lunch alone in the dining room. The Duke and Luis were playing golf at St.-Cloud. We discussed the dinner of the night before and how impossible it had been to get Paul Ferguson to talk. When I told her how well he danced and that he had been a hoofer before the war, she was indignant.

"Lockjaw could have at least danced with me to make up for not talking. Dancing is a plus for him, but so far that's all we have discovered about him."

We had to admit that the debut of our mission had been extremely unproductive. Nevertheless, the Duchess was determined

not to give up. She hardly touched the vichyssoise and only poked
at the filet mignon, which was the size of a quarter, while I, shame-
lessly, took three. She played a bit with the lettuce and when dessert
appeared, ignored the apple tart—but did justice to her favorite
green-and-white triangular mints. Below us in the kitchen were a
chef and three kitchen boys. I flirted with the idea of taking another
piece of Lucien's dessert.

"Never repeat," the Duchess said. "That's one of my rules. I
can't understand, Aline, how you stay so thin. It must be the exercise. I do none. Just walking around the garden bores me."

We discussed our dresses and headpieces for tomorrow's ball at
the Rothschilds' château.

"Anyone who is anyone in Paris will be there. I'll be on the
lookout for American officers, although I doubt if Marie-Hélène
has invited any. Do you know, the other day at dinner when I asked
a friend in the French secret service—now don't worry, I was most
cautious—if he thought any members of NATO were suspected of
selling information to the Soviets, he laughed and said that of the
several thousand employees, probably quite a few augmented their
incomes in that manner."

We had no time to make further plans because Luis arrived from
St.-Cloud with the car that was to take us to the Rothschilds' château
for the weekend: about twenty miles outside Paris. The invitation
stated arrival at five-thirty. There would be a shoot the following
morning and then the event of the season, the ball Saturday night.

We were standing in the Windsors' entrance hall. Outside, the
car was being loaded with our boxes and suitcases and guns for the
pheasant shoot Saturday morning.

"Leaving the poor for the rich," the Duchess quipped. "After
your miserable attic rooms, Ferrieres will seem like heaven."

Luis and I laughed. She rebuked us. "I'm serious. This house is
not especially large. It's just a home, and I hope a cozy one, but
there's not a palace, not a castle that compares with Ferrieres. Do
you know, in Guy's father's time, they say the wineglasses were
rinsed to prime them, to remove any trace of detergent, with the
same great wine that would be served in them later? Nowadays,
who can give a ball for two hundred guests where the footmen wear
powdered wigs?"

When we got into the car, she waved good-bye and said that she
would see us the next day. We were still amused by her remark

about leaving the poor for the rich. Of course, our apartment on her third floor was beautiful and extremely comfortable, but the Duchess was right. Ferrieres was the most luxurious home in the world.

Chapter 25
FERRIERES

Arriving at the Château of Ferrieres made me forget the disappointing results of the Duchess' and my espionage attempts the night before. Our car wound through the small town of Ferrieres and entered the walled-in three-thousand-acre Rothschild property through a massive iron gate. Then, after following a winding road through a forest of enormous trees, suddenly it was there—huge and romantic—a fairy-tale building of turrets and spires, of carved stone embellishments on roofs and balconies and elongated Gothic windows, with a curved double entrance of wide stone steps which led up to a grand portal.

Joseph Fouché, Napoleon's police minister, had been its owner before Guy's great-grandfather had purchased it in 1830 from Fouché's widow. The palace had not been imposing then, not until the famous English architect Paxton—the same man who had done the Crystal Palace in London—enhanced it on orders from the Baron James de Rothschild. In 1860, the Rothschilds inaugurated the fairy-tale château with a weekend pheasant shoot for Napoleon the Third and his Spanish-born Empress Eugénie. All Europe was astounded by the fabulous collection of art works and museum-like furnishings, the best Europe had produced during the past few centuries. And today the château held the results of three more generations of Rothschilds, who had continued to enrich that heritage.

It was tea time when we arrived. Instead of entering through the grand front entrance, we went in through a small side door, which was the custom, except on special occasions. We left our boots and coats there—the rest of the luggage had already been taken care of—and ran up the side stairway into a high-ceilinged red salon whose walls were covered with exquisite eighteenth-century tapestries and portraits of Rothschild ancestors. A large square sofa in one corner was piled with cushions which people could bunch up on; under an ornate six-foot-high mantelpiece, a fire glowed.

From there, we entered the still larger main salon, where tea was being served. Our handsome elegant host, Guy de Rothschild, approached, carrying a brown tekel, a mini dachshund, in his arm, and embraced us both. We patted the sleek, doe-eyed dog, an important member of the household whom we knew well. We had given Quinta to Guy several years before from our bitch's litter.

The men started to talk shop. "Luis, did you bring cartridges?"

Luis laughed. "You think we Spaniards expect our host to provide not only the birds but the ammunition as well?"

While they chatted, I looked around for our dynamic hostess, whose artistic genius was the engine behind every Rothschild festivity. Marie-Hélène was seated on a blue sofa talking to Audrey Hepburn. Her long-lashed aquamarine eyes smiled up at me. "You're late," she began and then, disregarding that detail, went on to say, "Tell me, did Luis bring the *jabugo,* the Spanish cured ham I asked for?"

After assuring her he had, we began to talk about friends from different countries who would be coming to the ball. Then she explained who some of the French guests were that neither Audrey nor I knew. She didn't mention either of the names Jupiter had given me, but I still hoped at least one would be present, since I knew she selected her guests from every spectrum of Paris life, to make her parties interesting. My blond, ebullient hostess possessed a penetrating mind, and at the same time an implike curiosity and directness that made her totally disarming. Also, thanks to Marie-Hélène's unparalleled good taste and energy, the château, which had been occupied by the Germans during the war and then abandoned for twenty years, had been completely restored.

Audrey was a beloved friend from Madrid, and I hadn't realized she would be at the house party. "I'm so excited," she exclaimed. "Do you know, I've never been to a ball before?"

Both Marie-Hélène and I were astounded. "How's that possible? You, of all people. Why, I've seen you in so many balls—in *War and Peace* and *My Fair Lady* and . . ."

She laughed. "That was only in the movies. I've never been to a real one." Audrey was, as always, totally honest and unpretentious.

The buffet table was loaded—brioche, tiny sandwiches, petits fours, small sausages, cakes, and tarts—all prepared in the enormous kitchen below, where on other visits I'd seen four chefs working. In the time of Guy's grandparents, the kitchen had been in a separate building two hundred meters away, with a small underground train to deliver meals to the main house so that the cooking odors would not reach the salons.

Elizabeth Taylor and Richard Burton came in about then—another example of how fabulous the guest list was. I had never met them before. Burton was attractive, but I was surprised to see that his face was badly marred by what looked like monstrous pockmarks: I must confess that I hadn't seen many of his movies. They remained together, leaning against the back of a sofa, looking tired, and neither seemed especially interested in partaking of the marvelous high tea. I was anxious to meet Elizabeth because both Ava Gardner and Deborah Kerr, close friends who also lived in Spain, had told me she was a wonderful friend and much fun.

An attractive couple from London were talking with the beautiful Vicomtesse de Ribes and debonair Guy de Bagneaux, while nibbling things at the tea table. There was a general fluster when the French Prime Minister, Georges Pompidou, arrived. He was an old friend and frequent guest of Marie-Hélène and Guy, and he had for years been director of the Rothschilds' Bank. He always pepped up any gathering with his jolly, unassuming manner and wit.

Claudine de Jorans, whom I recognized from the night before at the Windsors', was seated on a sofa in the far corner in conversation with our old friend, Klaus Fribourg. Seeing him in Ferrieres was a surprise. I didn't know Klaus knew Guy and Marie-Hélène, but he was one of the best shots in Spain. That was probably why he had been invited.

Ada Fribourg came over and sat down with us. She was definitely a glamorous addition to the weekend. Her abundant straw-colored hair was knotted at the nape of her neck and a few wisps of blond curls fell over the collar of the white cashmere sweater which hugged her still-slim, elegant torso. "What a fabulous place," she said to Marie-Hélène. "I fear my homemade costume for the ball will never do justice to these surroundings."

"Don't try to fool me," said Marie-Hélène. "I happen to know that your disguise was made by the best theatrical designer in Paris."

Just like Ada, I thought, to make certain her entrance would be sensational. Although her manner was gentle and shy, throughout the years she had proven to be a woman determined to excel. The partridge shoots Klaus gave, organized by Ada in their magnificent country estate near Toledo, were famous for the luxurious cuisine and the guests. Her two not-very-attractive daughters by her first husband had married well, and her teenage sons by Klaus were outstanding students.

When I got up to find something to eat, Ada came too. She stood next to me at the buffet table, with a teacup in hand.

"What do you think of that Jorans couple?" she asked. I was eating the delicious brioche, made that morning by Marie-Hélène's pastry chef, and couldn't answer, so she continued. "We've just met them for the first time. And I must say, it's hard to understand her success, don't you think? With those fat legs and that squeaky voice!" She chuckled. "But look at Klaus. He certainly seems to be fascinated. What surprises me is that the Jorans woman pays attention to him. Dear Klaus, although adorable, is not what he used to be."

No doubt about it, Klaus had never been outstanding for his sex appeal, and now he was not only short but plump and almost bald. The only abundance of hair was a gray fringe drooping unattractively over the back of his collar.

Ada had long since lost the nervousness of those wartime years, but she was still excitable off and on, and I suspected she had quite a temper at times. Now and then, I had heard her burst out at Klaus when he did something she did not like, which was embarrassing for all present. Undoubtedly she wore the pants in that household.

The afternoon was chilly, but sunny, and guests had begun to saunter out through the huge central doors, and down the broad curving stone steps to the superb park surrounding the château. Ada kept chatting as we finished our tea. "I've been told Claudine comes from a humble family in the wine area near Bordeaux. She got her start by being elected Miss Grapes or something like that—a minor beauty title." Ada laughed. "I guess in Spain we'd call it 'Miss Vendimia.' "

Listening to her, I was almost embarrassed. Years before, Ada had told me that her own beginnings were humble. It seemed strange she would bring up that point. Could she be jealous of Claudine? It didn't make much sense, since she had just met her.

From where we were standing in front of one of the high arched windows, I looked out at the magnificent view. On the lake on the other side of the lawn, graceful swans floated majestically, and in the woods beyond, we would shoot pheasant tomorrow.

Georges Pompidou joined us and suggested we go outside for a walk. We moved toward the door with him and down the wide granite staircase to the park, where long avenues of lawn, not yet green, stretched out on either side. Wide expanses of spectacular trees—still without leaves—led to the forest. Guy's great-grand-father had brought them from the far corners of the earth to provide a variety of color to the rolling landscape. As we strolled in the last rays of the winter sun, Elizabeth and Richard Burton could be seen strolling up a path toward a small Victorian gazebo on a hill in the distance. Monsieur Pompidou strolled ahead with Guy. Ada continued to chat.

"I suppose I've been unfair in my remarks about Claudine de Jorans. There's a reason. As soon as we were introduced this afternoon, when she heard Klaus say that we were going to the Feria in Sevilla in a few weeks, she told him they were going, too, for the first time. Then she added that they knew no one there. Frankly, I could tell she intends to convince Klaus, who is always so kind-hearted, to show them around and introduce them to friends. I'm sure they're nice, but it's such a bore to have to entertain foreigners during the Fair, don't you agree?"

Audrey joined us at that moment and, hearing us talk about Sevilla, said she and Mel would be there, as well. Her husband, Mel Ferrer, was busy doing a film in Spain. We walked together in the park until dark, at which time the guests who were not spending the night in the château left for Paris and most of the houseguests went to their rooms upstairs. A few stayed below to play cards.

By the time I reached our apartment, my clothes had been un-packed, pressed, and placed in a closet on one side of the room which led into the huge bedroom. Luis' clothes and our shooting gear were in a closet on the other side. The guns for the shoot had been left downstairs. Instead of a maid asking "Which dress for tonight?" at the Rothschilds', everything had already been pressed and hung in the closets ready to be worn.

The sumptuous bedroom had enormous proportions and incredibly high ceilings and two canopied beds facing an ornate chimney mantel flanked by windows leading out to a balcony. In a far corner was a large desk with all kinds of writing paper, postcards of the château, and pens and pencils. On the opposite side of the chamber was a ladies' dressing table. On either side of the fireplace were comfortable armchairs.

Luis was still downstairs engrossed in a game of backgammon, so I decided to bathe and be out of his way when he came up. In the bathroom a deep old-fashioned zinc tub encased in time-polished mahogany was drawn and waiting. Luxuriously, I settled into the leaden-colored warm water and enjoyed the smooth feeling of the polished metal, even warmer than the water, remembering that this sumptuous tub had been one of the first to be installed in France.

By the time Luis appeared, I was at the dressing table where a maid had prearranged my makeup. A Carmen curler and even fake eyelashes were also there ready for use. I laughed, remembering that I'd told Marie-Hélène sometime before about the fake eyelashes Imelda Marcos had in her guest rooms in the Malacanang Palace in Manila. She was amused and not to be outdone; evidently she had immediately added that detail to her already perfect guest quarters.

"That Claudine de Jorans plays a pretty decent game of backgammon. She's amusing, too," Luis said, as he took off his jacket and placed it on the men's clothes stand on his side of the room. The only place I'd ever seen Luis take off his jacket was in our bedroom. Although I'd been accustomed to my father's and brother's more informal American manners, I had soon learned that in Spain it was not the custom for old-fashioned Spaniards to remove their jackets on airplanes or in their living rooms, as Americans did. I turned around and told him about Ada's comments about Claudine.

"I'm not surprised," he said. "I suspect many women are jealous of her. But not Marie-Hélène. She told me Claudine was a most exceptional person. Evidently, when she was only fifteen years old she was in the Resistance in southern France, bicycling daily through lines of German soldiers, passing on messages for the Maquis and risking her life. Later, she came to Paris to work and to study. That's where she met Edouard. She was one of his students."

"Ada said someone told her she met Edouard in Bordeaux and that she married him for his money."

"I don't think that's correct. Marie-Hélène said Jorans didn't have any money when Claudine married him."

An hour later, we were seated at the large oval table in the dining room. Six liveried footmen served the eighteen guests. The menu in front of my place was lengthy. Marie-Hélène had seated the table according to French protocol, of course, but everyone had at least one interesting dinner partner, because guests were picked for their wit or their attractiveness or their fame or their power or simply to have a mixture of nationalities. The stimulating atmosphere made people be at their best.

The Jorans had gone back to Paris to sleep, but would return for the ball the following evening. The differences of opinion about Claudine had awakened my interest in her. During dinner I asked Guy, who was next to me, what he thought of them. His opinion on any subject was always unbiased and intelligent.

"Claudine's a delight," he said. "Edouard's another story. There's no doubt he's first-rate at what he does, as an art critic and writer. They say he paints quite well, too. So on one hand he's what I would call gifted. But I'd say he's also obscure—enigmatic. At one time, there were rumors that he had been a collaborationist, but Claudine was a heroine of the Resistance—so I doubt she would have married a man she would have considered despicable."

After dinner Marie-Hélène, her glamorous mother, Maggie van Zuylen, Pompidou, Luis, and others played gin at one end of the large blue salon. At the opposite end of the room, Guy, the handsome French Minister of Finance, Giscard d'Estaing, and the rest of us chatted, laughed, and helped ourselves to drinks from a table nearby. We also looked at gigantic picture books of Ferrieres house parties dating back to the year 1860. Then we went to bed early to be ready for the next day's shoot.

For me, accustomed to rough hilly Spanish terrain and rustic customs, shooting at Ferrieres was like shooting in someone's salon. Everything seemed so pristine and neat in comparison—the beaters dressed in white jackets to avoid being shot at, the trucks which transferred them from one drive to another so they wouldn't have to go on foot. Even the pheasants contributed to the orderly atmosphere by flying in on a straight line and making a convenient racket, so one had time to be ready, unlike the sneaky, fast Spanish partridges. Guy was generous about giving me a butt, unlike the English who rarely offer a stand to wives. I found myself next to stiff, formal Giscard d'Estaing, whose good looks charmed the women, and who was also a good shot, and Pompidou on my other side. I wasn't as good a shot as some Spanish women, but I still got more birds than Pompidou, and we both laughed about that. Pompidou was witty about everything and kept those of us near him in high spirits all day.

Luis and Klaus were top shots and used to the competitive Spanish custom of noting the number of birds each gun downed. The nonchalance of the French, I knew, left them disappointed—the French moved on after each drive and left the beaters to pick up the birds, not even asking how many pheasants each gun had downed. Klaus's butt was nearby and I walked over to kid him about nobody being aware that he had downed twice as many birds as the French. The group was about to break for the small midday snack out in the field, and some of the women who had slept late were just arriving to join us. Ada was with them and came directly to her husband's butt. She was a vision in a long dark suede coat lined in mink, a matching hat, an elegant antique walking stick and high fur-bordered boots. Klaus was busy sharpening his hunting knife and never looked up to salute his beautiful wife, who could have gone to anyone else's butt first instead of to his. For the first time, I felt sorry for Ada and marveled that she had remained faithful to such a dull, unaffectionate man all these years.

Since we were not supposed to spoil our appetites for the high tea, the snack was restricted to steamy consommé, tiny sausages, and hot red wine spiced with cinnamon to ward off the chill of the day. While we lunched I commented to Luis about Klaus's indifference to his wife.

"Not at all." Luis lowered his voice. "He's always been in love with Ada. But—she's got somebody else and he suffers a lot." He looked at me and grinned. "He's being very generous. I wouldn't put up with that kind of situation for a minute."

Chapter 26

When we returned, the château was undergoing a metamorphosis. Boards, brightly colored cardboard slats, wire, light bulbs, tools, carpenters, painters, and decorators cluttered every entrance. On the second floor, boxes, headdresses, and costumes raced by; also hairdressers, masseuses, dressmakers, and servants—everyone running back and forth. Guests were bathing or being curled and primped. Antoine, the famous hairdresser, with two boxes of dark curly hair pieces, bumped into me on his way to Elizabeth Taylor's room. Someone looking like Brigitte Bardot entered the room next to mine. I looked again. It was Brigitte Bardot. In Spain she was famous for the first bare-breasted film, *And God Created Woman,* which had almost been prohibited there. This heterogeneous cast and fabulous decor was run-of-the-mill for Ferrieres parties. We rushed around in the typical last-minute frenzy before a ball in a grand château—probably just as had happened before at balls and house parties in other French châteaux centuries before.

A few hours later, when the house guests were frizzed, perfumed, jeweled, and bedecked, carrying walking sticks, swords, animals, horns, and masks, we were directed to the Grande Entrance, so that we could experience the thrills which the guests arriving from Paris would go through on their way into the ball. Their first view would be the château, with candelabra shining in every window. Then as they ascended the main staircase, lackeys in gold and red brocade, their faces painted black or with cats' heads, would greet them from the banisters and the landings. Then they would be obliged to enter a long, endless, dimly lit tunnel, which had been constructed to wind in curves and twists inside the huge palace, a labyrinth of black ribbons, phantom animals, giant cobwebs. We all passed through the whole fascinating interminable adventure, amused by the sounds of chains and groans, pushing away the shadowy cobwebs, laughing at the ghoulish dummies swaying overhead and the wispy ghosts dangling from invisible cords. Our screams rattled through the ancient building. On emerging, Guy and Marie-Hélène, in a headdress of a hind weeping diamond tears, were standing there to greet us.

We admired each other's costumes and toasted with champagne. The excitement of the ball had begun.

The Duchess of Windsor was resplendent in a white satin-and-diamond mask sprouting feathers, with more feathers bursting from her ornate coiffure. The Duke was not wearing his kilt, after all, but instead wore a tuxedo and a black silk mask, which also served to protect his weak eye. Audrey Hepburn wore no mask at all, but had a wicker birdcage over her head, with little colored stuffed birds glued to it. A small door opened in front of her mouth, so she could eat.

Claudine de Jorans was among the first of the guests to arrive without a mask. She carried a basket of live white pigeons on her head, which complemented her white Balenciaga dress—I realized, to my dismay, it was exactly the same as mine. I had a white sequin headdress concocted by a Spanish stage designer to resemble a sea urchin. Luis wore a monstrous mask with painted ghastly cockroaches and strange stars like a surrealist painting.

The music began as soon as the guests emerged from the tunnel, and a few people in the adjoining room started to dance. Someone tugged on my sleeve. I turned around and saw a tall man whose head was encased in a furry wolf's head, a shiny black mask; he was in a tuxedo with a tiny dead rabbit dangling from the handkerchief pocket. With no explanation, he took my arm and pulled me toward the other room.

Although I tried to get him to talk, he danced in silence, while directing our steps to an isolated corner. When we were at a prudent distance from the others, he lifted his mask for a split second. My surprise was complete. The last person I had expected to see!

"Divina," he said in that familiar squeaky voice, "you always said I was a wolf in sheep's clothing, but frankly I don't like sheep's clothing, so I came as my real self." The unique accent and giggle alone would have given him away.

It had been years, but it was as if we had said good-bye yesterday. "For heaven's sakes, Edmundo, get rid of that dead rabbit in your pocket. It's just under my nose and smells terrible." I couldn't help laughing. "What in the world are you doing here?" I asked.

He ignored my question. "Let me tell you, my pet, that you are beautiful. More beautiful than before, more alluring and more sophisticated. I always knew you had great promise."

"Oh, Edmundo. You're just as preposterous as ever. Flattery won't do you any good with me. Now be sensible and tell me how you happen to be at this ball."

Again he disregarded my inquiry. "Well, take a look." He stretched at arm's length from me, turning his head from side to side so I could admire his headgear. "How was I going to miss a chance to show my true colors?" He pulled on one of the sharp fuzzy ears.

I couldn't hide my amusement. I had missed my old friend all these years. "I didn't know you were a friend of the Rothschilds," I said.

"I'm not. Never met either of them." He shrugged. "But I don't see what that has to do with my being here."

"How did you get in? No one is allowed to enter without an invitation. And there are place cards at the tables."

"You still talk like a beginner, my pet. Since when have documents of any nature been an impediment for my work?"

"Then you're still working for . . . our friends?"

"You ask such discourteous questions. Still a child." He brushed off my request.

"But where are you seated at dinner?"

"I'm not staying for dinner." He snickered. "To avoid any embarrassment for the hostess, of course, I'll absent myself for a while. You may see me later, however."

Despite the mask I could see that the years had changed Edmundo very little. His face was fuller than before, but he had the same thin slit of a mustache and it was as black as ever, although the bits of hair escaping from under the huge wolf's head appeared to be pepper and salt. Yet the sparkling smirk, the Aztec cheekbones, the swagger, carried the same sophisticated exotic air I remembered so well.

"We may be interrupted," he said. "Be sure to call me. I have a small pied-à-terre in Paris, although my base is London. Here's

the number and address." He slid a paper into my hand. "If I'm
not in, leave a message. Ask for Jacques. That's my name for the
time being."

"Then you are working." Again, I prodded him.

But Edmundo didn't answer. He continued to hold me in a tight
grip despite the stinking rabbit. The tune ended and he relaxed his
embrace. He began to speak, then cocked an ear toward the music
and his voice trailed off. I realized why. A few piano strains of
"Avignon." We listened, both remembering the tune from our war
years, when those strains had announced the beginning of a secret
message on the regular radio broadcasts from southern France. As
the band swung into a new song, he waltzed our way among the
other couples to the bandleader. In a few words, he convinced the
fellow to change the tune. At the piano, I realized, was the same
man who had been playing at the Windsors' two nights before. A
few seconds later, Top Hat's snaky movements and wild twists
distracted me from concentrating on anything else. His tango was
still fun, but his wild dips and slinky steps began to attract attention.
I marveled that the wolf's head stayed in place, but we lost the
rabbit. Then, abruptly, Edmundo straightened up and stood still.

"Sorry, *Divina*," he murmured, dropping my hand. "Our dance
ends now. Don't tell your husband or anyone else you've seen me.
I've got to leave."

Before I had time to ask why, my partner had disappeared. I
stood next to the band, stunned. To see Top Hat after so many
years, for such a short time! There were so many things I wanted
to ask him.

I went back to the other room where the last guests were emerging from the tunnel. As each new arrival tumbled out, there was a
whoop of acclaim. One man was carried in on a long coffinlike box,
stretched out on top like an effigy, sprayed with something that
made him appear to be sculpted in stone. A woman entered with
two heads; the wax one above her own was so identical that it was
hard to tell which was real. Ada and Klaus Fribourg arrived—Ada
in a spectacular black glittery headpiece with huge shiny antennas
depicting a black spider. The black eye-makeup enhanced her pale
blue eyes; the long black silk crepe gown had tiers of black fringe,
which also hung from the sleeves and shoulders. Next to majestic
Ada, Klaus looked smaller than ever in a long white wig which hid
his bald head, and a white mask. Salvador Dali appeared with his

wife, Gala, his stiffly waxed mustache twisted, as usual, into two sharp points on either side of his face. The dazzling flashbulbs concentrated on the famous Spanish painter as he was rolled in a wheelchair through the crowd. But what made the atmosphere more amusing was that few guests were recognizable. How was the Duchess going to find any American officers, I wondered? What a perfect setting for anyone who did not want to be recognized!

During dinner the music ceased so that the service would not be interrupted, and we took our places at round tables set with Surrealist hand-painted place cards and centerpieces inspired by a Surrealist painter or poet. The menus were made up of humorous double meanings and crazy phrases, so no one had the slightest idea of what was going to be served. When the dessert arrived, on the menu referred to as "The Dessert of the Barbarians," it was so spectacular that everyone applauded. Eight footmen supported a huge platter holding a nude woman reclining on a bed of roses. It was entirely confected of edible spun sugar.

I was delighted to have Edouard de Jorans seated at my side and we talked about his plans for going to the Sevilla Fair.

"I am ashamed to say," he remarked in his French-accented English, "that although I've been all over Europe and the Near East, this will be my first trip to Spain. Claudine's, too."

I asked what had made him decide to go, particularly to the Feria.

"I'm going for the bullfights. I'm a real aficionado. *Corridas* have always interested me. During my youth on summer vacations in southern France, I got to know some of the best Spanish matadors. Meeting them during those summers developed an admiration . . ." His voice trailed off and his forehead folded in deep creases. The thick black brows closed down over his eyes, which were now two narrow slits. In one second, my handsome companion's aspect had become sinister. For a moment, Edouard maintained gloomy silence, and then, as if coming back from another world, he turned to me. His expression again was warm and showed concern, probably because of my consternation.

"Forgive my rudeness," he said. "But I've just seen something very disagreeable." He jerked his head in the direction of the table. "Do you see that plump man with the mustache, the Argentine?" I nodded. "Not long after my brother drowned, that man appeared in St. Jean de Luz in his impressive yacht and decided he was attracted to my mother. He pursued her relentlessly. She was very beautiful . . ." His voice trailed off and then resumed. "My mother was so upset about my brother that she didn't know what she was doing. She ended up leaving my father for him. My father couldn't take it—losing his wife and his son too. He became an alcoholic." Jorans glanced again at the man. "It's all the fault of that monster. We never saw her again, and he didn't even marry her! We heard later she died in Buenos Aires."

For the remainder of the dinner, Edouard was his usual charming self, but I was aware he was making an effort. Again he spoke to me about the luncheon he was planning for his American friend and asked if I thought it would be too much to have chamber music.

The Duke of Windsor was at the next table, engrossed in Princess Grace's conversation and actually gobbling the delicious dinner. Since he never had lunch, I knew that by this hour he was starving. Luis was at the same table and gestured to me to dance with him. I got up, but Ada got there first and pulled him to the dance floor. For the rest of the evening, Luis was so busy dancing that we didn't have a chance to talk. While I danced, I kept looking for Edmundo, hoping he would reappear.

After dinner, I tried to get close enough to the Duchess to ask if she had seen anyone, but she danced for a long time with ex-King Umberto of Italy and then with our host. At the beginning of the evening the Duke, despite his bad eye, was on the dance floor as well, doing everything from the twist to his old favorite, the Charleston. I knew the lights bothered his eye. There were many candles and flashing camera bulbs.

The Duchess never stopped dancing. Luis was one of the best dancers there, and for comfort's sake had long since discarded his monstrous head mask. Now he was dancing again with Ada, whose tiers of fringe enveloped her like masses of black spaghetti as they swirled around the floor. The music was continuous; one orchestra stopped, another took its place. We enjoyed an orgy of polkas, cha-chas, rumbas, waltzes, and just plain old-fashioned fox trots. As I passed the Duchess on the dance floor, she leaned close and whispered into my ear, "I'm dancing with every man here to see if I can uncover our mole."

When finally I saw her sitting down, I went over to ask if she'd recognized anyone. She grimaced. "No, but I've done my best. But don't worry, I'm going to invite Maureen Ferguson to go shopping with me. I'll work it out. Her husband may be better-looking, but she's a lot more talkative. David will be astounded at my sudden interest in this woman, but I can handle him." Then she lifted one white satin-slippered foot in the air. "What I don't do for my country! I'd prefer the front lines in a battle." She slid her foot out of the shoe. "The doctor says I'll either have to stop dancing or have these bunions operated on." Almost before she had finished speaking, Edouard de Jorans appeared and dragged her to the floor again. To watch her laughing and whirling around, no one would dream that her feet were killing her.

Ada was still attracting attention with her black spaghetti dress, now swirling around Edouard de Jorans. The night rolled on. Battered headdresses and costumes were strewn about on chairs and sofas, masks discarded. People drank, flirted, danced wildly, and gossiped. The Duke's eye bothered him and he went to bed around one, but the Duchess stayed on. Claudine danced with everyone from Richard Burton to my husband and . . . Paul Ferguson, who only became recognizable around one A.M. When I saw him, I was shocked. How had we both missed that tall, thin frame? I looked for the Duchess and managed to get two words with her. She had just become aware of him, as well. "I saw him remove an Arabian headdress and mask a few minutes ago," she said. "But I haven't seen Maureen Ferguson, and with those hips, I don't see how we could miss her."

We had no opportunity to comment on Ferguson's presence. Could he be the NATO mole after all, transmitting a message? But to whom? It wasn't enough just to see him, we needed proof he was passing information. From then on, I never took my eyes off him, and I noticed the Duchess doing the same thing. But the proof, I realized, would be impossible to get. At any moment, he could have slipped a message into someone's pocket without our being able to tell, even while we were watching.

And Top Hat did not reappear.

It was almost three when I wandered into the red room to grab one of the candies from the table bar. Edouard de Jorans and Ada Fribourg were in conversation on one of the sofas next to the fireplace. They had certainly become good friends quickly, I thought. Beyond them in the open doorway, but in the shadows, someone waved to me. When I got near, I was startled to see Edmundo. He pulled me into the hall and then to the entrance of the tunnel through which the guests had arrived. Inside, it was dim and the flimsy remains of ghostlike figures and eerie masquerades above banged my head as he yanked me along.

"What's the matter, Edmundo? Why are we going through this thing?" He continued to tug, but he didn't answer.

Finally, I pulled my arm loose. "Stop for a minute and explain."

"I need your help," he gasped. "I have to get out of this place without being seen by the guards. I must get to the parking lot where I left my car."

"This tunnel will take us to the main entrance where there'll certainly be police or guards," I explained. "But at this hour, I don't see that it makes much difference. Nobody will stop you from leaving the building."

"No, no." He shook his head. "Isn't there some kind of a side entrance?" He was obviously upset. "Take a look at this." He rolled up his sleeve. Despite the shadows, I could see a thick stream of blood running down his forearm. "This guy wasn't fooling, Aline." He pulled the sleeve back over his arm and I saw that the black cloth was sliced through. "I don't want any more problems with these people," he added.

Despite my asking what had happened, he gave no explanations. In order to help him, I suggested he break through the cardboard tunnel wall so I could lead him to a side door. When we emerged, we found ourselves on the second floor hallway which circled the glass rooftop of the château's rectangular center salon. He followed me to a corner balcony; from there I knew we could look outside and get our bearings.

Silently, we both stepped out. The entire facade of the house was still illuminated with torches which shed light around the château. Below, two men in guard's uniform were talking.

"I can't go out here. And that's not where I left my car anyhow," said Edmundo. "How do we get to the other side?"

We returned to the wide hallway and took a few steps. Abruptly, Edmundo grabbed my arm. For a moment I thought he had lost his head. Everything he had done that night was preposterous, even for eccentric Edmundo. But then I understood why. At the end of the long, dimly lit gallery, a tall, thin man stood looking at us. Something about his stance was menacing.

"We've got to get out of here—fast," Edmundo whispered.

He spun around. In the silence came the resounding crash of breaking glass. I looked down. The carpet was sparkling with hundreds of pieces of splintered crystal. Edmundo had dropped something he had been concealing under his jacket. It hit me at once. My old friend was still a kleptomaniac!

He started to run toward the hole in the tunnel wall and I turned to follow him, but my heel caught and I stumbled. Top Hat turned and whispered. "Get out of here quick! Don't let that guy see who you are. Take the opposite direction and I'll go through this thing. He's bound to follow me and you can get away. I don't want you mixed up in this."

In the confusion of the moment, I couldn't understand his reasoning, but I didn't stop to figure it out. Not only Edmundo's tone, but the recollection of the ghastly knife slash in his arm, and his blood-soaked sleeve, convinced me I was in danger.

In the distant dimness, the tall man started to advance. I sprang up and instinctively did as Edmundo advised, running down the hall to look for a stairway that would let me escape into the protection of the festivities below. To my dismay, when I reached the corner, I saw that the staircase I had expected to find was not there. I looked behind. To my astonishment, the man was following me instead of Edmundo, who had disappeared into the tunnel. My heart began to throb. The high heels on my white satin evening slippers made running difficult, but I turned the corner and kept going as fast as I could. Obviously, I had lost my bearings, but most likely the stairway was at the end of this corridor. Now I was passing the doors that led to the guest rooms. The man's heavy tread resounded as he, too, took the turn behind me, and I realized there would not be enough time to find the stairway and reach the bottom floor safely.

The best way out would be to find my own room, lock the door, and telephone for help. My bedroom had to be only a few doors farther on. While I ran, I wondered if the man chasing me could be the enemy agent. Could he be the man who had murdered Magic in such a horrible way? My premonitions made me run faster and faster. The footsteps on the thick carpet behind me seemed to become closer each moment. Just in time, I reached my door, opened it, and once inside, turned the key. My heart was beating like a tom-tom.

Then, just as I was beginning to relax a bit, from the silent room came a familiar voice. When I heard it, I realized, to my horror, I was in the wrong bedroom.

"Is that you, darling?" the man's voice called out.

I froze. I was in the Windsors' bedroom. From the frying pan into the fire. The Duke would never understand any explanation I might invent for stumbling into their room, which was on the far side of the house from my own. Could I pretend I was drunk when he knew I never drank! Strange actions on my part might make him wonder about his wife's long conversations with me and the reason she had invited the Fergusons.

Again, his voice. "Darling, darling. Put the light on."

I stood paralyzed next to the door. Could he hear my pounding heart? Would he get up? I hoped the man outside would disappear if I waited long enough. The Duke was so close I could hear the rustle of sheets, the mattress squeaking. He was trying to sit up in bed. In a second, the light would be on. I turned the key again and slipped out. This time the hall was empty. I breathed a sigh of relief. Now I knew where I was. With skirts in the air, I raced until I reached my room.

When I called the switchboard, nobody answered. It rang and rang. I was completely puzzled about what had happened to Top Hat. He could have been chased by guards because of the object he had stolen, but that would not explain the gash in his arm. Again, I wondered if he was still working for the Company and if he might be on the same mission as I. That seemed the most logical explanation. The Duchess and I certainly weren't the only ones working on it. I had a vision of the enemy agent wandering at large around the château, hidden among the guests or maybe even more anonymously among the waiters, musicians, electricians, or guards.

Since my dress was torn, I changed into another, refreshed my makeup, and then went downstairs. The ball was still going strong. Waiters, footmen, band players, and guests all appeared to be involved in amusement only.

Neither Edmundo nor anyone resembling the man who had followed me—I had only gotten a blurred view of his face—was in sight. I looked for the Duchess. She must have just left. I wondered what she would have thought if she'd seen me coming out of her husband's room. Luis came rushing to the doorway. "Darling, where have you been? I've been looking all over for you."

At that moment, I wanted to tell him everything. I needed someone to lean on, someone to share the anxiety. But instead I told him that a waiter had spilled coffee on my dress and that I'd gone upstairs to change it. I was afraid that even mentioning having seen Edmundo would make him think of espionage.

Luis took me in his arms and I felt safe again. We began to dance.

"Why are you shaking?" he asked.

I squeezed him and laughed. "Because I'm dancing with you, darling."

In a few minutes, my fright of the past half-hour had almost faded. Claudine de Jorans danced by, obviously having difficulty with her partner's clumsy steps. When he turned his head our way, the puffy lips as red as Claudine's lipstick told me who it was, despite his white mask. She saw me and, leaning over Fribourg's shoulder, called out.

"Cherie, you've changed your dress. Two other women this evening are wearing the same one. We seem to have chosen the most popular number in Balenciaga's collection."

Until that moment, it hadn't occurred to me that at a distance, and in a dim light, Claudine could be mistaken for me. White dress, dark hair. I wondered if the other woman wearing that dress was also tall with dark hair and started to look around. But by this time many had already left and I could not find another woman in a white gown like mine. Perhaps any one of us could have been the target of the harrowing chase. But why? Had the man chased me only because I was with Edmundo, or did Edmundo have some mysterious relationship with a dark lady in a long white dress? I remembered how upset he had been when the crystal ashtray or plate, or whatever it had been, had crashed to the floor. The object had probably had little value; I knew he usually grabbed things for the excitement, not for their worth. For him, kleptomania was like an alcoholic's urge for liquor. When things got too tense, instead of a drink, he had to steal something. But I could not believe Edmundo's kleptomania would encourage a security guard to chase a woman in a white evening dress or attack him with a knife!

Luis and I remained until the end of the ball—about six A.M. By the time the last guests left, it was dawn, and as I fell exhausted into bed, I still wondered what had happened to Top Hat.

Chapter 27

L ate Sunday afternoon, I rode with Luis to the airport. I had
invented a flimsy excuse to stay on in Paris, so that the Duchess
and I could continue our project. I could tell that he was
peeved about this, and my distraction as we zigzagged between cars
on the crowded highway seemed to make things worse. I was
preoccupied with Top Hat's fate and my lack of progress, but I
could not speak of these things to Luis. He felt my distance.

When he kissed me good-bye, he added, "You'd better be back
soon. I get very lonely by myself." He gave a half-hearted laugh.
"Really, Aline, you have nothing very important to do here. The
Duchess is spoiled and too accustomed to getting her own way. By
staying on, all you do is indulge her."

The most he could extract from me was a promise to return home
two days later. Though I hugged him tightly at the airport, I could
see that he was confused and hurt, and I felt a pang over the chaos
espionage missions always caused in my domestic life.

The Duchess was as good as her word. During the Rothschilds'
ball, she had managed to find Maureen Ferguson and to entice her
to join her on a shopping spree Monday afternoon. The reason
neither of us had seen Maureen was that she had also been dressed
in Arabian attire, an all-enveloping Moroccan jellaba with hood and
veil. Of course, she had accepted the Duchess' invitation happily.

After lunch, on her way to pick up Maureen, the Duchess
dropped me off at The Drug Store on the Champs-Elysées, where
I used a public telephone to call Jupiter in Washington. Calls from
the Windsors' house went through the central switchboard in the
gate house, and the Duchess often complained that this arrangement prevented her from placing a call herself. We had decided

that, when possible, calls relating to espionage would be safer if made from outside.

When I reached Jupiter, he was delighted to know that the Duchess was continuing to help us, but when I told him about seeing Top Hat at the ball and asked if he could help me with Operation Magic, he seemed taken aback.

"Aline," he said, after a moment's silence, in his slow quiet voice, "he's already on the project. That Mexican fools everyone. Sometimes even those he shouldn't." I sensed an undertone in his voice, but couldn't figure out what it meant. "But you're right, you should work together. I'll contact him to let him know. You two should meet immediately to plan your strategy."

So Edmundo *was* working on Operation Magic! I wondered who else was working on the mission. It gave me an odd feeling to be part of a mostly invisible structure, like glimpsing a shadow from the corner of my eye, yet finding nothing there whenever I turned to look. Still, I was very glad to be working with my old friend again. I just wondered what I had heard in Jupiter's voice.

Later that afternoon my taxi happened to pull into the curved gravel drive of the Windsors' house at the same time as the Duchess' car. The instant I saw her in front of me, I felt a jolt; I had forgotten to remind Jupiter that no one, not even Edmundo, was to know about her. I would have to hope that he remembered. The Duke, animated by the warm springlike day, was on his knees digging around his favorite bushes, and the Duchess leaned out the window, calling to him as she passed by. Georges was at the foot of the steps. Germaine had advised him of our arrival by ringing a bell when our cars entered the gate. As we entered the hall, the pugs made their usual racket, and I stopped worrying about my call with Jupiter. The Duchess and I installed ourselves in the boudoir where one pug peered leery-eyed at us from the depths of the Duke's chair and the other nestled on her lap.

There was an enigmatic glint in her lavender eyes. "Well," she began, "I've had quite an afternoon. Eye-opening, you might say." Her blunt fingers toyed with the single strand of pearls around her thin neck. On her wrist, the green eyes of a David Webb frog bracelet blinked, and matching earrings glittered on either side of her face. For a moment, I think, she simply relished creating an atmosphere of suspense. Then Georges interrupted, carrying a large box.

"Where would Her Royal Highness suggest I send the pieces of broken crystal?"

"Oh, just take them away for the time being, Georges. I can't bear to look at them. I'll have to find out if anything can be repaired." She turned to me with an expression of dismay. "Do you know, we've had the most ghastly tragedy." She pointed to the vitrine next to the door. "One of those shelves caved in all of a sudden and at least five of the most valuable goblets in the world were destroyed—priceless heirlooms of the royal family. David and I are absolutely distraught. Can you imagine anything so heartbreaking?"

For that moment she seemed to have forgotten espionage completely, but as soon as Georges was out of earshot, she whispered, "What Maureen confided to me this afternoon, however, is so bizarre as to almost make me forget this calamity of the crystal, although it is awful, just awful." She spoke in her brisk, staccato way, as if conversation were a matter of clipping words with a pair of sharp scissors. "Paul Ferguson is a mysterious man," she added, "and that's putting it mildly. I now think he could very well be the one your friends are looking for." Lowering her voice again, she said, "While Maureen and I were in the fitting room today, waiting for the vendeuse—you know I offered to help her choose her spring wardrobe, let's hope she looks a little better for my effort— she revealed that she worries for her husband's safety. Do you know why? Because he carries a revolver, Aline, and makes frequent *secret* trips out of town." The Duchess looked at me quizzically. "Now what do you think that indicates?"

I shrugged. "Hard to tell. Did she mention anything about Colonel Chandler or any other NATO officers?"

"No. I questioned her as cautiously as I could, but she said they had few American friends, that they saw mostly French people. She said the only NATO people she meets are those who go to concerts."

"Wait." I leaned forward. "That could be significant. Jupiter told me that documents might be transferred during concerts." I told her how Magic's KGB boyfriend had been a pianist and that she had thought he sometimes picked up the location of dead drops at concerts.

The Duchess' eyes widened. "Listen! Do you know, Maureen said that the pianist we had here for our dinner last week often plays at affairs given by Manlio Brosio as well." Brosio was the Secretary General of NATO.

I felt my heart race and told the Duchess that the same pianist had been in the band at the Rothschilds' ball. She said she had seen him too, though she had not given his presence any importance then.

"The same musicians work at all the affairs in Paris," she noted. "At my dinner party, he was a substitute for our regular pianist, who was out of the city. Do you think he might be able to tell us which NATO officials attend these concerts?"

"The ideal solution would be to have him work for us," I said. "But it would be too risky to try. For all we know, he could be already on the enemy's payroll."

I asked her to give me the fellow's name and address, so Edmundo could put a shadow on him. She picked up the phone and called her secretary downstairs to ask for the details and after quickly jotting them down, she leaned back in her chair and smiled enigmatically. I realized she had some news for me that especially amused her.

"What I have to tell you, Aline, may or may not have importance. Let's see what you think."

She tapped the arms of the Louis Seize chair. There was no doubt that she was more animated this afternoon than I had seen her in a long time.

"On the way home from our shopping spree," she began, "when we were on the Avenue Miromesnil, Maureen asked if Martin"— the Duchess' chauffeur—"could stop while she picked up something for her husband. When she returned to the car, she was still trying to stuff a rather fat envelope into her small handbag. I realize this could mean nothing, but it was an art gallery, and you said that Jupiter was interested in all aspects of the suspects' lives, so I wrote down the address as soon as I got home."

The Duchess reached out to the table next to her chair and picked up a triangular green mint. Sometimes it seemed to me she lived almost exclusively on candy mints. Then she plunged her hand into the pocket of her blue Givenchy suit and retrieved a paper. Her pencil-thin eyebrows lifted as she handed it to me. "It seems to me an art gallery could be the kind of place, like bookstores, where spies pick up messages." Her laughter echoed through the room. "At least that's the way they do it in some of the books I've been reading." In the familiar long snaky strokes, were the words, "Philippe Mazerolle."

The maid entered the boudoir with two red clay pots of orchids fresh from the hothouse, one of which she placed on the desk before continuing on with the other into the Duchess' bedroom. "Now, let me tell you what else I learned. Maureen was born in Georgia, but had an aunt who lived next door to my grandmother's house in Baltimore. During the war she was a pilot—can you imagine; ferrying fighters for the U.S. Navy Air Corps. That's how she met her husband, on leave in London. She said he was devastatingly handsome and she fell in love with him immediately. But it was not until ten years later that they were married . . ."

The sound of the maid closing the back servant's door leading from the Duchess' dressing room to the gallery reached us. The Duchess paused until the footsteps disappeared along the gallery outside. Then she spoke freely again. "Now here's the part that nearly made me fall out of my chair. I tell you I think I've missed my calling by not becoming a spy much earlier in life. It justifies the most shameless curiosity! Life is so much more interesting when you feel a mystery lurking under the surface. Anyway, Maureen claims that her husband had an identical twin, who was killed in the war. Also a West Pointer—very brave and the pride of the family. The brothers had been in different war zones. Paul Ferguson was in G2, translating French behind a desk in London most of the time. The brother, Lt. Peter Ferguson, went through the entire campaign in Europe and was killed just before the war ended. Maureen said her husband hated the idea of staying in the Army after the war, but because of his brother, he felt obliged to carry on the family tradition. Evidently, they were the third generation of Army brats.

"That's not the most amazing part of this story," the Duchess went on. "Maureen told me sometimes she has the uncanny feeling . . . that she is married to the dead brother. *And* for good reason. Her husband apparently has periods of depression during which he takes on an entirely different manner, which everyone tells her is just like the dead brother. She didn't know the brother herself, because he was at the front in Germany when she met her husband and of course, he never came back. But, she said, according to their pictures and what the family tells her, they were absolutely identical. Maureen says that during these times her husband's voice becomes deeper and he dresses differently, in bright colors and wide-brimmed hats. He does violent exercise like squash and box-ing—things he never does otherwise. Normally, she says, he likes music, walking, painting."

"How appalling! What do his friends think of this?"

"None of their friends knew his brother. They're mostly hers. She's the social one—very ambitious—and he lets her organize their lives. They have one daughter about ten, I believe, the only one who has any influence over him. He's away from home of-ten—I told you that. Do you know, Maureen says that sometimes she dreams that when he goes away, he visits his brother who is not dead at all, and sends Peter, the brother, back instead!"

"Their family life sounds terrible."

"It's all that and more. Maureen is determined to follow her husband the next time he goes away to discover exactly what hap-pens. She's obsessed with the notion that the brother is still alive."

"It sounds to me as if one of them is crazy, if not both. Unless, of course, the whole thing is a smokescreen to cover his work with the KGB."

"Well, if it is a smokescreen, Paul Ferguson gets top marks for imagination. What a story!"

Her skin, which was normally pale as milk, had flushed in excite-ment. She sat up straight in her chair, as if fascinated by the dark underside of "normal" life she had just discovered. And as I lis-tened to the familiar hush of the house nestled among the sprawling trees of the Bois, I could hardly blame her. Nothing had changed here for years—the brocades and the crystal, the furniture carefully dusted and arranged at the same meticulous angles—an ornate, gleaming cage in which the Duke and Duchess were imprisoned and which they would probably inhabit until the end of their days. Nothing would change, there would be no surprises, no excite-ment, and no return to England. What it lacked was the unknown, and it was this unknown which so beguiled the Duchess now.

At that moment, Georges entered the room to announce a call for me from a Monsieur Jacques. It was Edmundo. He was brief, simply instructing me to meet him for dinner at eight in a restaurant in Montparnasse.

Chapter 28

The place was huge and quite full. Top Hat was at a table in the far corner, and he stood up when he saw me wending my way between customers, most of whom seemed to be middle-class businessmen, some with their families. Caramel fingers grasped mine, he flashed his sparkling teeth. The creases around the eyes reminded me again that years had passed, yet the feeling of sitting down beside Edmundo in a crowded restaurant was so familiar that for a moment I felt confused.

"*Divina,* how long has it been since we were at a table plotting mano-à-mano like this?"

I asked him what had happened after he disappeared in Ferrieres, if the man had been chasing him because of the glass object I had seen fall out of his jacket. He made no bones about the glass dish, and for the first time spoke openly of his kleptomania.

"At least you understand what happens to me. You've seen it happen before," he confessed. "There's nothing I can do to stop it when I'm overwrought. This is a trying time, though unfortunately I can't tell you why."

When I told him the fellow had chased me, Top Hat looked upset. "I'm sorry about that. *Divina,* he mistook you for someone else. Soon I'll be able to explain that, too, I hope. Don't ask me now. As for my escape from the fiasco, I found a side door and reached my car with no further mishap."

I relayed all that the Duchess had learned that afternoon: the piano player, the connection with Maureen Ferguson, and NATO concerts. Though his eyes widened with interest when I told him the particulars of Paul Ferguson's odd behavior, he was not optimistic about him being the mole. "A professional would be more cautious with such a talkative wife," he said. "It sounds like a housewifely neurosis, rather than something more sinister." He agreed to trail the pianist.

Then he explained the set-up. "NATO has thousands of employees, as you know," he began. "Our colleagues are investigating the backgrounds of most of the officers in the military section and even some minor posts. This is delicate and must be handled cautiously, without arousing suspicions. Very few of them have access to such high-level stuff, and if Jupiter considers these men on his list suspicious, he must have reasons. Your royal friend is a definite advantage. Unlike ourselves, she can meet anyone and ask questions without being suspected."

I shuddered. Now there was no doubt that Jupiter had disclosed the Duchess' identity! At least Top Hat was an old-timer in the business and thoroughly reliable. But if she knew!

Edmundo went on. "After all, being American herself, she has the perfect excuse to invite any American official to her home. Tell her not to be finicky about asking them, because even if she hasn't met them, inviting them to dine would simply appear a patriotic gesture on her part. Any light she can shed on these fellows' habits or social tastes could be useful in putting this puzzle together."

"I'm afraid she wouldn't invite someone she didn't know," I said, still fretful about Edmundo knowing her identity. "Do you suppose Jupiter has divulged her name to anyone else?"

Edmundo scoffed at my misgivings about the Duchess and dropped the subject. I was anxious to hear about his life during the years we had been out of touch. Although he spoke of it freely, I also sensed a sadness, a hint of misgivings—perhaps just the inevitable disillusionment of unmet expectations. He told me Renata had divorced him, he had married again, and now he had three children from another wife. At the mention of the children, his face became animated, and he was again the Top Hat I remembered from twenty years ago.

"My children are exceptional, the only worthwhile thing I've accomplished in my life," he cried. "I'm proud of them, but the role of husband is not for me. I've already had three divorces. And you," he said, winking at me slyly, "have married just the person I hoped you would. From the moment I first saw the two of you together, I heard bells. I knew Luis was too clever to miss grabbing the smartest and best-looking girl in Madrid."

Though I spoke happily of my life, I felt a pang at the mention of Luis, who I knew was anxiously awaiting my return. It frightened me to think of his reaction, if he could see me here, plotting with Edmundo.

Edmundo was tight-lipped about his own progress on Operation Magic, but a bottle of Burgundy relaxed him enough to tell me about the work he had been doing for the Agency before that.

"I helped uncover a KGB network of disinformation specialists," he said. "Fascinating stuff. Their specialty was to buy, blackmail, or fool journalists and writers into producing anti-American propaganda all over Europe in the media."

This was the kind of conversation which fascinated me. Listening to Edmundo, I realized how much I'd missed being in the know about all that went on under the surface. After a while he veered back to the Duchess, and each mention of her name sent tremors of anxiety through me. True to character, he was delighted to be the colleague of a royal highness. "You can be sure with such a team we'll find the traitor," he enthused. "I'd love to meet her."

"No way," I said. "She doesn't even want to meet Jupiter. She's afraid of involving her husband, who doesn't know she's helping us. In fact, Luis doesn't know either."

"You're absolutely right, my pet. You and the Duchess must not let anyone suspect you are working with me. Why, if the press ever found out . . ."

Suddenly, Edmundo lunged, grabbing me in a passionate embrace. I was so stunned that I remained limp instead of collaborating in the pantomime. Without releasing his embrace, he whispered.

"Two guys who have been shadowing me for days have just come in the door. I don't want them to suspect you."

For the rest of the evening, we played the role of lovers, while making plans. I told Edmundo about the art gallery, and although he dared not jot down the address while the thugs were watching, I knew his good memory would suffice. He agreed that the gallery was worth looking into, and he said that he would also examine counterespionage files for material on the gallery and its owner.

"Don't go near the Company's office in the embassy again. At least one member of that staff could be on the Soviet payroll. Anyhow, the KGB watches everyone entering and leaving the building. There are so many surveillance spy teams operating in this city that anytime you're in touch with one of us, you could be suspected. Both the Soviets and the Americans employ the same system." He snickered. "Their local teams protect their agents and chase our teams who are protecting our agents. It's a real merry-go-round." He began to sing in a tone much too loud, "Round and round we go." No doubt the Burgundy he had consumed had something to do with the notes he was bellowing out. The KGB thugs looked at us, startled.

Edmundo lifted one hand and waved. The enemy agents looked embarrassed. Like puppets, their faces took on their former dead-pan expressions, and they returned their attention to their drinks.

"Look," giggled Edmundo, "you see, we all know each other. We're what you might call friendly old enemies."

As we drank our coffee, Edmundo continued to hold my hand after every sip. Those watching had to believe we were in love. We talked and talked, hoping the KGB surveillance team would give up, but they were conscientious and followed us from one night club to another. I dared not return to the Windsors' until we'd managed to shake them. Finally, in desperation I went to the ladies' room and exited through a window, wrecking my stockings and ripping my new suit. Then I jumped into a taxi while Edmundo remained inside holding the men at bay. But Top Hat and I had mapped out our future strategy.

Chapter 29

The next morning the Duchess told me that she had invited Maureen to lunch with us at Maxim's. Martin dropped us at Rue Royale number three just before one o'clock. The Duchess' entrance was always an event. Albert, the maître d', smiled with pleasure and bowed deeply, and his staff made the usual fuss. We were led to our table amidst a flurry of smiles, nodding heads, white damask, and sparkling crystal to the front of the restaurant near the lace-covered windows.

"Her Royal Highness' table," announced Albert. Once we were seated and the salutations and smiles had ceased, the Duchess leaned toward me.

"While you and your friend Top Hat unravel the mystery in a more professional manner, I hope I can be useful here on my own turf. Entertaining really is a sort of profession for me and maybe this experience will finally serve some useful purpose. I might be able to uncover the culprit in a few simple luncheons or dinner conversations. It could happen, you know."

"We would still need to catch the man in the act of passing the information on to an enemy agent."

"But wouldn't knowing who the guilty one is make it easy to prove?"

"That's only the beginning. A professional agent is extremely cautious. He notices every inquiry, recognizes immediately when he is being tailed. Getting legal proof is sometimes the most difficult part."

Yet I was aware that the Duchess' talents had so far extracted more information about the Fergusons than I had.

As Maureen approached our table, the Duchess whispered, "You'll see how easily I get her to talk."

Maureen had barely sat down when Claudine and Edouard de Jorans entered the restaurant, accompanied by Enrique Paredes. Claudine was wearing a red Dior suit with matching hat and a huge diamond pin on her lapel. They stopped by our table before proceeding on to the corner to join a flashy blond woman and a heavyset, gray-haired man with a plump pink face.

A few minutes later, as we looked at Edouard's well-cut gray and white pin-stripe suit retreating across the room, the Duchess commented. "He does dress well, but really he studies the whole thing too much. You know what I mean. For him, dressing well is not something that comes naturally. Charlie Beistegui said that when Edouard de Jorans came to visit for weekends, he had more suitcases than any woman. My David has such a knack for putting things together that, believe it or not, he travels with very little. Most of that luggage you see accompanying us is mine. Edouard de Jorans wouldn't think of wearing a shirt that wasn't custom-made in England. David even wears American ready-to-wear. He gives an American manufacturer ideas and they send him free shirts, which delights him."

"Ah," exclaimed Maureen, eyeing the group the Jorans had joined. "That's Adelle Chandler and her husband. He's one of Paul's colleagues."

At the mention of Chandler, the Duchess and I snapped to attention. Quickly, she pounced on the opportunity. "Ah, that blond woman is quite striking. Are you close friends?"

I pressed my lips tight to hold back a grin. I realized the Duchess had chosen the word "striking" carefully, to hide her true opinion. The woman was overly made up and dressed in the worst taste. To the Duchess, I knew, she appeared extremely vulgar.

"No, not really. I see them only at NATO social functions."

"I suppose," said the Duchess, "those NATO dinners are held in that huge building near the Etoile."

"Never," answered Maureen. "The security is too strict. I've never been there. Even employees are rigorously checked going in and out. But still there are quite a number of social affairs going on. Sometimes at the different embassies."

Desperate not to let the conversation drift from Colonel Chandler, I said the first thing that entered my head. "Is that man another military officer?"

"Yes, not a West Pointer—but he's regular army, nevertheless," said Maureen. Then she returned her attention to the menu, which obviously interested her more than the Chandlers.

The Duchess looked at me. We had to tackle it now, or getting back to the topic later would be difficult. Imperceptibly, I nodded. Then the Duchess asked. "What does Chandler do in NATO?"

"He's a colonel, though you'd think he was a general, with the airs they give themselves. But he's basically a scientist, I believe. And she works for NATO as well, in the political section. She's Belgian, I think. They've only been married about a year. Mike Chandler has been divorced twice, and she's been married before, several times, I believe." Mrs. Ferguson placed the menu down firmly on the table. "That's only one of the reasons I don't like her." Then she picked it up again. Before she studied it anew, she added, "In fact, I don't think much of either of those women at that table."

"What a pity," said the Duchess. "I was about to say how much I enjoy meeting Americans and to suggest that you introduce me sometime to the Chandlers."

"Oh, I doubt you'd like them. That woman is very common. I know much nicer couples I could introduce you to."

The waiter appeared to take our order. NATO and the Chandlers faded into the background as Maureen chatted about menus and the Rothschilds' ball.

Though I racked my brain for a way of steering the conversation back to the Chandlers, I could think of none. Apparently, the Duchess couldn't either, and she poked restlessly at her chicken salad while Maureen remarked on how difficult it would be to tolerate America, after the splendors of France.

That brought an indignant reaction from the Duchess. "Splendors of France, indeed! You'll be lucky to live in America! Don't mistake me, there's much I admire in this country. Paris is the most beautiful city in the world. But it's only our lawyers' advice about taxes that keeps us here instead of living in America." Then she added, as an afterthought, "And, of course, David wants to be near England."

After lunch, as we were driving along the Champs-Elysées on our way to drop Maureen at her home, the Duchess pointed to the long lines waiting in front of a movie house. "How David and I have always wanted to go to one of those movie houses," said the Duchess, looking longingly out the window.

"Well, why don't you?" asked Maureen.

With an expression of bewilderment, the Duchess looked at her. "Well," she stammered," how do you suppose we could get in there without being mobbed? And the security guards! They wouldn't permit it."

"You mean you've never been to the movies?" Maureen was astounded.

"Since I started to see the man who became my husband, no. And I'm afraid David has never been to a public movie house ever, except for special occasions, when they would have obliged him to have bodyguards. It's such a pity. Imagine what fun! To be able to go where one wants to, without coming out in the press, and being criticized for not behaving like Royal Highnesses." Her lips curled. "Especially when one doesn't enjoy the advantages of such status."

Maureen remained in awed silence until we dropped her on the Avenue Kleber, and then we continued on through the Avenue Foch into the Bois. The Duchess was clearly disappointed that today's rendezvous had failed to produce the dramatic results of yesterday.

"What a bore it is to have lunch with someone who neither amuses nor says anything important," she said.

I explained that espionage more often consisted of fruitless encounters like today's, and that one could never be successful in this business without patience.

"I'm sure you're right, Aline," she said, looking at me. "The problem is, having lived so long as a dilettante, I've lost my ability to stick with things." For a few moments, she appeared troubled by this thought and said nothing. Then her mood changed. She pepped up and began to amuse herself and me, too, by inventing code names.

"In the books I read, spies do those things, Aline. Let's begin with Claudine. Everybody talks about her, she's the tops nowadays, like the song," the Duchess said. "We'll call her the Cat's Meow."

"Code names are supposed to be short," I explained, "so they can be enciphered easily. The ideal is five letters; messages in code are sent in blocks of five letters."

"Then we'll call her husband Romeo because he's so good-looking. And your friend, Señor Paredes, who looks like a baby elephant, can be Dumbo from now on." She paused, "Oh, I've got one for Maureen Ferguson. This one has to be long, whether you like it or not. What did you think about that terrible blue rinse she uses? Blue Sails in the Sunset. That's the name for her. By the way, don't you think she looks years older than her husband?" She laughed heartily. "And wasn't that suit with those huge checks something! What it did to those floppy bosoms! And that derriere was even bigger than the first time I saw her!" She laughed. No one enjoyed the Duchess' jokes more than she did.

"We'd better give the Duke a code name," I suggested.

She laughed. "That's easy. I can just see how those blue eyes and that turned-up nose would look if he knew I was doing espionage. There's nothing like that adorable face when he gets upset. He'll be Grumpy, like Snow White's dwarf."

She turned to me. "And don't I get a code name?"

"Of course," I answered. "Actually, Jupiter has given you one already. He's named you Willy."

"Willy?" she repeated. "I don't know if I like that. Willy? That makes me sound Willy-nilly. Wishy-washy, sort of. Doesn't sound like me."

"That's just the point."

"As long as nobody knows who Willy is . . ." She laughed as the car swung around the Château de Madrid, and the gates to her house came into view. I thought again that working on the mission had made her happier. She was less formal, less stiff.

Chapter 30

I t was not me but the Duchess herself who decided that we should do more about the art gallery than simply leaving the matter in Top Hat's hands. And because a visit from the Duchess might attract attention, we decided that I should be the one to go.

I took a taxi so that no one would recognize the Duchess' car, and got out several blocks away. It was a dim day, and although no longer raining, tiny rivulets had formed on the windows of the art galleries which lined the street. It was clearly a neighborhood which specialized in fine art, and for a while I simply shopped, entering stores and glancing at the paintings and sculptures. Then, gradually, I wandered into the Rue de Miromesnil, not far from the Elysée Palace. There, at the address I had been given, was the prosperous-looking gallery with the name "Philippe Mazerolle" in large letters over the door. Inside, it was quiet. The only customer was a lady with white hair in conversation with a slim, middle-aged Frenchman whom I presumed to be the owner. The fact that he was engaged gave me the opportunity to wander about.

A Bonnard "View of the Place Clichy" was on the *cimaise* of the gallery, and an intimate Vuillard, "Femme Cousant dans un Intérieur," captured my eye on the wall to my left. The works were a mixture of styles and periods, but I was impressed by the fine taste and quality. An open doorway led into a breezy office, where a woman was typing. A young fellow on a ladder was painting the woodwork. There were two wooden crates on the floor, and several empty frames piled in a corner.

The woman at the typewriter glanced my way and, after removing her glasses, stood up and came to me. I explained that I was interested in obtaining a large *bodegon,* a hunting scene, which would be suitable for a dining room. By this time, the owner had finished with his client and crossed the salon to where we were standing.

Philippe Mazerolle was the classic art gallery proprietor, cultured, soft-spoken, gently probing while he judged the new client. He led me around the salon and chatted amiably while I studied the paintings. There seemed nothing suspicious about either the gallery or Monsieur Mazerolle, and since he said there were no paintings similar to what I had in mind, I turned to leave. Though I did not know what I had hoped to find there, I was still disappointed. I searched for any small detail which might indicate a cover for agents, but the place had the aspect of an authentic, serious gallery and nothing else. As I said good-bye, the owner detained me, and bent over to pick up a canvas which had been on the floor leaning against the wall.

"It's too bad you want a large painting, because at this moment, a few very worthy Impressionist paintings have just arrived. Of course they are not what you wanted, but I can give you an excellent price, because I'm selling them for a private collector who wants a quick sale."

The canvas he placed in front of me was a winter scene in the Seine valley by Sisley. Intrigued by the lovely painting and wanting to prolong my visit, I waited.

"This is one of a group I received only a few days ago." Noting my interest, he continued, turning over two more and placing each on a *chevalet,* so that the light from the street could illuminate them. "Two are believed to be by Cézanne. There's also one Pissaro and a sketch by Lautrec. They will all bring magnificent prices. Decide for yourself if they are not lovely. One better than the other."

I stepped back to view the paintings and experienced such a shock that I felt weak. There it was! A couple in nineteenth century garb, seated at a rustic table, surrounded by wicker baskets filled with fruit, and in the lower left corner . . . a small yellow dog! Though I had never before seen the painting, it had the strange familiarity of something I had dreamed repeatedly. For several moments, I simply stood there, unable to speak. After all the danger and disappointments that had surrounded my search twenty years ago, here was the painting, resting demurely in this quiet gallery.

I pointed to it. "What is the price of that one?" I managed to say.

Monsieur Mazerolle was pleased with my sudden change of

mind. "Since I've just received it, I haven't yet calculated the price. And I must confer with the owner. I can telephone you tomorrow about this."

I feigned indecision and tried to prolong the conversation. I learned that the paintings had arrived from a foreign country, but that was all Monsieur Mazerolle would tell me, and I dared not appear overeager. I told him that it was difficult to reach me by telephone and that I would either call or return the next day. Then, still in shock, I staggered out of the shop and walked several blocks to calm myself before calling Edmundo. Fortunately I reached him right away, and we met about thirty minutes later in a small bar.

Breathlessly I described my discovery. To my chagrin, Edmundo wasn't as excited as I. He swirled his Don Pepe for a moment. "You know," he said, "that gallery is probably completely legitimate."

"I'm not saying it isn't," I cried. "I doubt the owner has the slightest idea that the painting was originally stolen."

There was silence. Then Top Hat said, "How can you be sure you recognize a painting you've never seen? Especially after twenty years have gone by since you even heard about it?"

When he saw how disappointed I was at his skepticism, he promised to go to the gallery himself. Pleased, I reminded him not to show interest in the same painting, for fear of arousing Monsieur Mazerolle's interest.

"But I can't spend too much time on this, my pet," he warned. "We have to concentrate on that mole—Jupiter would insist on that. Operation Magic is urgent and my reputation right now depends on solving it. If I don't get to the bottom of this, the Agency might drop me entirely. I've had some . . . run-ins lately with Washington." I pressed him to elaborate, but he wouldn't. "The NATO job is difficult enough, let's not get involved in some wild goose chase involving someone who interested us twenty years ago. If it's waited this long, it can wait until this is solved."

He delivered this speech with a note of impatience. I attempted to improve his humor by telling him about the code names the Duchess had invented. Also they might be useful during future telephone conversations which went through the Windsors' switchboard. Edmundo laughed as he jotted the names down.

"Neither the KGB nor the CIA, nor any other agency, could make anything of this list, but they do give a clue to the personality of the particular Duchess who chose them."

"That's one more thing," I said. "We can't keep referring to the Duchess by her name. The only request she's made is that no one know who she is. From now on, please call her Willy. That's her code name."

"All right, *Divina,* don't nag. But it is heartening to know one is working with a Royal Highness."

When I arrived at the house in the Bois, the Duchess was sitting at the desk in the corner. She was an avid letter-writer and had a whole array of colored stationery: Yellow with a blue monogram, blue with white, gray with white. She amused herself designing these details and was good at it. I sat down in the Duke's chair, removing the stack of foreign newspapers he had left there—the dailies from London, the *Herald Tribune,* and journals in Spanish and German. I wondered sometimes what he did with the vast store of information he absorbed each day, other than use it in dinner conversation. She folded her letter and moved from her desk to the chair facing mine.

"You've discovered something," she said, seeing my face. "Tell me."

I recounted my bizarre experience of stumbling onto the painting. Having no idea that the painting was in any way related to espionage, the Duchess was puzzled by my excitement at first, but very intrigued by the coincidence. She agreed that my description of the painting sounded like the one she'd seen in Madrid. "I thought that painting had been sold to someone else," she said.

With a pang of remorse for talking about a secret mission I had never mentioned to anyone, except Luis, and also for involving her in something that had nothing to do with the NATO matter, I briefly told her about my work on Operation Safehaven. I stressed the potential importance of this discovery and the incredible coincidence that she had been the one to discover the painting.

"Of course," I said, remembering my conversation with Top Hat, "even if the painting is the same one I was looking for in Madrid so long ago, following it up now would sidetrack us from Operation Magic. I've been warned not to spend much time on it, but that's difficult." I sighed. "The possibility of it being the same one is so tempting."

The Duchess had listened with rapt attention. "But Aline," she said, "doesn't it seem likely that the two missions could be connected?"

I smiled at her naiveté. "Do you know how great the odds of that are?" I asked.

"You're not thinking clearly, you're too close to the situation. Now step back a moment. You go to a gallery looking for something suspicious, because you believe the gallery could have a connection with a possible NATO mole. You immediately stumble on what you know is stolen merchandise. Now, how can you tell me those things aren't connected? If you look for one thing and find another, chances are that those things have something in common."

I had to admit that she had a point, and I even wondered how Top Hat had managed to convince me so easily of the opposite.

Enthusiastically, the Duchess continued. "One of the advantages of being a novice is that I lack the preconceptions that come with experience."

"Well," I finally agreed, "that's an amusing way of looking at it. I don't think Jupiter would agree with you, but who knows, now and then that may be the case."

"How can I get this boring Maureen to talk about that gallery? I'm sure that painting is the one I saw in Madrid."

In a burst of energy, she stood up and paced twice across the room. It crossed my mind that if she stuck with espionage, she might even lose her dislike for exercise. I suggested she tell Maureen she needed paintings for a new room at The Mill, her country house, and ask her if she had any ideas about where she could find high-quality art.

"I must be careful not to do anything that would be embarrassing for David. Imagine if his relatives in Buckingham Palace got wind of what I'm doing! They're always looking for something to criticize us about. Cookie would be delighted."

"Who's Cookie?" I asked.

"My terrible sister-in-law. We call her that because she always looked like a pudding dressed up." She laughed and continued. "David, of course, would forbid me to continue. That's why I can't tell him a thing. He's so boringly honorable. He would never allow me to be involved in anything that could be considered even slightly indecorous for his family—no matter how ghastly they've been to him."

I warned her that unless we quickly discovered some evidence that the two missions were linked, we would have to abandon the painting for the time being and concentrate on meeting more

American officers. For my own part, I knew I wouldn't be able to resist following up on the painting, no matter what, but I did need the Duchess to focus on her job.

"Paul Ferguson is guilty until proven innocent, I say," she went on, her eyes sparkling. I noted that the moment I suggested a problem she became more determined to push on, forgetting her concerns about Buckingham Palace. She was such an unusual woman, I thought. There she was, facing me in her perfectly tailored Dior suit, flawless hair and makeup, the best-dressed woman in the world, according to the yearly list, wearing jewels that were different from yesterday's and carefully selected to enhance her outfit, yet attacking this job with a professional's sense of responsibility. "Besides," she continued, "I think it's strange that your friend Edmundo is so discouraging at the outset, before he has reason to be."

Her words astonished me, for once again she had struck a chord. I remembered how years ago, when Prince Lilienthal had been shot at the Yebes shoot, I had harbored suspicions about Top Hat. I didn't mention my doubts to the Duchess, however. Instead, I asked a question which had occurred to me several times that day.

"By the way, how did you happen to hear about that antique shop in Madrid where you tried to buy this painting? It was so out of the way."

"That was thanks to Cat's Meow."

"Claudine? Not Claudine de Jorans?" I was astounded.

"Of course, it was Claudine de Jorans. Who else? Why do you find that so strange?"

"Because Edouard told me she'd never been to Spain. It's unusual that she would know of a place I'd never heard of myself. Even Luis didn't know about it, and he visits all the antique shops in the city."

"I could call Claudine and ask her."

"No. If the place is fishy, and if she's involved, this would be just the wrong thing to do. We'd better wait until we hear if Top Hat uncovers anything." Again, I felt a pang of worry—would Top Hat really investigate thoroughly?

The Duchess was thinking about Claudine. "She never told me she had *not* been to Madrid, and I took it for granted that she had. The strange part is, that shop was the only address she gave me."

I asked what she really thought of Claudine.

"She's not what I would call brilliant," she began. "But she is an asset at a dinner party and I do believe she is a kind, well-meaning person. But the interesting person in that ménage is Edouard. At first he appears better than Claudine, but now I'm sure he's just a fourflusher."

I wanted to ask her what she meant by "fourflusher," but she kept on talking. "They live in luxury, despite the fact that the salary of a professor at the Sorbonne does not go far, nor the fees of an art critic either. Edouard must have a large private fortune. Claudine orders more clothes than any woman I know. She says he encourages her to buy the best." The Duchess laughed. "Imagine, it's usually the reverse, isn't it?" She looked at her watch. "Speaking of clothes, I must dress for dinner in one of my 'overpriced' gowns." She added, "Mind you, David also expects me to look perfect . . . a case of wanting to have his cake but not anxious to pay too much for it, I'm afraid.

"What a pity you have to go back to Madrid tomorrow," the Duchess lamented. She handed me a small box from Hermès. "A little present. Something that reminded me of you when I saw it, Aline. I hope you like it."

Impatiently, I opened the box. Inside was a brooch—a lovely gold horse with small diamonds sprinkled on its mane. Just the thing to wear on the lapel of my new black suit.

"It's beautiful. How can I thank you? I'm the one who should be giving you a gift, with all you're doing to help me."

"Not at all. You've provided me with something worthwhile and interesting to do. The gratitude is mine, Aline."

It was already Thursday and I had promised Luis that I would be in Madrid last Tuesday. I had become so involved in this mess that I was forgetting my husband, my children, my real life, which had nothing to do with this. In order to communicate while I was in Madrid, we invented more codes that could be used by telephone or telegram. We made lists of substitute names for places—London for Paris, Rome for Madrid—very amateurish stuff, but good enough for the time being.

Before I left for Madrid the next morning, Top Hat called. "You may have uncovered something after all," he said. "There's nothing suspicious about the gallery or about Mazerolle. But the fellow you saw painting the woodwork was quite talkative, once I placed a few francs in his hand. He told me that the new canvases had been delivered a couple of days before by a fat, middle-aged man in a beige Bentley—the latest model. And listen to this. The car had a Spanish license plate. Try to track that down in Madrid, my pet," he said. "But don't go back to that shop."

"That already tells me something about the man who delivered the paintings," I answered. "Spaniards accustomed to owning large expensive cars usually order black. So if he's Spanish, he'll be flamboyant and easy to find."

As he hung up I was filled with relief. Top Hat had not only been helpful, but after learning that the painting had come from Spain, he was enthusiastic now, too. His reaction removed my old suspicions.

Chapter 31

On the Iberia DC-9 to Madrid, I thought about Edmundo's news concerning the Spanish license plate. There was now little doubt in my mind that the painting was the one the Duchess had tried to buy, and the one Luis had seen twenty years before at the Rastro. Whether Top Hat liked it or not, I would ask Jupiter for permission to buy that painting. That would give me an excuse to go back to the shop. I was not going to pass up the opportunity to discover something about Safehaven, no matter how much time had gone by.

An hour later, I arrived in Madrid. The terminal building was under construction, and passengers waiting to depart on the Iberia plane for Barcelona were seated in the disembarkation room. The customary group of bored travelers were smoking, sitting on benches, or standing looking out the window. My glance happened to fall upon a long, dark brown suede coat with a mink lining, exactly like the one Ada had worn to the shoot. The woman wearing it was seated on a bench in the corner, invisible behind a wide-open newspaper. When I stretched my neck to see who it was, I was astounded. It was Ada! And she was trying to hide—from me! I kept on walking, pretending I hadn't seen her, and left the terminal with the other passengers. But I remained mystified by her behavior. Why? Why would I care if she went to Barcelona?

Pepe, my driver, was waiting outside the terminal. As I got into our car, I asked whether my husband was playing golf or if he was at home.

"The Señor Conde is in Barcelona," he answered. "He left just two hours ago."

A chill climbed my spine. Could that be the reason Ada had been hiding from me? Was she on her way to Barcelona for a rendezvous with my husband? It would never have occurred to me if she had saluted me normally. Or if Luis had not made that remark about Ada putting horns on her husband. Or if Luis hadn't commented about how "lonely" he got by himself. But no. If Luis were the "other man," he wouldn't have mentioned Ada's infidelity in the first place. What was I thinking of? Espionage was making me paranoid, ridiculously suspicious of everyone, even my own husband. It was a recognized malady of the trade.

Luis called from Barcelona that evening, and I was ashamed to mention Ada and my doubts. He wasn't coming back for a few days, so I had time to get in touch with Jupiter in Washington. I wanted to get permission to follow up on the Cézanne. He was out of the country, however, and it was not until a couple of days later that I reached him. His answer was ambiguous. Safehaven was a closed issue for the Agency. There were no funds available for the purchase of a painting which related to a mission of over twenty years ago. At the same time, however, if my pursuit of the yellow dog painting did not distract from my work on Operation Magic, I was free to go ahead. He was definitely interested in Ferguson, and the fact that there was some connection between the gallery and Ferguson made Jupiter more willing to let me follow up on the painting. In fact, he had some news of Ferguson for me: recent reports mentioned meetings between Ferguson and an unknown contact in obscure hotels and pensions. He also told me that Top Hat would be calling me with a minor change in plans.

I called the Duchess immediately after hanging up with Jupiter, and was pleased to discover that her obsession with the painting now rivaled mine. She announced that she was determined to buy it, regardless of Jupiter's opinion. "And tell him I've just spoken to Colonel Chandler's vulgar wife and will be having them for dinner next week. That should sweeten the pill," she added.

No sooner had I hung up than Top Hat called.

"Sorry, my pet, you'll have to get along without me for a few weeks. I've got to go back to London to take care of some urgent business. It won't be for long." As he spoke, I could hear the announcements of airline flights in the background. He was undoubtedly in an air terminal. "I'm sure you'll survive without me, although of course you won't have as much fun." He attempted a giggle, but I could tell that he was harried. "Jupiter knows about this. We have a temporary replacement for you, a case officer in the Madrid office who can keep you in touch with the Paris office while I'm away. Normally, this wouldn't be necessary for such a short period of time, but things may begin to pop about now. You'll continue to be the only go-between with Willy . . ." The line cut.

He didn't call back for a half-hour, and when he did he explained that he'd been obliged to change phones. "There's a fellow trailing me and he's hard to shake. By the way, I've been following Chandler. Willy should invite him the soonest possible. Tell her to find out who his friends are, where he goes, what his hobbies are. Everything she can think of. Including where he was on February first."

Hastily, I began to tell Edmundo that it was a French friend of the Duchess' who had recommended the shop in Madrid where she had first seen the painting. When I had given Edmundo the Duchess' code names the other day, we had not discussed the people themselves. I was about to explain about Claudine when the line cut off again. This time, he didn't call back.

I went upstairs feeling concerned. Not only did it worry me to switch partners in the midst of a mission, but I worried about the urgency of Top Hat's situation. Mulling these matters over, I wandered to my dressing room and took off my earrings and ring, placing them on the shelf with the other jewels. In doing so, I noticed that the small velvet box which held the Duchess' horse pin was open and empty. Thinking my maid must have put it someplace else, or that I had misplaced it, I searched my drawers, even poking under the dressing table and getting down on my hands and knees to see if it had fallen. Finding nothing, I began to feel nervous, and called for my maid. When Angustias raised her hands in a gesture of ignorance, my nervousness turned to panic. How would I face up to the Duchess, having lost her gift so soon?

What could have happened? Nothing else had been taken. Why would someone pass over more valuable things and take only this pin? The only reason I could imagine was one I did not want to contemplate: someone knew the Duchess was working on the mission and wanted to scare me.

My palms were damp as I ran downstairs and gathered the servants together in the kitchen. I described the brooch in detail. After a moment's silence, Pepe stepped forward. He said he had seen such a pin in my son Miguel's hand when he drove him to school the day before. I was astounded. Why would my ten-year-old son be interested in that pin? I leapt into my car and drove to Rosales. Miguel was the only one at school in Madrid this year. Alvaro and Luis were in school in England.

I found my child on the football field, his white and blue uniform streaked with mud. I waved to him from the sidelines and he came running over. When I asked him about the pin, a guilty smile sneaked across his face.

"It was so beautiful, Mama, I gave it to my girlfriend," he admitted.

"Your girlfriend!"

With a frightened Miguel in tow, I scoured the halls for little Victoria. When I finally found her, she said that she'd lost the pin yesterday when she was playing with it in the sand on the banks of the little stream that ran next to the school. We all went to the riverbank and searched until dark, but to no avail. The Duchess' brooch was gone. I felt terrible, wondering how I could ever explain. But at least the episode had no relation to our secret mission. I bawled Miguel out thoroughly for stealing and promised suitable punishment. Then I waited to find out what Top Hat's replacement would be like.

Chapter 32

Although switching colleagues in the midst of a mission worried me, at first the transfer seemed to occur without a hitch. The new case officer identified himself as Stanley Baker, and said John Derby had given him my number. We set up a meeting for the following morning in an out-of-the-way bar.

The moment I saw my new contact, I realized that he would pose another kind of danger for me. He was about my age, strikingly handsome with lots of light brown hair, an athletic build, and a charming manner. I knew it would be impossible for me to meet such an attractive man frequently in any public place without friends finding out and gossiping. As there was no divorce in Spain, marital tensions were eased in other ways. Madrid society, accustomed to and amused by illicit affairs, would talk. And my husband would inevitably hear about it.

Rather than advance such an awkward conversation with a man I was meeting for the first time, I merely suggested that, in the future, we meet in back streets in his car or mine and make our conversations the briefest possible. Stanley Baker ran his hands through his hair, confused by what he obviously considered an exaggerated concern, and asked me why I felt compelled to such secrecy. Politely, I tried to explain that new CIA agents operated very differently from the way I had been trained in the OSS. There, secrecy had been of prime importance. He said nothing, but our methods clearly were destined to clash. Stanley's offices were inside the American embassy, which meant that everybody there knew who the CIA officers were, including the Spanish personnel. He could be followed each time he left the building. That alone made me uncomfortable. Not only Luis, but everyone else in Spain would soon know I was working for the CIA.

One of the first matters Mr. Baker addressed was my salary. "Jupiter insists that you receive a regular monthly payment," he told me, sipping his coffee.

I wasn't so sure about that. "Although I understand his reasoning—people always feel more obligated if they are accepting money for a job—it's uncomfortable for me to receive a salary. I dislike having my name on lists that may be leaked," I explained.

"Jupiter had another idea. He said to ask if you would like permission to shop at the PX store at the American air base in Torrejon?" Torrejon was on the outskirts of Madrid. "Of course, I'd love that," I said, "but people would see me and find it strange that I had a right to shop in a place reserved for military and official personnel."

My colleague nodded, then snapped his fingers. "How about my doing your shopping for you? You can give me your list. You can say an American embassy friend has offered to get you things from the PX."

So that became the solution, better for me than a salary. Twenty years in Spain had not quenched my taste for American pancake syrup, cottage cheese, frozen cakes . . . My mouth watered just thinking about such things. Maybe Stanley Baker was not so bad after all. We parted on better terms.

In the late afternoon of my third day home, Luis returned from Barcelona. I heard his voice talking to Benito, the butler, downstairs and rushed to my mirror to refresh my makeup. It was not just seeing Ada at the airport which had made me ill-at-ease, but the fact that so much had happened in my own life since Luis and I were last together. For the first time in our marriage, I worried that there was a disturbing distance between us.

When his familiar steps resounded on the stairs, I rushed out to the landing to greet him. The instant I saw those cool green eyes, the distance vanished. There was the man I had fallen in love with: tanned and athletic, dressed in a dark gray double-breasted suit and stiff collar, moving with the graceful elegance that never failed him.

"My my!" he said, smiling at me coyly. "What a surprise to find you at home."

I paid no attention and put my arms around him. Despite his

wariness, he seemed genuinely glad to see me too, and we clung to each other as tightly as if we had been separated for weeks.

It was an unusually warm night for this time of year and we both went downstairs and out into the garden. Benito went to get Luis a whiskey and me a Coca-Cola. The lilac bushes and the jonquils were in bloom, and the air was filled with a sweet, rich aroma. I leaned back in my chair and took Luis's hand.

"Tell me what you did in Barcelona," I said, in a tone I hoped appeared innocent.

Luis said he'd met with the manager of one of his companies, had been to the racetrack, bought a stallion, and played golf with Felipe Bertran. He'd had a busy schedule. Yet I couldn't help wondering how he had spent his evenings. My heart was pounding again.

"Where did you go for dinner?" My voice failed to sound as light-hearted as I'd intended.

He gave me an odd look. "One night with Felipe Bertran and . . . look, after all, I was only there three days."

"That's true," I said, feeling ridiculous. "It just seemed longer to me." I sipped my drink and stared at the sky which was now beginning to glow with a pink phosphorescence from the street-lights that had just come on. To change the subject, I added, "Until I see all those lights go on, I forget that we live in the middle of a great city. It's grown so much since I arrived here."

"Speaking of activities outside Madrid," he said, ignoring my change of conversation, "what exactly were you and the Duchess doing in Paris?"

Though I had prepared an answer to this question, my preoccupation over Luis and Ada had wiped it from my mind entirely. I found myself looking at him in dumb silence. "Well," I stumbled, "the usual . . . lunch at Maxim's, shopping . . ."

"And the nights?" He was laughing, but eyeing me, enjoying my discomfort.

I shrugged. "We just had dinner at home and talked."

"That's strange," he pursued relentlessly. "The Duchess is not one to stay home at night often."

"Well, she had a toothache or something and the Duke's eye was bothering him." I was annoyed with myself for sounding so preposterously guilty. "Oh, yes," I remembered. "We did go out one night to dine at Margot Muni's." That was true, but in my nervousness I had forgotten about it.

"There," proceeded Luis. "You see. You suspect me of keeping secrets because you know that you are doing exactly the same thing. Isn't that right?" He spoke in a half-joking manner, and I seized on this opportunity to make light of it.

"That's right," I said, laughing blithely. "Just think how dull it would be if you knew everything about me."

"Oh, I doubt that. I suspect it would be quite interesting. Why not try me?"

I looked into his eyes and saw, of course, that he was deadly serious. The smile withered on my face. "Luis," I said, "give me a few more days and I promise I'll tell you everything."

"It must be very entertaining, if a few more days mean so much to you."

"It's—entertaining is not quite the word. Look, it's not another man—"

"Enough," he said, rising from his chair. "Not another word until you can be honest with me. I just want you to know you're not dealing with a fool."

He took me by the hand and led me back toward the house. I suspected then that he had guessed my secret was espionage but was sensitive enough to know that breaking off a mission before it was completed would be difficult. I leaned my head against his shoulder and marveled at what a wonderful husband he was. Luis was right; it was the fact that I was concealing something from him which had made me suspicious. Worries about Ada Fribourg vanished from my mind.

Two days later, Stanley Baker called again. This time it was urgent to meet him right away—something important had come up. I had just begun to dress for a formal dinner at the British embassy and Luis, who was still downstairs, was astounded when he saw me rushing out at nine P.M. I mumbled some excuse and continued down the steps to my car, aware that this meeting might upset the fragile balance we had regained. The fact that I was putting my marriage in jeopardy was beginning to worry me more than the mission.

Luis was indispensable for my happiness, yet I was eroding his trust. Who knew what he might do to retaliate . . . or what had already been done! Dizzy with these troubling thoughts, I drove recklessly to the Calle Lagasca where Stanley Baker was waiting. As the dim streetlights spilled across my windshield, I thought that

John Derby failed to appreciate the sacrifices I was making for my country. So far I had proven to the Spaniards that their dire predictions about American wives were wrong, but the slightest bit of scandal could reverse years of effort. Also, scandal or no scandal, Luis would be the first to see through my flimsy justification of a few moments ago. Although serving my country seemed like an acceptable reason to me, still I was lying to him and going against a promise I had made, and I hated it.

"Jupiter has bad news for you," were the first words Baker said when I got into his car. Although he had told me during our first meeting that he had a wife and four children, I still felt uncomfortable seated beside this handsome man in the murky darkness. Somehow it didn't seem normal that Jupiter would send me a colleague who looked like a movie star. Apprehensive, I waited.

"He asked me to deliver it personally," he went on, looking as ill-at-ease as I was. "I'm sorry to be the one to inform you . . ." His voice broke off. I thought he was embarrassed to tell me that I was being taken off the mission. Well, don't be, I practically cried aloud—nothing could be more convenient. At any rate, I was totally unprepared when he finally blurted it out. "Your friend Top Hat was found dead a few hours ago." For some reason, I reached for my earring and found I wasn't wearing one. Top Hat dead! His words left me numb. None of this was true. Me, in a dark car on a dimly lit street with a handsome man I hardly knew—listening to this! No, something was wrong. This was not real.

Gently, Stanley explained. "He was found with his head inside an oven with the gas turned on, in the kitchen of his apartment. It was clearly suicide."

"That's impossible," I cried, overtaken by a burst of fury. I turned to Stanley Baker. "I spoke to him about four days ago. He was completely absorbed in the operation we're doing. He did not commit suicide. This is a mistake. They must mean someone else."

"No, no chance of that," he said. "Our case officer in London verified everything."

For some time, we sat in silence. More than once, I turned to Stanley, prepared to argue, but I was unable to speak. Finally, I said, "Please send a message to Jupiter. Tell him that in my opinion someone faked the suicide. The last time he contacted me by phone, Top Hat was being followed closely. Before that I'd been in touch with him daily and never found him despondent. On the contrary, he thought he was getting close to the mole." I avoided mentioning Top Hat being worried about his job, knowing the Agency might seize on it as evidence of his motive for suicide.

"I know it's hard to lose a colleague," my companion said, with infuriating solicitude. I had the impression he was humoring me and had no intention of sending my message to Jupiter. Abruptly, I got out of the car and ran along the street to my own, trying in vain to make myself believe that Top Hat existed no longer.

I drove like a madwoman, wondering all the way home how I would be able to carry on a conversation at the table later on, with such terrible news weighing on my mind.

Luis was waiting in his black tie, ready to leave for the dinner. He looked at me, but said nothing. That was his manner. He would never lift his voice or endure my doing so, and if I began a quarrel, he would simply turn and walk away. I had never won a disagreement with him, unless I had reason to. Though I dressed hurriedly, we were still going to be late for the dinner. During the three minutes' ride to the British embassy, neither of us spoke.

The fact that I was leaving the next day for the Feria in Sevilla now struck me as a nightmare. I would be left dangling with no further news of Edmundo, not to mention leaving Luis on bad terms. He would not be meeting me there until Friday, because a new stallion was arriving from Deauville and he wanted to be certain it arrived in good condition.

I blundered through the dinner in a daze, a smile pasted on my face. Luis and I drove home in silence. The next morning, he left early for the golf course. I took advantage of his absence to telephone Paris and tell Willy about Edmundo's death. I had to tell someone, and I dared not mention it to Luis without concocting some logical explanation of how I had found out—an explanation he was bound to see through. I wasn't up to that, particularly after not even having mentioned Edmundo's presence at the Rothschilds' ball.

The Duchess was shocked, and for a moment her silence made me think that the line had gone dead. Then she said that, although she'd never met Top Hat, she'd come to feel that he was a friend. Again there was silence on the line, and I suspected she was getting cold feet. I assured her that I would understand if she wanted to bow out. She insisted that she was more anxious than ever to help. When I told her about my new colleague in Madrid, she reiterated that no CIA agent or anyone else should know her identity, and an uneasy feeling swept through me. I felt ashamed to tell her that Jupiter knew, Top Hat had known, and that I suspected Stanley Baker knew as well.

Chapter 33
SEVILLA

Pepe had left for Sevilla the day before with my bulky luggage—starched flamenco dresses, lace mantillas, high combs, riding boots, leather chaps, wide-brimmed riding hats. I took the afternoon plane. When I left for the airport, Luis was still not speaking to me.

There was no way I could have canceled the Duchess of Alba's invitation at the last minute. Cayetana to her friends, she'd asked me to help her with Jackie Kennedy, who would be one of her house guests this year, and whom she'd never met. Antonio Garrigues, Spain's ambassador in Washington, had suggested Cayetana invite the former First Lady to the Feria to distract her from the horror of her husband's assassination only two and a half years before.

Cayetana had called me before I left Madrid to ask if I would mind Luis occupying another room at the end of the corridor, since he was coming later in the week, so that she could put Mrs. Kennedy in a room connecting with mine.

"Mrs. Kennedy doesn't know anyone here. I don't want her to feel lost. If you're close by, she'll have someone to solve her problems."

I had told Cayetana that would be fine. There was little else I could say. I added that I had packed an extra riding costume for Jackie. She told me that Fermin Bohorquez, the *rejoneador*—bullfighter on horseback—was sending Nevada, his most spectacular mount, for her to ride in the daily parade and that among the twenty-two houseguests were some of the most attractive men in Spain. She'd done everything possible to assure that her illustrious guest had a good time.

In previous years, the prospect of going to the fair had kept me in a state of anticipation for weeks before. This April, however, as I looked down at the rugged landscape between Madrid and Sevilla, the stony mountain tops, the rugged forests of evergreen, oak and olive trees, the yellow and orange tilled fields, my spirit was gloomy. I couldn't accept Top Hat's suicide. In my mind I went over everything he had said during those last telephone conversations. Nothing had indicated he was despondent. The more I thought about it, the more convinced I was that someone had murdered him. I worried that the person could have been the same one who had killed Magic. Maybe the assassin could kill me or, God forbid, the Duchess!

The plane was packed with passengers in a holiday mood and when we filed out, the scene had a hectic, festive air. Masses of young girls in bright flamenco dresses, women with red carnations in their hair, black-eyed gypsies carrying guitars, luggage of all sizes and sorts, cluttered the small Sevilla air terminal.

As I threaded my way to my car outside, it seemed that I was the only one not rejoicing. Pepe was standing next to my car just in front of the entrance, enraptured by the colorful crowd. When he saw me, he hastily opened the car door. I fabricated a smile and was about to get in, when a huge Bentley, especially noticeable because of its color, rolled out of the parking lot in front of us. The license plate on the light beige car was from Madrid.

"Pepe," I screamed, jumping in, "follow that Bentley, no matter where it goes, and don't let it out of your sight."

When we reached the outskirts of Sevilla, trailing the Bentley wasn't easy. Children and grownups were dancing and singing in the streets, inattentive of the traffic. The girls' long ruffled dresses grazed the sides of our car as we passed, and Pepe had to slow down not to hit them. When a carriage drawn by four horses bedecked in colorful ribbons came out of a side street, our way was blocked and we lost precious time. Fortunately, two blocks farther on, a group of horsemen had obliged the beige car to slow down too, and we were able to catch up. The car followed along the Guadalquivir River and past the Torre de Oro, the Tower of Gold, so-called because the gold from the New World had been deposited there. The Bentley seemed headed for the Hotel Alfonso XIII.

The tall, graceful palm trees in front of the hotel were waving gently in the breeze when the Bentley pulled into the circular drive and parked behind an ancient Rolls. While the driver jumped out, carrying a briefcase and sprinted up the marble steps, Pepe struggled to find a spot to park. Men in black, wide-brimmed felt hats accompanied ladies in high heels and silk print dresses in and out of horse-drawn carriages. Little girls in bright ankle-length gypsy costumes pranced around, doormen in elaborate livery with ropes of golden braid draped from their shoulders shouted orders to porters carrying luggage.

"Pepe," I said, pointing to the Bentley, "please go into the hotel, and ask the concierge who that car belongs to."

"Oh, Señora Condesa, I can tell you that. It's Don Enrique Paredes' car."

The news hit me like a blow. Paredes fit to a tee the description the painter had given Edmundo. I remembered that Enrique often drove by car to Paris because he was afraid of planes and disliked traveling by train. So Enrique Paredes was also connected with the yellow dog painting! What relationship did he have with Claudine? Had he had something to do with Safehaven in Spain? I had to let someone know about my discovery. If only Top Hat . . .

On the way to Las Duenas, Cayetana's beautiful palace, I could think of nothing else. Neither the clip-clop of the horses' hooves, nor the jingle of the carriage bells, nor the castanets resounding through the narrow streets distracted me. I tried to remember things from those war years so long ago, things that pointed to Enrique Paredes as head of the Nazi organization. How amazed Luis would be when I could tell him! I regretted more than ever having to keep my work secret from him.

We arrived at Las Duenas. With his usual welcoming smile, Juan, the guard, opened the huge iron double gate. Our car proceeded along the yellow sand driveway, flanked by rows of blossoming orange trees, toward the beautiful Arabic-inspired fifteenth-century palace. The facade and balconies were covered with flaming red bougainvillaea. To one side, in front of the stables, two carriages, a landau and a break, waited. Their perfectly matched, pure Spanish-Cartusian horses were bedecked in pompoms and silk ribbons. The coachmen wore costumes of the period of Goya. The Alba carriage and horses, too, were in the family colors—blue and yellow. Looking at the other carriage, which was in blue and white,

I realized Tomas Terry, an old acquaintance, had arrived. Guests sometimes brought their own maid or valet, but Tomas had come with his coachmen and carriage.

Already, the enchantment of the old palace had cast its spell on me. I jumped out of the car, anxious to see again the beautiful central patio with its tall graceful columns and magnificent high arches. Running through the arched entrance, I stood enthralled, enjoying the symmetry, the exquisite delicate artistry of the Arabic structure, and, in the quietness of it all, the magical, fanciful sounds of trickling water and birds singing. Pencil-slim palms climbed high—higher than the sculpted lacy stone balcony, where a fountain of color shouted out in red carnations, pink bougainvillaea, scarlet roses—up, up, to the blue heaven above. Around me, green plants and pristine calla lilies filled the patio garden. The ancient fountain spouted thin sparkling streams of water high in the air, creating a delicate music of its own.

Suddenly, I was engulfed again by the realization that this Feria was spoiled for me. What a pity! Last year, April had been cold, unusual for Sevilla at that time of year, and at night we women had been chilly in our light summer dresses while sitting in the *casetas* listening to flamenco. But this year I could see that even the weather was going to be perfect.

After a few minutes, I tore myself away from the hypnotizing view and turned toward a side stairway, which went up to the second-floor guest rooms. As my heels clicked on the ancient tiled floors, I thought of their history. Almost five hundred years before, on his return from the New World after having conquered Mexico, Hernando Cortez had mounted these same stairs when he'd come to this palace to visit his daughter. Much later, and many times, the Spanish-born Empress Eugénie of France had walked these steps when she visited her sister, the Duchess of Alba.

I knew Juan, the gateman, would advise Cayetana that I had arrived and that she would contact me when convenient, so I went directly to my high-ceilinged Victorian bedroom. My clothes were already hanging in the old-fashioned armoire, and my boots and chaps had been polished and placed next to the sofa at the foot of the canopied bed. From the open balcony, I looked down at the flower-choked garden and breathed in the scent of orange blossoms. Life could be so beautiful if . . .

Then I remembered. I'd better let Willy know that the man who had delivered the Cézanne paintings to Paris was Enrique Paredes. The fact that Claudine had recommended the shop now held greater significance. The only telephone in my wing of the house was in the salon just outside my room. Juan, who was also the switchboard operator, told me the call would take a few minutes. I sat down to wait, leaning on the table, gazing at Cayetana's ancestors who were staring at me from the walls. Some of their ghosts had been inhabiting this palace for several centuries. Where was Top Hat's ghost right now, I wondered? He should be here. The fair would be just to his taste. The ring of the phone startled me out of my reveries.

Paris was on the line. Shouting, because of the bad connection, I told the Duchess about Paredes' car and suggested she not go to the Mazerolle gallery.

"But I've already been," was her answer. "I'm trying to buy the painting." The line had so much static I could barely hear. I tried to tell her about Claudine and Paredes, but she couldn't hear me any better than I could hear her. It was useless. Fortunately, no one else could have understood, either. When I hung up, it occurred to me again that if she continued to pursue the painting she might be in danger.

When my next call, to Stanley Baker, came through, a colleague in his office answered instead. The man told me that Stanley had left for Sevilla by car an hour ago, because he had an important letter to deliver to me. The colleague went on to explain that it was a message in code that their machines had been unable to decipher. "Obviously it's a private code, that only you can decipher," he said. "Mr. Baker will be telephoning me later on to ask where he can meet you tonight, about one A.M. or maybe a bit later."

I told him I would be in the Ybarras' *caseta* and described how Stanley could find it.

"Please wait there for him. Since he has to go by car, there's no way we can be certain of the time," the voice said. "By the way, he told me to tell you the letter is from Top Hat." The CIA case officer either hung up or the communication was cut off again.

Was I misunderstanding everyone? How could I have a message from Top Hat if he was dead? And why would he send a letter to me to the CIA office instead of to my house? Probably so my husband wouldn't open it and find a letter in code. My confusion was complete.

"An-da-aaaaaa." From the garden below my window came the low guttural voice of a coachman and the snap of a whip. I rushed to the balcony. Blond, lovely Cayetana, resplendent in high comb and ancient yellowed white lace mantilla, was in the open carriage ready to leave for the bullfight with two of her five sons. Placing a hand to shade her eyes from the sun, she called up to me.

"I was worried you wouldn't get here in time for the *corrida.* Tomas' carriage will be leaving in a few minutes. Dress quickly so you won't keep them waiting. You have your *barrera* seat, and Mrs. Kennedy won't be arriving until later."

Cayetana's words brought me back to reality. Claudine and Edouard de Jorans would probably be going to the bullfight. Seeing them might help uncover something. That would make the bull-fight twice as important for me today.

As I dressed hastily for the fight, I thought of my hostess, a Duchess of Alba who would probably become even more famous than her ancestor, the other Cayetana, the one painted by Goya. Cayetana had masses of long, silky, honey-colored hair, a clear golden skin, an upturned nose, warm brown eyes, a perfect figure and a spirit that was shy and brave and daring at the same time. She danced flamenco better than the professional gypsies, was an expe-rienced horsewoman, a connoisseur of art, an *aficionada* of bull-fights, a Duchess who preserved Spanish customs and traditions, and who understood and loved her *pueblo.* Her husband was tall, dark, handsome, and distinguished. With their five young sons and baby daughter, they made an impressive family.

I slid a high comb behind my head and down under my chignon, pinning it firmly so it wouldn't wobble. Over that, I draped my long black lace mantilla which reached from my head to my knees, using a hairpin to hook it to my hair in front of the high comb, so the lace shawl would drape becomingly over my hair. I used a simple straight pin to secure the black lace to either shoulder of my dress. This took the weight off the top of the head and made it easy to turn my head comfortably from side to side without pulling on the comb. Then I took a large diamond brooch, with which I gathered folds of the lace behind my head and pinned them securely to the back of the pronged high comb. That also took some of the man-tilla's weight from the top of my head and gave a graceful fullness behind. From the dressing table, I grabbed three red carnations and pinned them behind my left ear. When I stood up, the red of my dress brought out the delicate flowery design of the lace, which also framed my face. The red carnations contrasted well with the black mantilla and my black hair. The effect was exotic and fun. Breathlessly, I rushed down the steps ready for the promenade in the beautiful open carriage.

It was a glorious feeling to ride in the Terry landau with the harness bells jingling and echoing through the beautiful, narrow, twisting streets of Sevilla. The clatter of the horses' hoofs clip-clopped in rhythmic cadence over the cobblestones. People waved as we went by, enjoying the sight of the magnificent carriage with its five perfectly matched pure Andalusian horses. The coachmen also commanded admiration, sitting straight and correct—superb in blue silk bandanas, colorful short jackets, and glossy boots and chaps. The pair of lead horses were sleek dark gray and the three wheelers behind almost identical. This type of harnessing was typical of southern Spain and was called *Media Potencia*—words and customs which no longer existed in any other part of Europe, but which here, during the Feria, gave the nostalgic atmosphere of times long gone by.

At the entrance to the bullring, we in the carriage—Tomas, Angelita Almenara, Bunting Teba, and I—waited in a queue of other splendid carriages, relishing the atmosphere around us, waving and saluting to friends in carriages nearby. The horses, impatient and nervous, shifted hooves constantly, making all the little harness bells jingle with a hundred different tones. The mass of people near the entrance gates exuded excitement and anticipation. Castanets clacked, hawkers shouted their wares, and women selling red carnations called out. And since it was very hot, tiny improvised stalls were doing a record business in hand-painted fans, and icy cool water was being sold in paper cups from old-fashioned red clay *botijos.* Men peddling cushions for the hard cement seats of the bullring couldn't move fast enough to attend to the crowd of customers. The tension in the air augured a great bullfight.

In the midst of this excitement, while I sat enjoying the spectacle around me, I saw the beige Bentley arrive and stop on the other side of the street. What luck, I thought, as Paredes got out, and, dodging carriages and cars, crossed the road to join the throng at the main gate. I observed him standing in the queue, while he glanced around. It astounded me to think that this man, whom I had known for twenty years, could possibly be the criminal I'd been looking for during the war. At that moment he spotted us and waved, making gestures to indicate that he would like us all to join him for a *copa* in the Alfonso XIII after the fight. Tomas said we were also invited to the Fribourgs' yacht at the Club Maritimo, but that we would go to Enrique's cocktail first.

Just on time, a bit before six o'clock, we entered the Maestranza, Sevilla's famous ancient bullring. The sandy arena glistened like gold in the hot sun as we stepped down to the ringside. Over the *barrera* in front of my seat, I stretched my red and black embroidered *manton de Manila,* which I had been carrying over my arm, and then I looked around the plaza. What a glorious spectacle! Above, crowning the round arena under a narrow, red-tiled roof, was a circle of lovely aged granite columns where in small boxes were seated beautiful women of all ages, ravishing and dramatic, in high combs and delicate lace mantillas. Some wore white mantillas, others black, and all had carnations in their hair and fluttered lovely painted fans. Their fringed silk shawls, draped in graceful curves over the splendid grated railing, made splashes of bright color here and there. Behind the ladies stood handsome men in dark suits, waving and calling to friends while sipping sherry in long narrow glasses. The plaza was packed and the atmosphere was electric. In a few moments, the greatest matadors of the season would enter the ring and the bulls were said to be over five hundred kilos each.

The public's attention was concentrated on those boxes above. "Everybody's trying to see Princess Grace," explained Tomas. My obsession about the mission had made me forget that the Rainiers were going to be at the fair this year.

Next to us was the famous flamenco star, Lola Flores, with her husband. We chatted for a few seconds. Farther down, also in *barrera* seats, was Audrey Hepburn, absolutely stunning in a great white straw hat, with Mel Ferrer. Then I saw Claudine. Her beautiful red Dior dress and wide-brimmed red and black silk hat made her stand out in the crowd. In true Spanish style, she was fluttering a black lace fan and looking around the plaza, obviously also enjoying the colorful scene. Edouard de Jorans spied me and waved. At that moment, Enrique Paredes, looking bigger and heavier than ever, was just stepping down into the seat next to Claudine. I wondered if that meant Claudine was flirting with Enrique—and all the while I had believed they'd met at the Windsors' party. I still couldn't understand how Claudine would be flirting with such an unattractive man, when her own husband was so much better-looking. There had to be another explanation.

A few seats to my left, also in a *barrera* seat, was my old bullfighter friend, Juanito Belmonte. Beyond him, a ray of sunlight made Klaus' bald head gleam. Ada was at his side, more glamorous than ever in a blue print Balenciaga dress, her golden hair tied in a neat chignon under a wide-brimmed blue straw hat, which she had pushed back to enable her to use the field glasses with which she was scanning the plaza.

And then I had an incredible surprise! At quite a distance behind them, almost invisible in the crowded upper rows, I recognized a blowsy blond woman and a man with bushy, unruly graying hair. Only because I was perusing the assembly for friends did I chance on the Chandlers in the midst of the mob. What were they doing here? Obviously, it was my destiny to be involved in this particular drama: the cast seemed to go everyplace I did!

The bulls were brave and Antonio Ordonez had one of his fabulous days, with the tension of sudden gory death ever present. His fearless graceful passes, the bull's horns grazing his body each time, absorbed my attention totally. Until the fight was over, I forgot about Operation Magic.

Later, at the Hotel Alfonso XIII bar, it was not easy to talk to Claudine, but I was able to suggest that she and Edouard accompany us to the Fribourgs' yacht. On the way there, I asked her about the antique shop she had recommended to the Duchess in Madrid.

Claudine displayed no visible signs of uneasiness. "It was the only shop I knew of in Madrid," she answered calmly. "The owner used to come to Paris now and then, and sometimes he brought paintings for Edouard to see. Then Edouard recommended art dealers who might be interested." She shrugged. "I don't understand anything about painting, but that's Edouard's specialty, you know. So when the Duchess asked me if I knew where she could get some nice but inexpensive paintings, I thought of that place." She looked at me. "Why do you ask?"

I tried to sound nonchalant. "The Duchess asked me if I knew the shop, but I couldn't tell her anything, since frankly I'd never heard of it."

Then I changed the subject. "By the way, did you know your friends the Chandlers are here?"

Her expression changed completely. For one second, I thought she looked frightened. "The Chandlers in Sevilla?" she said in a voice that did not disguise her astonishment. "Are you sure? Where did you see them?"

"At the bullfight."

Recomposing her manner, she said, "They must have made their minds up at the last minute when they heard us talking about coming here, but they never told me."

Until then Claudine had been carefree. Now we walked in silence. She was quiet and pensive, until a gypsy woman jabbering at my side attracted her attention. She asked me why the woman was following us. I told her not to pay attention, that the woman only wanted to tell our fortunes.

"Oh, I'd love to have my fortune told. And by a Spanish gypsy! It would be so fun," said Claudine.

I told her that this woman was undoubtedly a fake, and that having heard us speaking in a foreign language, she'd probably calculated we were easy bait. But Claudine paid no heed to my warning and, despite people jostling us on either side, she insisted on stopping in the middle of the street and offered her palm to the gypsy.

The wizened old woman took Claudine's right hand and then her left. Dramatically, the long dirty fingers traced circular motions while she jabbered a gypsy chant. Even when I translated the woman's humdrum tale about love and money and fame on the way, Claudine didn't lose faith. Then abruptly the woman paused, dropped Claudine's hands and indicated she had seen something too terrible to reveal. It was an old trick, but to Claudine the gesture had the desired effect and, now more intrigued than ever, she begged the gypsy to continue. The old woman refused. Claudine insisted again. Only after giving her a large *peseta* bill did she get the woman to comply.

She shifted her eyes from my friend to me. "This lady is in danger," she mumbled. "Her friends are enemies. I see the hands . . ." I told Claudine again to pay no attention, that this was part of the woman's regular act, but Claudine stood without budging, attentive to every word. Without taking her eyes off the gypsy, she cried, "No, no, she must tell me all."

"Oh, please, Claudine. Pay her and get rid of her," I begged. "Don't you see, she's inventing that story because she thinks she'll get more money if her tale is dramatic."

Tomas and Edouard, who had been walking ahead, were now threading their way back, looking for us.

"We'll be late for everything, if you girls don't hurry."

Claudine opened her bag and took out some *pesetas* for the woman.

"It's a pity I can't hear the rest," she said. "This gypsy has clairvoyance, no doubt about it." Tomas and Edouard were walking in front of us again. Claudine lowered her voice to a whisper. "You could never imagine, Aline, what problems I have at this moment. I must learn what's going to happen." Reluctantly she handed the money to the gypsy who grabbed it and scurried away.

We made plans on the Fribourgs' yacht to meet after dinner at the Ybarras' *caseta,* where rumor had it that the best flamenco of the night would take place. I had to go there anyway, because I had given that address to the case officer.

Back at the house, dinner was scheduled for midnight, the customary hour in Las Duenas during Feria. Arriving at the fairgrounds before the flamenco was in full swing was pointless. We usually left the *palacio* around one and straggled back between four and eight in the morning, then slept until noon. While we had been at the bullfight, Jackie Kennedy had arrived from Madrid in the embassy plane with the American ambassador, Angier Duke, and his beautiful wife, Robin. The large double doors between our rooms were closed and I assumed Mrs. Kennedy was resting for the long night ahead, and I decided to do the same.

About eleven forty-five, in a long red and white polka-dot flamenco dress and Luis' grandmother's red silk Manila shawl, which I took to protect me from the chill of the early morning hours, I walked along the wide second floor *galeria* on my way to join the others in the red salon. My ruffled, stiffly starched gypsy skirt swished so loudly that I didn't realize that Jackie was behind me until she appeared at my side. She was ravishing, in a short Oleg Cassini white shantung sheath with an embroidered red, white, and blue bolero. Two white carnations were placed on either side of her glossy dark brown hair. As we reached the grand staircase, Luis Miguel Dominguin and Antonio Ordonez, the two most famous matadors of the fair, were coming up the grand staircase. After introductions, we all walked into the high-ceilinged drawing room together. The walls were covered in ancient red damask, and two tiers of family portraits circled the room. A fireplace was blazing. We chatted about horses, bullfights, and flamenco until, a bit after midnight, Gregorio, the major-domo, announced dinner.

In the dining room, the oval mahogany table, flickering in the candlelight of four massive silver candelabra, was set for twenty-four. On the walls was an equestrian painting of Cayetana and one of her aunts, the Duchess of Santona. Jackie was placed between Luis Alba and the Count of Teba, who were soon enchanted by her. Everyone's attention was concentrated on her.

"You know, Aline," my dinner partner said, "that gesture Mrs. Kennedy has of sliding one hand up and down her arm while she speaks may appear innocent, and perhaps it is, but the effect is extremely sensuous."

The woman on his other side added, "And have you noticed? She pays unwavering attention to the man with whom she's conversing. Combine it with that low sultry voice and that delicate alluring air of hers, and the men become mesmerized."

By the time we got up from the table, the men were all under her spell and we women were trying to learn how she did it. She was not only beautiful, we agreed, but, more important, very dignified. However, I couldn't spend all my time thinking about Jackie. The prospect of meeting Stanley Baker in the next couple of hours, and reading Top Hat's letter, occupied my mind.

When dinner was over, and Jackie claimed she was too tired to go to the fair, I left with the first guests who were on their way there.

At night, the sky above the narrow streets harboring the mass of little *casetas* glowed with a million colored lights. On both sides of the narrow dirt road, Japanese lanterns illuminated the small terraces of the canvas shacks which resounded with the music of guitars and the stomp of dancing feet. We strolled along under the arch of glowing paper globes in a crowd composed of Sevillian matrons in their most fashionable ensembles, young girls in long ruffled dresses, prancing children in costume, and gypsies beating intoxicating rhythms on tin pans. At this hour, all the flamenco parties were in full swing. For the entire week, the city of Sevilla, rich and poor, would be laughing, singing, and dancing—dedicated to gaiety alone.

When our group arrived at the Ybarras' *caseta,* it was jammed, but Antonio Ybarra saw us and beckoned toward the front seats. A gypsy boy, about eight years old, occupied the small stage, dancing and gesturing, his little feet beating out the rhythm of the guitar music in professional style. One after another, artists and some guests who were expert flamenco dancers, jumped onto the platform doing *bulerias, fandangos,* and gypsy-rumbas. For everyone in that small room, time stood still, but I was impatient and kept one eye on the entrance.

Chapter 34

S tanley Baker didn't arrive until two. When I saw him appear in the doorway, I got up and wiggled my way out of the crowd, to meet him in the street. He suggested going someplace where I could decipher the letter without being observed. We found a bar which, although crowded and noisy, was not conspicuous and neither of us exchanged a word as he handed me the envelope.

The stamp showed that the letter had been mailed the day Edmundo died. His normally neat letters were sloppy, but in the usual coded five-letter blocks. Obviously he'd been in a hurry. Stanley handed me a pencil and, standing at the bar, I went to work.

"This could be a suicide note," murmured Baker while I decoded. "Probably the last thing he wrote."

The message was short. Some time had passed since I'd decoded messages regularly, and it took quite a while for me to decipher. Stanley waited patiently at my side, scanning the words as I wrote them down:

ADVISE WILLY TO ASCERTAIN IF CHANDLER IN PARIS FEBRUARY FIRST BUT WARN HER TO BEWARE STOP CATSMEOW IS LINK STOP PROCEED WITH CAUTION IN SEVILLA STOP ABRAZOS.

Stanley Baker looked at me. "What do you make of that?"

"That Top Hat didn't have suicide on his mind when he coded this." I tapped the paper. "And do you know, Chandler and his wife are here in Sevilla right now?"

Stanley seemed sincerely astonished. "Who is this Chandler? Who are these code names?"

I looked at Stanley Baker. "Hasn't Jupiter told you the names of his suspects?"

"Frankly, no," he answered. "To tell you the truth, I've never met Jupiter. My part in this operation is only to be your contact with our Paris station chief."

I was barely listening. What puzzled me was what Edmundo meant about Claudine being a link. Did he know her? He hadn't said so when I gave him the Duchess' code names, which included Claudine's. What a pity I'd never told him that Claudine was the one who had recommended the shop in Madrid. What did he mean about Cat's Meow being "the link"—to what? Could that indicate a link between the two operations? Jupiter had told me there was no possible connection between Operation Magic and Operation Safehaven. "One had to do with the Germans and this is a KGB operation," he had said.

Stanley and I continued to discuss the enigma. It seemed to me Edmundo had suspected Colonel Chandler of some involvement in Operation Magic. That word, "link." He was linked to Claudine in some way. Claudine was connected to Operation Magic. Maybe, I thought, the Duchess was right when she said the two operations could be related.

Stanley thought that the warning to proceed with caution in Sevilla was because Top Hat knew Claudine would be there. He also said he would send a copy of Top Hat's message to the Paris office. For me, Operation Magic had become more confusing than ever.

Stanley had to drive back to Madrid immediately, so he made a copy of my translation, and then suggested taking me back to my friends. I insisted that I return alone, so my friends would not see me with him. Jamming my translation of the message into the farthest corner of my handbag, we left the bar in opposite directions.

I wandered through the dim and almost deserted streets in the direction of the *caseta* where I had left my friends. The thought that this had been Edmundo's last message depressed me. I ambled along, almost oblivious to the guitar music and the gaiety echoing from behind the striped canvas walls of those *casetas* that were still open. It was getting chilly and I wrapped my *manton de Manila* closer around my shoulders.

I don't know when I became aware that someone was following me. At first, I thought nothing of the shadowy figure about forty meters behind. There were plenty of inebriated farmers and gypsies and other fairgoers at this time of night, but rarely had anyone been accosted during the fair. It was an unwritten law to be on good behavior that week. People drank, but no one rolled in the streets drunk. People had fights, but it never developed into anything serious. For decades, the Feria in Sevilla had been a place where respectable women could go alone without risking their reputations.

I arrived at the *caseta* and lifted the canvas curtain to peek inside. The flamenco was still going on, but our group from Las Duenas had left. Then I wandered over to the next street and looked inside the Lapiques' *caseta.* They weren't there, either. Walking for so long in high heels had made my feet ache, and Top Hat's message upset me. Suddenly, I realized I was tired. I wound my way to the end of that street and then zigzagged through the little roads looking for an exit where taxis might be waiting. That's when I realized the person behind was making the same twists and turns. Still, I wasn't frightened, although now I was in the last row of *casetas,* the public ones, where hoodlums, stray drunks, and prostitutes were apt to hang out. But when I saw there was no taxi, I turned around, hoping to find a carriage for hire. The person behind did the same. I began to feel uncomfortable. After all, if the fellow was a gypsy who wanted *pesetas,* he would have asked me by now. If the man's intention was something else, he would have approached me long before. From a low-class bar at the end of the street, lights glimmered. I quickened my steps. Inside, bedraggled men were dawdling over their last drinks of the night. The place was filthy—empty bottles and cartons were strewn on the dirt floor. Some chairs and a table had been turned over, as if a fight had been going on. The stench of old sherry and of urine was overwhelming. Since the customers were eyeing me lewdly, I hastily looked around for a telephone, but there was none. I dared not ask any of these hoodlums for help.

When I went back into the street, the now-familiar silhouette was still there, standing under a street lamp not far away. Although I couldn't see his features, the bushy gray hair rang a bell. Then, for a moment, he turned his head, and the lamplight shone directly on his face. I recognized him immediately. No one could have terrified me more. Michael Chandler was following me! Struggling to control my fear, I considered going back into the bar, but changed my mind. The men there were dangerous also.

I tried to convince myself that I was being foolish, that there were still hundreds of people at the fair who could appear at any moment. As I walked, the dust from the dirt road seeped into my sandals, making them more uncomfortable than ever. The silence was such that the swishing of my starched skirt sounded like a drum marking my pace. Maybe it was because Top Hat's words of warning were still so recent, or maybe it was the memory of Magic's gory death; at any rate, I was now thoroughly frightened, and I had no means of self-protection. Needless to say, I hadn't even thought about carrying my Beretta with me for years.

No one had introduced me to Chandler or his wife that day at Maxim's, so I had no idea if he had seen me or knew who I was. Rapidly, I tried to remember the details of the luncheon. If she'd been asked that day, Claudine would probably have mentioned that Luis and I were a couple from Spain—that was about all she knew. She might have known that I was American-born, but neither she nor anyone else knew I had been doing espionage for the United States. So from that point of view, I consoled myself; I had nothing to worry about. He had no reason to involve me in his problems, even if he was the traitor. But what about Baker, I wondered. Was he entirely reliable? Could there be someone on his staff working with Chandler, one who knew that I was working for the CIA?

I realized that Chandler had been trailing me for the last fifteen minutes, at least. Never had the streets of the fairgrounds appeared so desolate. The shacks, which during the busy hours of the day and night sold mementos and candies, were closed. The lanterns illuminating the streets of the fair had been turned off an hour before. It was probably about three-thirty or maybe even four by now.

The footsteps behind became louder. I could near nothing else. A moment later, Michael Chandler caught up with me and gripped my arm. Trying to free myself, I avoided looking at him and kept walking. My gilt metallic evening bag was hard and quite heavy.

I wondered if I could knock him out with it. Twenty years ago, I would have been ready for this type of assault, but I was out of practice.

He walked by my side without loosening his clutch. "What are you doing alone in a place like this?" His voice was coaxing. The case officer in the CIA office in Paris had shown me Chandler's picture and a short case history, along with those of other suspects they had been investigating, but nothing had indicated that Chandler was a womanizer. By his addressing me in English, I understood immediately he knew who I was. Americans at the fair usually mistook me for Spanish, and if they spoke to me at all, did so in whatever Spanish words they knew.

Nevertheless, I decided to act as if I had no idea who he was, and once more I tried to jerk my arm away. As I did so, I glanced at him again. The same bushy overhanging eyebrows, the thick bulbous nose, the height about five-eleven. There was no doubt. This man was Colonel Michael Chandler.

"Now, now," he said, "no need for alarm. I saw you talking to that fellow in the bar a while ago, so I know you're not shy."

He was pretending that he didn't know who I was. How long had he been watching us? Had he seen me transcribing the message Stanley handed me? He had not been in the bar or I would have seen him. The thought that Chandler might have trailed Stanley, knowing full well that Stanley was a CIA agent or that Stanley had come to Sevilla to get me to decipher a message, gave me goose bumps.

In my handbag was Top Hat's transcribed message. If Chandler was the mole, that would give him reason enough to finish me off, perhaps even as he had my friend Magic. I suspected the worst. Somehow I knew he wasn't just trying to pick me up.

Again, he pressed on my arm, and this time it hurt. "Come off it. You're as American as I am. You can't pull this act with me." His voice was no longer cajoling.

When I saw a group of people stumble out of an alleyway about ten meters away, a wave of relief swept over me. I called to them in Spanish. But they were making such a racket they didn't hear. Chandler's grip kept me from running to them.

"They're only drunks," he said. "Nobody can help you, except me." He yanked me toward him in a brutal embrace. The ugly face close to mine, the pain of his grip and the stench of sour alcohol infuriated me. I struggled, trying to kick him with my knee, but his hold tightened. I never knew what his real intentions were, because at that moment someone attacked Chandler from behind and suddenly I was free.

"Señora Condesa, get out of the way." The rasping voice of Tomas Terry's coachman bellowed out as he struck Chandler. The American fell to the ground. The coachman came to my side, peering at me in the semidarkness, his voice filled with concern.

"Are you all right?"

"Yes."

Chandler was on his feet again and in his hand was a thin, shiny blade. I screamed as he made a dive for Ramon, who dodged the blow just in time. Kicking the knife from Chandler's hand, Ramon, young and powerful, attacked him with his fists. The American turned and ran toward a small alleyway between two dark *casetas.* But the coachman was after him. I picked up the knife, noticing it was the kind gypsies in southern Spain preferred, not the three-blade regimental type we had been trained to use. I worried that Chandler might also carry a gun, but Ramon returned almost immediately.

"That *hijo de—,"* he cursed, "has escaped and I can't continue to try to find him. It would be imprudent to leave the Señora Condesa alone." He shook his fists. "But if I ever see him again, I'll get my hands on him . . ." He looked at me.

"Are you sure, Señora Condesa, he didn't harm you?"

I nodded. "But if you hadn't appeared, Ramon, I'm not sure what would have happened."

"I was on my way home. When I came around the corner, I could see that fellow meant no good. Thing is, I didn't know the lady was yourself, Señora Condesa. The fellow has to be a foreigner. A Spaniard wouldn't attack a lady like that during the Feria."

When I got back to Las Duenas that night, despite being exhausted, I couldn't sleep. Evidence was mounting, but it confused me. Was Chandler the traitor? Or was he just a drunk trying to make a pass at me? Did he connect me to the CIA and did he know they suspected him, or that Top Hat had suspected him? Questions raced through my head. What would Luis say if he knew I was involved in a mission that had taken the lives of two colleagues—

and that I could have been the third? Each day, the new developments made it more difficult for me to confess to Luis that I had lied to him.

In my mind, Operation Magic and Operation Safehaven had to be connected in some way. How well had Edmundo known Claudine? And what exactly had he discovered about Michael Chandler? His suggestion about caution in Sevilla probably indicated I should carry a weapon as we used to, but where would I get a pistol in the middle of the fair without arousing suspicions? Edmundo was not likely to suggest that the Duchess concentrate on Chandler, if he knew him to be the mole we were looking for. He had had his doubts about that when he sent me that last message. It irked me that my old pal had not given clearer explanations. But, of course, Edmundo never expected to die. He probably thought he was about to solve the mystery himself and reestablish his record.

The only one who could clear things up now was Claudine. Talking to her would be my objective for the following day, which, as I glanced at the slivers of light sneaking through the thick curtains, was today! I grabbed my eyeshade and plugged wax in my ears to eliminate the early morning sounds of horses and carriages being washed directly under my window, and I turned over to sleep.

Chapter 35

bout four hours later—noon time—everyone was waking up. Boots were being polished, chaps tied, clothes pressed. Ladies who intended to ride sidesaddle were calling from one room to another, asking friends to help them with cummerbunds, calling for hairdressers to fix their chignons. Men were struggling with the brims of their Cordobes felt hats which had become misshapen during the trip. The staircase resounded with the echo of steel spurs ringing on tile. In the patio, horses' bells jingled. Coachmen were still buffing a harness or relocating a pompom. Everyone was in some stage of preparation for the daily parade of horses and riders. Chandler's attack of last night faded like a bad nightmare.

We rode in the Albas' carriage to the fairgrounds. The air was hot and humid, and I was already damp under my green velvet jacket. Jackie was wearing my red velvet riding jacket, striped pants, and embroidered chaps, and she was beautiful.

When she mounted the majestic white Nevada, she created a sensation. With our wide black hat brims tilted over one eye, our hair in large chignons, our embroidered chaps tied snugly under the thighs, a striped horse blanket across the pommel of our wide Andalusian saddles, we initiated the slow formal Spanish trot. Then we broke into a cadenced canter.

"Aline, this Spanish horse is a beauty." Jackie glowed with pleasure. "So powerful and yet so gentle." She sat her horse like the excellent horsewoman she was, something Sevillians recognized better than most. People stopped to watch her, and some came into the street to get a closer view.

"Tell me how to do those fancy steps this horse is trained for," Jackie said, trying to ignore the growing crowd. "Those slow motion high steps and turns. I've seen that in Vienna with those Lippizaner horses, but I've never ridden one trained for that before."

I leaned to one side and pressed my horse's flank with my spurs, and then did the same on the other side. The horse began to trot, lifting his forelegs high. No sooner had Jackie started to do the same, than photographers and admirers pushed closer, crushing our horses so that her efforts became impossible.

"Oh, I do hate mobs," she cried in desperation. "And I'm so fed up with the photographers! No matter where I go, they make it impossible for me to enjoy myself."

The Marqués of Atienza's spectacular carriage, drawn by four pair of white horses with one lead horse on an invisible nylon cord, was just behind us. Normally, the crowds stood back and gazed in awe, but today everyone wanted to get close to the famous Mrs. Kennedy. The jostling crowd encircling us became more oppressive each second. Our mounts became nervous and skittery. To make things worse, advancing toward us, also with difficulty, were Audrey Hepburn and Mel Ferrer. Both were astride horses belonging to Angel Peralta, the country's top *rejoneador.* I could see that Audrey was frightened. She'd been thrown in a film a few years before and had broken a lumbar vertebra. So she wasn't having any fun either.

With difficulty, we moved slowly through the crowd toward the judges' stand. I wondered if Colonel Chandler was lurking in that mass of people, ready to do something evil.

The sophisticated Sevillians were demanding in judging the riders. Any mistake in dress or posture was noticed and prizes were given to those who fulfilled the rules. No one—not even the First Lady of the U.S.A.—would be awarded a prize if there was the slightest error in her attire. Our striped pants were wrong—my maid had packed them by mistake instead of solid black—but fortunately, Jackie didn't know, and I was too upset about Top Hat's death and the possibility that an assassin was in our midst to care.

But the parade of carriages and riders was spectacular. Behind some of the horsemen, sitting sidesaddle on the rump of the horse, *a la grupa,* were girls with carnations in their hair, their ruffled, long polka-dot gypsy skirts spread decoratively over the animal's rump. Some of these handsome riders were the week's star bullfighters, which made the parade still more glamorous and exciting for all.

Little girls in brightly colored cotton costumes were perched high up on the back of the carriage seats. Long, thin glasses of icy sherry passed from one carriage to another, and now and then to a rider nearby. Guitar music came from the *casetas,* and inside, groups of girls in multicolored costumes danced, their arms lifted in the air, writhing and twisting to the classical movements of the "Sevillana." People laughed and chatted and waved at friends. Carnations flew through the air.

The crowds surrounding Jackie finally made it impossible for her to move. And dangerous, too. Like knights in armor on powerful steeds, Fermin Bohorquez and Alvaro Domecq appeared and miraculously saved her from the mob. I knew they would take her to the Parque de Maria Luisa, where they could all canter in peace, away from the crowds. I stayed in the fairgrounds, advancing with difficulty along the dusty dirt road, looking for Chandler, and Claudine too. Pedestrians carelessly brushed against my horse, and I worried it might kick one of them. A violent tug on my chaps made me look down. At first I had a twinge of fear, half expecting to see the dreaded Colonel Chandler. Instead, peering up at me, squinting in the bright sunlight, was the wrinkled face of yesterday's fortune teller. Her hand was not out begging for money this time, but she obviously wanted to say something to me. I couldn't hear her and leaned over to catch the words. As I did so, she changed her mind and abruptly turned around. Before I could say anything, she had disappeared into the crowd. That was strange, I thought. What did that woman want?

Neither Chandler nor his blond wife, nor the Jorans, were at the fair this morning, or so it seemed. About a half-hour later, I left my horse with the groom, in front of the Aero Club, and went inside to join friends and to cool off. Eventually, we were all reunited, and about four o'clock we climbed into Cayetana's carriage to return to Las Duenas for lunch. There was no set hour. One of the luxuries of staying there was that each guest could arrive when convenient. Today, however, TV trucks and the press blocked the streets surrounding the palace and it was almost five when we straggled in. The footmen were waiting to serve a delicious buffet, which was stretched out over the long dining room table: Gazpacho; Mediterranean seafood—crayfish and baby shrimp from El Puerto de Santa Maria—*chanquetes,* minute baby eel from Malaga; fresh fat white asparagus from Aranjuez; smoked ham from Montanchez; cold sliced veal from Salamanca; sweets and fruit. However, those of us who were going to the *corrida* barely had time to eat.

While a hairdresser was adjusting Jackie's mantilla and high comb, I asked Juan if there was a message from my husband. Normally, Luis would have called at least once a day, but Juan said there had been no calls from him, probably because the switchboard was besieged with calls for Mrs. Kennedy. However, he said, another call had come for me from Madrid and the person had left a number where I was requested to call back. When I did, it was the Madrid station chief. Stanley had arrived, and they had made inquiries as a result of Top Hat's message.

The voice read to me their findings. "The antique shop has been rented since 1943 in a building belonging to Klaus Fribourg. The shopowner, Felix Martos Sanchez, died in January, leaving the business to his niece."

The man went on to tell me that their call to Paris so far had not revealed anything of interest on Claudine de Jorans or Michael Chandler. He told me the DST had been requested to investigate Claudine de Jorans, but that I should "not place too much importance on Top Hat's warnings. He was prone to exaggeration, you know." And then he hung up.

Although I was indignant about the reference to Top Hat, I had to resign myself to the idea that Chandler may just have been trying to pick me up in a particularly disgusting fashion. Yet Stanley Baker's message did convey some worthwhile news. Klaus Fribourg would certainly tell me all he knew about the shop and its owner, when I asked him.

Jackie was on her way downstairs when I came out into the hall. The horses were impatient, and many guests had already left for the bullring. When we finally got moving, our carriage had difficulty getting through the narrow street clogged with television trucks and press. Fortunately, we arrived just in time. The public stood up to watch Mrs. Kennedy as she entered the box we were going to occupy this afternoon. Princess Grace, striking in a white mantilla, was in another box a bit farther on. As before, Cayetana and I draped our embroidered Manila shawls over the railing. This had the effect of adorning the plaza, but it had a more practical purpose as well—those below could not see up our skirts. Down below, Claudine was seated in the same *barrera* seat she had occupied the day before. Her husband was on one side and again, Enrique was on the other. I took my field glasses and searched the *tendidos* for the Chandlers, but if present, they were invisible in the crowd.

Antonio Ordonez did two great *faenas* and got an ear for each; one he threw to Grace and the other to Jackie. Photographers were not allowed to take pictures during the fight, but when we left the bullring, nothing distracted them from trying to get more shots of our famous houseguest—not even a car accident, in which a woman was run down, trying to get across the street. Sevillians were even making bets on which of the two American women was most popular. Houseguests at La Duenas decided that the winner was Jackie, and although the day before they had been flattered to be in the same house with such an important international personality, they were beginning to resent the inconveniences.

That night, instead of going to the fairgrounds, we went to a large ball in the Casa de Pilatos, another magnificent Arabic palace belonging to the Duchess of Medinaceli. I missed Luis and tried to get him on the phone before leaving for the ball, but the line in Las Duenas was always busy and I never got to call. Another day with no news from Luis worried me.

I was quite certain the Chandlers would not be at the ball and hadn't mentioned my encounter of the night before to anyone. But the Jorans were seated nearby and I hoped I could get Claudine to talk about them. I didn't have to make much of an effort, because as soon as people began to mill about, Claudine came to me.

"That gypsy woman!" she said. "I must find her. She's right about everything she told me. Danger does surround me. Do you know that the woman who was run down by the car after the bullfight this afternoon was standing next to me! That car was aimed at me. I'm sure of it. It's a miracle I wasn't killed, too."

I didn't even know the woman had died. I tried to convince Claudine that it had to be a coincidence, but as I did, I remembered the gypsy soothsayer's expression when she tapped on my saddle that morning. I decided not to tell Claudine that she had wanted to say something to me.

"Speaking of the bullfight," I said, "were your friends, the Chandlers, there today?"

She looked at me suspiciously. "Why are you so interested in the Chandlers?"

I made an effort to sound nonchalant. "I'm not interested in them. I don't even know them, but they are friends of yours."

"They may be friends, but they're the last people I want to see in Spain. I can see them in Paris." Then abruptly, she went back to her original topic. "You can't imagine how important it is for me to find that fortune teller. I had a real rapport with her. She understood me. I'm an excellent medium. All my friends tell me that."

Her next words made me wonder if she did have supernatural powers after all. "Edouard is so jealous," she sighed. "I didn't dare mention this to you in front of him, but ever since I met you, I've wanted to talk to you about a mutual friend we have." She smiled slyly.

"Oh, yes. You did say something about that. Who is it?"

No name she could have mentioned would have surprised me as much.

"Edmundo Lassalle," she said.

Claudine noticed that her words shocked me.

"What's the matter?" She asked. "Don't you like him? I thought you and Edmundo were good friends?"

"Claudine, I hate to tell you this, but Edmundo is dead."

Under the heavy makeup, her face turned pale. "That's impossible." Her words were barely audible. "I saw him only a week ago." Her expression revealed disbelief, then terror. My news about Edmundo more than stunned her. She was petrified.

"This happened in London." I added.

"I was in London," she whispered. "Please don't tell anyone. I was in London. With Edmundo." She placed both hands on her decolletage and breathed an anguished sigh.

I struggled to hide my amazement. Claudine, I guessed, had had something to do with the sale of those looted Nazi paintings, but being in London with Edmundo definitely connected her with Operation Magic as well. That's what Top Hat must have meant when he referred to her as the "link." And now I realized that Claudine herself might lead us to the mole in Operation Magic.

Making an effort to regain her composure, Claudine asked. "How did it happen? Who told you?"

"They say it was suicide. He was found with his head in the oven in his apartment and the gas turned on. It appeared in the London papers. An Englishman here at the fair mentioned it to me; he must have heard about it on the telephone or seen a paper someone brought in." This was a lie, and a dangerous one, that she could catch me on, but I had to take advantage of the moment. Claudine, the link, was in a mood to confide.

"When was the last time you saw him?" I asked. I knew I had to be careful now. If she suspected me in any way, she would not talk freely. I remembered Edmundo's words: "caution in Sevilla."

Instead of answering my question, Claudine grabbed my arm and pulled me from the table, away from the ornate patio where guests were dining and dancing, to another that was almost empty. "You must help me," she whispered, as we walked across the ancient stone floor. We found an isolated bench and sat down. The night was warm and sticky and I could see that Claudine was perspiring heavily. She grabbed a cigarette from her evening bag. Trying to light it, her hand shook so much I had to hold the match.

"Edmundo and I began a romance a few weeks ago," she babbled. "Last week I had the opportunity to go to London, and since he had an apartment there, we decided to spend a few days together. Only two days! But we had a lovely time. Edmundo is . . . was . . . so special." She rubbed a tear from her cheek. "On the way back to Paris, I stopped to buy things, you know, to make Edouard believe I had gone to London for my usual shopping." Claudine was sobbing now and speaking in spurts. She was either sincerely distraught or a great actress. "We stopped in Harrods on the way to the airport," she gasped. "Edmundo and I. He wanted to take me to the plane . . . so thoughtful, so affectionate." She looked at me through the tears. "But do you know, he did the strangest thing in Harrods! Almost got me into terrible trouble, too." She dabbed her eyes with a hankie and took two nervous puffs on the smoldering cigarette. "While I was looking for my husband's favorite English sausages, Edmundo picked up something and put it into his pocket. Two cans of sardines, I think it was. The store police saw him and actually put handcuffs on him. I couldn't believe it. It must have been some sort of mistake."

"He was a kleptomaniac," I told her. "Had been all his life—he even 'lifted' a glass plate or ashtray in Ferrieres during the ball. By the way, did you see him there?"

"Of course. I was the one who told him about the ball. You know how Edmundo loves elegant affairs. I didn't dare ask Marie-Hélène for an invitation for him, so he put on a disguise and gate-crashed."

"Where did he find that dead rabbit? It was still limp."

For a fleeting moment, she smiled. "His car hit the rabbit entering Ferrieres." Her mascara was running in little black lines down her cheeks. "Do you know what he said? He said it was in his pocket for his next snack." She shook her head. "Always so amusing!" She began to sob anew. Tossing her cigarette butt onto the stone floor, she opened the bag, taking out the damp handkerchief. She dabbed at her makeup again.

My thoughts went back to Edmundo's kleptomania. I knew that indicated he had been under strain. "What had happened to make him especially worried that day in London?"

"Nothing that I could see," she babbled.

"And what made him nervous at Ferrieres?" She was no longer listening to me. I had to ask her twice.

"Nothing that I knew about there, either." She looked guileless enough as she answered. "But he did have the crazy notion that we were being followed all the time we were in London. I knew my husband was in Paris and busy with his own affairs. That's why I could go to London." She shook her head. "I can't believe Edmundo's dead. I just can't believe it," she repeated.

"Do you think he was upset enough to commit suicide?" I asked.

"Oh, *mon Dieu.*" She dabbed at the corners of her eyes. I noticed her fingernails were bitten to the skin. Claudine had been jittery for some time before tonight. "Never. He was wildly happy with me."

"Do you think someone could have murdered him?"

My words hit her like a blow. She cringed, and little wrinkles appeared around her eyes and forehead. In a gesture of despair, she threw her arms around my neck and hung there. "Don't you see how necessary it is for me to talk to that gypsy again," she whimpered. "So many terrible things are happening all around me. I don't know what to do. Edmundo protected me. Now that he's gone . . ."

"Protected you from what?" I asked, gently pushing her away.

Behind the bench was a tiled wall, and she leaned against it. "From Edouard. You see, he's so jealous, he frightens me."

"But why?" I implored.

She shrugged her shoulders, and although I plied her with questions, she didn't answer. Guests from the party entered the patio and were coming our way. I hastened to take advantage of the last second. "Claudine, what do you think of Colonel Chandler?"

Claudine's hand touched my knee to silence me. I turned around and saw that Edouard was walking toward us with friends. A moment later, he was at our side and the opportunity had passed. Although it was obvious that he had noted Claudine's state, he said nothing.

We all walked back to the large salon together. Edouard, making an effort to cover up for his wife's distress, chatted constantly. I think no one noticed anything unusual. Inside, the music was not very good, but nevertheless, Edouard asked me to dance.

"Claudine is upset lately. You must forgive her. She's not strong and always tries to do too much," he said. "I worry about her. I hope she hasn't been boring you with her wild tales. She has a great imagination, you know."

I assured him that she had been quite amusing, telling me how much she enjoyed the fair. We bounced around the floor to the tempo of a *pasadoble.* His smoldering black eyes belied his words about worry. He was furious. "I hope Claudine is in better spirits when Mr. Worthington arrives in Paris. He's seventy years old and I need her help—not only during my luncheon, but for the entire week."

For a moment I was puzzled. Who was Mr. Worthington? Then I remembered Edouard had mentioned it to me—it was the American he had saved from drowning. He went on. "It is even possible President de Gaulle himself may come to the luncheon. You know how badly our President and the Americans are getting along lately. My dream is to use cultural affairs to improve relations. It could be the outstanding accomplishment of my life." Edouard's dancing, usually better, had become routine, even out of step with the music. "I expect Their Royal Highnesses to attend"—I realized he meant the Windsors—"and your friends the Rothschilds also."

I told him I had seen the Chandlers at the bullfight.

The minute I mentioned the name, his body stiffened. "You must have mistaken them with someone else."

"Not at all. In fact I saw Colonel Chandler again last night wandering around the fairgrounds. His wife must have gone to bed, because he was alone. Could you tell me if he is often drunk?" By now, Edouard was a good friend, but I decided against asking him how he would judge Chandler's attack of the night before.

My partner was no longer listening to the music. His steps had become mechanical. "I haven't the slightest idea. The Chandlers are not among my closest friends."

That was all he said. My charming friend had become a taciturn stranger this evening. I wondered if he was aware that Claudine had had an affair with Edmundo.

But I felt sorry for him again when we returned to the table. Claudine, making an astonishing recovery, I thought, was flirting with the handsome Spaniard sitting at her side. I excused Edouard's attitude because I knew he was upset and very much in love with his wife. Not only did her affairs worry him, but, I now realized, her demeanor could be a handicap for his most coveted aspiration—impressing Mr. Worthington, the man whom he had admired for thirty years.

When we sat down, Ada Fribourg leaned over and whispered, "Your compatriot is not very kind." She nodded toward Jackie, who was surrounded by admirers. Ada's frown caused her blue eye makeup to crease in a manner that would have upset her if she'd been in front of a mirror. "Do you know, I crossed the room to speak to her, and she ignored me. Can you imagine! It's not as if we hadn't been introduced. Have you noticed? She never bothers to be nice to women, but she certainly puts on the charm with men."

Ada's remark surprised me, just as her criticism of Claudine had. She hadn't been like this before, I thought. Her attitude and remarks this past month made me wonder if her former benevolence had been only a role she'd played.

Claudine was drinking one glass of champagne after another. Klaus Fribourg joined us and sat down next to me. His thin, gray hair stuck to his bald head and the pencil lines he had carefully marked to make his hair appear fuller were now mixed with perspiration and oozing in little stripes down his forehead. He, too, was looking at Claudine. In an irritated voice, which for him was rare, he murmured to me.

"That woman is dangerous. She creates problems wherever she goes."

His words were a surprise. In Paris, he'd been charmed by Claudine. Was Ada influencing him against Claudine out of jealousy, I wondered? And if so, jealousy of whom? Ada's recent streak of resentfulness had made me see her in a different light. There was certainly no love lost between Ada and Claudine. A few minutes later, Edouard took Claudine home, and soon after that we all left. I had no desire to go back to the Feria without Luis, who was arriving tomorrow, so I went back to Las Duenas early, about three. It was going to be my one full night's sleep.

The next day, my doubts about Claudine and my preoccupation about Chandler were mitigated by my anxiety to see my husband. We had hardly spoken during the entire week. I knew he was still annoyed by my prolonged visit to Paris and the knowledge that I was keeping something from him. If this mission was not resolved soon, it could spoil my perfect marriage. I rode all over the fairgrounds, but by three o'clock there was no sign of him. Then I experienced a wave of delight: there amongst the masses of carriages, riders, and pedestrians cluttering the hot dusty streets, Luis was making his way to our usual meeting place, the Aero Club.

I rode as close as I could and called out. He looked my way. There was no smile, no word. He merely nodded and calmly continued on his way. He was not as happy to see me as I to see him. A new fear overcame me. Something had happened. It wasn't like Luis to be disagreeable. He rarely lost his temper and was always in a good humor. Hastening to the club to dismount, I had to wait for the groom to arrive to take the horse before I could join Luis at the bar.

When I did, he was engrossed in conversation with Ada, who was more glamorous than ever, in a white linen suit with a bright green chiffon neck scarf. Finally, he turned to me with an icy stare and propelled me to a far corner of the bar.

Hardly opening his mouth, he said, "This morning I met a friend in the airport on his way back to Madrid who said he saw you alone in a bar in the Feria with some American. You haven't telephoned me all week. When I went to Las Duenas, I find that Cayetana has put me in a separate room. What happens?"

Friends interrupted and I was able to avoid explanations he probably would not have believed. The fear that my husband had already fallen out of love with me made me weak. When the carriage was ready to take us back to Las Duenas for lunch, Luis grabbed Ada's arm and said they were going to Poli Maza's ranch for the afternoon and would not be back in Sevilla until the evening. I knew there would be a *tienta* and a party there that afternoon. That meant he was not going to the bullfight with me either. I couldn't believe that he really was flirting with Ada, but I realized with a stab of fear that, if he were, she was serious competition.

I tried to console myself with the thought that, without Luis there, it might be easier to look for Claudine and to get her to talk. But I was engulfed by despair.

Maybe Luis' absence would also give me more time to call Stanley Baker and to advise Jupiter about Claudine having been in London with Top Hat just before he died. Perhaps by now Stanley would have some information for me. But that afternoon I couldn't reach him, nor did I see Chandler or Claudine.

That night, General Franco came for dinner at Las Duenas, and as soon as he departed, we left in a group for the fair. Luis went in someone else's car with Jackie, who had been disguised with dark glasses and a scarf. Nevertheless, the admiring mobs recognized her, and she was obliged to return to the house. The rest of us wandered from *caseta* to *caseta* looking for a good flamenco.

About three in the morning, we met the Jorans and the Fribourgs in the Lapiques' *caseta.* When we entered, the flamenco was at its height, with the four famous Pelados—the great gypsy dancers—hypnotizing the audience. The captivating guitar music and the beat of the *palmas* held everyone enthralled. At first, it seemed Claudine had recovered from her shock of the night before. She was beautifully dressed and her smile was happy and relaxed when she waved, indicating to me that there was a seat next to hers. But as soon as I sat down, she leaned toward me.

"Since your news about Edmundo," she whispered, "I haven't slept a wink."

I pressed her hand. "It's made me very sad, too," I answered. "Especially since I'm sure it was not suicide, but murder."

If Top Hat thought she was the link, I had to get her to tell me more than she had last night. "It would be only fair to him," I added, "if we could prove that he had not killed himself."

She didn't say anything. The Pelados were ending their *buleria.* The *palmas* became louder, the beat faster, and the rhythm almost hypnotic. I was drawn into the spell of it all. I thought Claudine, too, was absorbed in the stimulating flamenco before us, but after a while, she nudged me, murmuring, "I'm afraid it was my fault."

"What was your fault?"

"His death."

I looked at her. She was lighting a cigarette with the stub of the last—Claudine was a chain smoker. Her eyes held tears as she searched in her handbag and brought out a lipstick and began to spread a thick layer of vermilion on her lips. Meanwhile, Cari Lapique was dancing a *rumba flamenca,* a gypsy rumba, on the small wooden stage and had the audience entranced. Antonio Ybarra jumped onto the stage to join her. That was the moment I heard the loud gasp at my side. I turned to look. Claudine's face was contorted, and before I could ask what was the matter, she had fallen to the floor.

Luis and Klaus, who had both been standing nearby against the wall, picked her up and carried her out to the street. A crowd gathered and some chairs were supplied to rest her on. We took for granted that she had fainted. It had been very crowded and close inside the *caseta.* When she didn't come to, however, Klaus went in search of Dr. Larrizabal, whom we had seen a few moments before. Someone in the crowd produced smelling salts. I thought she might have had too much to drink and said so to Edouard, who had just come out of the *caseta.* He said he had never known her to faint before and that she had not drunk much that evening. By the time the doctor appeared, Claudine had still not come to, and we were all quite alarmed.

Dr. Larrizabal took her pulse and opened her eyelids. By this time, Ada had also come out of the *caseta* and was pushing her way through the crowd. The doctor was kneeling down in the street next to Claudine, still taking her pulse and opening her eyes, but she remained unconscious. After a few minutes, he looked up at us, and slowly stood up. His expression was very sober.

"Where is this woman's husband?"

Edouard stepped forward.

"I'm sorry to inform you, señor, but your wife has suffered a massive heart attack." He spoke in a low voice, so those who had collected around could not hear. "She is dead."

Edouard de Jorans became frantic. Someone sent Klaus for an ambulance to take the body to the morgue in the hospital. We waited and waited next to Claudine's body. None of us could believe that she was dead. All the time, Edouard held her embraced in his arms, crying inconsolably.

Claudine was dead! There was nothing we could do, except help

Edouard, who was almost prostrate. When we got to the hospital, he was told Claudine's body could not be removed without an autopsy and without permission from the authorities, which would be impossible until Monday. When finally we persuaded Edouard to return to his hotel, Ada was effective in getting a nurse to give him an injection which enabled him to sleep.

When we walked down the steps of the Alfonso XIII, Luis put his arm around me. We were both moved by the drama we had just been through.

"All I can think of is how lucky I am that something like that didn't happen to you," he said. "You're the most important thing in my life. And I want you to know that."

"Oh, Luis," I said. "I've been thinking the same. I wouldn't know how to live without you."

By this time, we were in the car. He leaned over to kiss me. "No more secrets, *guapa,*" he said. "And no more misunderstandings."

As we drove through the quiet streets, the pale blue light of dawn was replacing the shadows. A few fairgoers were still straggling home on foot. I told Luis why Cayetana had put him in a separate room, and I also explained that Stanley Baker was merely an American from the embassy whom I had tried to show around the fairgrounds, that I hardly knew him.

"Don't worry," said Luis. "I've always trusted you. But it does put me in a bad humor when people gossip. We love each other and that's what counts."

That night, despite my exhaustion, I twisted and turned for what seemed hours. Not only was I shocked and sad about Claudine, but at the same time, I realized I had lost the only person who could have led to the mole! I wanted very much to finish this mission.

When we awoke, it was Sunday. Jackie Kennedy's departure was creating the expected excitement. Luis and I were not able to say good-bye because we went back to the Alfonso XIII to see what we could do for Edouard de Jorans. Few guests at La Duenas had met Claudine, and most left unaware of the tragedy. The death of an unknown Frenchwoman during the last hours of the fair did not distract the attention of the press nor the fairgoers from all the celebrities.

But, at least for a short time, Claudine's death brought peace to our marriage. Traveling back to Madrid in the plane, Luis held my hand and we were happy again. Without speaking more about it, we were both determined to repair our differences. I longed for the moment I could tell him all.

Chapter 36

On arriving in Madrid, I called the Duchess, principally to tell her about Claudine. She had already heard the news. "I'm shocked," she said. "And for such a young woman to have a heart attack is a real tragedy. She probably never dreamed she had a heart problem. What a sad thing."

I also told the Duchess about Claudine's confession that she had been in London with Top Hat and that she was having an affair with him.

"Nothing about that poor girl would surprise me anymore. She's had many affairs, I fear." Then she switched topics. "The Chandlers are coming for dinner tonight. Let's hope that may turn up something. I'll let you know how things go."

Claudine's death had almost led me to forget about Michael Chandler. The truth was, right now I wanted peace with my husband more than I wanted to solve the mission. However, the Duchess' words reminded me of the danger involved. "Beware of Chandler," I advised. "He was Top Hat's candidate and he attacked me in Sevilla. I can't tell you about that now; I'll explain it all later. But be careful you don't let him know that I told you. Try to find out if he was out of Paris on the night of February first. And of course, I know you'll try to find out what kind of a relationship he had with Claudine."

She called the next morning. "What an exhausting dinner. Do you know that Michelle de Bragotti arrived late. Well, I didn't wait. Everyone was invited for eight and we sat down at eight-thirty. How was I going to spoil Lucien's soufflé! Such bad manners and, do you know, she came in after the doors were closed? Completely unconcerned, making a grand entrée. I really don't think I'll invite her anymore. This has happened before. You know she's always late." I realized the Duchess was making light conversation to discourage anyone who might be listening in, because a moment later she began to tell me what had been her reason for calling.

"Sorry, but I found nothing incriminating about Colonel Chandler, other than learning that he has bad table manners, likes to ski, speaks French, and is interested in music and bullfights. He told me that he and his wife had gone for two days to the fair to see Ordonez and Dominguin fight. When someone mentioned Claudine's death, he said he had not seen the Jorans there, due to the short time they were in Sevilla, and that he didn't learn about the disaster until they were back in Paris. The Chandlers spent the last week of January in St. Moritz. Alexis de Rédé, who was also here, confirmed having seen them on the slopes. We got along easily enough. He wasn't uncomfortable at all, and in fact he's quite witty." Before hanging up, she added, "I'll be dining with them again next week and I have a few other ideas. I'll call you when there's something worthwhile." The Duchess limited her long distance conversations to save money and hung up as soon as she had transmitted her news.

As I hung up, I wondered again if Colonel Chandler had simply been drunk and was trying to pick me up that night in Sevilla; if, after all, I was only suffering from trade paranoia. I was discouraged. Progress was minimal, and I considered advising Jupiter that I was going to give up the mission entirely. Then I could confess to Luis the reasons for my behavior. His attitude with me was still a bit distant. It also disheartened me that neither Jupiter nor the CIA in Madrid seemed to give any special importance to Top Hat's suspicions about Michael Chandler.

However, when the Duchess called again two days later, I forgot all my good intentions. "Aline, you'll have to come here immediately. You've gotten me into this mess and so many things are going on, I don't know what to do. This time, I can't say anything over the telephone."

When I told her Luis would be furious, she suggested I take a morning plane and return that same afternoon. I had another reason for going. Stanley had left for Washington and called to say that the CIA case officer in Paris had information I should pick up. At home, I said I would be having lunch at the Club del Campo and riding all afternoon.

Usually, I took Iberia to Paris. Air France had so many mishaps that we called it "Air France, Air Chance." But this morning I took their eleven-ten plane, hoping I would see fewer Spaniards. Leaving the house any earlier would have startled my household, not to speak of my husband.

Chapter 37

I arrived in Paris just in time for lunch. The Duke was playing golf, and once again the Duchess and I sat facing each other at one of the two small round tables in the dining room. The lovely Chinese wallpaper and the two corner balconies, their antique musical instruments decoratively placed—the Duke's idea, according to the Duchess—always gave the room a cozy atmosphere, even when, like today, we were only two. Yellow jonquils from her garden placed in green Portuguese porcelain vases separated us. Beyond the French doors, the wide expanse of lawn was now green.

Georges moved in and out of the pantry like a cat, so we were careful when we spoke. The Duchess concealed her impatience less well than usual. I hoped she'd been able to hide her nervousness better from her husband and wondered what it was she had to tell me. At first, Georges was unaware of our desire not to be heard, but after a while he caught on and dismissed the footman who had been assisting him. Before I could discuss my experience with Michael Chandler, or the details of Claudine's death, the Duchess began.

"There's no doubt about the painting in the gallery. It is the one I saw in Madrid. But, you won't believe this—it's a fake!" She described her visit to Mazerolle's gallery while I enjoyed the prosciutto and melon. She said the Fergusons had been out of town, so she had not asked Maureen for suggestions of galleries, as we had originally planned. Fearing someone might buy it in the meantime, she'd gone to the gallery herself. When she'd entered the shop, she'd recognized the painting immediately. She decided to buy it on the spot, but Monsieur Mazerolle quoted a price so high that she knew she couldn't make the purchase without consulting the Duke.

"Shylock," she said. "That's what I'll call him from now on. He's a real bandit. What prices! But despite my complaints, he suggested I take the painting home and think about it. I guess he thought that once it was in the house, I would like it enough to meet his price. But alas, when David heard the cost, he was astounded. The man was asking ten times more than the Madrid shop. And you know, Aline, my romance has never been willing to spend much money on paintings. This time he was adamant—said we couldn't afford it. So I asked my decorator to take a look at it to give me an idea of what I could offer Monsieur Mazerolle. That's when we discovered it was a fake. Now what do you think of that?"

She played with her fork. "Shylock was very surprised when we sent it back, with the explanation that it was a phony Cézanne. But he did not lower the price, not one franc." She returned her attention for a moment to her plate and took a chip at the melon. "Instead, he told me that the painting came from the private collection of the most reliable Impressionist expert in France. He said the man had sold part of his collection at a low price because he needed quick liquidity, and that it was extremely unlikely that the painting was not authentic."

The Duchess said she asked him if he was referring to Monsieur de Jorans, since it was known that Jorans was a great specialist in Impressionist art. The dealer neither affirmed nor denied it, saying he was obliged to maintain the anonymity of his source.

"If Mazerolle's source was Edouard de Jorans," I exclaimed, "that would explain Claudine knowing the address in Madrid. But how would Jorans be in possession of looted World War Two artworks?" We were both puzzled.

"The worst thing is," continued my hostess, "instead of lowering the price and sending it back to me, he said that he would have to talk to the owner—that he refused to sell copies or fakes in his gallery. He said South America had been flooded with fake masterpieces after World War Two, but that in France, they were very cautious about such things." She patted the table. "My decorator says it's very fishy that the owner of such a gallery wouldn't recognize a fake. Maybe since it had just arrived, he hadn't taken a good look. At any rate, I still don't have that painting I loved so much. Actually, if the price had been the same as in Madrid, David and I wouldn't have minded about it being a fake."

We decided that Edouard must have bought the Madrid shopkeeper's stock of paintings, perhaps from the niece after the shopkeeper's death, and had not known he was being cheated. Edouard certainly would not buy fakes. Had the others been fakes also? The late Madrid antique dealer had to have known who the head of Operation Safehaven was. If Stanley did his investigation well, he should be able to discover something in the shop's books. Now Claudine's explanation of how she had known about the obscure shop was understandable. For years, perhaps, the Madrid dealer could have been supplying Mazerolle with paintings which had been looted during the war.

Georges appeared to serve the salmon with dill sauce and unfortunately remained at attention, as he was supposed to, near the pantry door for the remainder of the luncheon. So I was not able to tell the Duchess about Colonel Chandler and Top Hat's warning until after lunch. When we got up, I tried to convince her into taking a few turns around the garden, but that bored her. "Exercise and I do not agree, Aline. It's useless, I'll stay thin starving myself instead. You know I've never been fond of sports." I laughed about her considering walking in the garden a sport, and we took the little elevator up to the second floor instead.

We retired to the boudoir. Small white orchids in terra-cotta pots from her greenhouse were scattered around the room. The Duchess sat in her chair; next to it on the floor was a stack of books. She continued on about the painting.

"Can you beat it!" She enjoyed using American slang expressions. I think it made her feel not only more American, but younger as well. "Monsieur Mazerolle asked me if Paul Ferguson had been the one to recommend his shop to me." She glanced into the bedroom behind her to make sure Maria, her maid, had left. "You can imagine my amazement." Her eyebrows lifted. "He said that he knew the Fergusons were friends of mine and that Colonel Ferguson often sent customers to him. Right there I realized that Monsieur Mazerolle must give Ferguson a percentage of sales for buyers he sends. At least that could explain what Maureen picked up there that day."

She was called to the phone, and I looked at the pile of recent best-seller novels on the floor next to her chair. They were in English, and fresh from Galignani's, the bookstore in front of the Tuilleries Gardens on the Rue de Rivoli—her favorite. There were two spy novels in the batch. Behind her on the shelves of her small corner desk, where she wrote her letters, were lines of red-bound books, some in French: those were the ones she didn't read. On the large table jammed with photographs, I noticed that the pictures of the Duke's childhood, which had been in the back row on my last visit, were now in the front.

The Duchess returned to her chair. Her sapphire eyes were intense. "I shouldn't have taken that call. It was a pushy American businesswoman who always calls when she comes to Paris, so that I'll invite her and get her invited to things." She settled herself more comfortably, which consisted in straightening her spine against the back of her chair. She was not one to slump. "Let me tell you about my dinner party the night before last. Our pianist mentioned something about Claudine that has left me astounded. You must realize, Claudine's death is the topic of conversation everyplace these days. Well, the pianist said he often played at the Joranses' dinners."

The Duchess crossed her legs and smoothed a wrinkle in the skirt of her navy suit piped in beige. "What left me amazed," she continued, "was that he said Colonel Chandler must be especially upset about Madame de Jorans' death because they were—his exact phrase was—'such intimate friends.' " The Duchess clasped her hands. "Now, I ask you, Aline, what do you make of that?"

I felt my temperature soar. In great part, this explained Top Hat's message and again connected Claudine to Operation Magic. Chandler could be the mole. But how? Things were becoming clearer and more confusing at the same time.

"I wanted to talk to you about Michael Chandler," I said. "He attacked me in Sevilla, and ever since I've been in doubt about whether he knew I was working to uncover him or if he was merely trying to pick me up." I briefly described the incident. "It was scary, because Top Hat's message hinted that he was suspicious of Chandler. That could mean that he suspected him to be the mole we're looking for and a killer, besides."

My hostess took a deep breath, but waited for me to continue. "Top Hat called Claudine 'the link.' I didn't know what Edmundo meant, but now I think it could be that she was the link to everything. To Operation Magic and to Operation Safehaven as well. It seems to me that both operations are in some way connected through Claudine, just as you said so long ago."

"Then the pianist's implication," interrupted the Duchess, "that

Michael Chandler and Claudine were having a liaison, fits in perfectly?"

I shook my head. "It doesn't make sense. How could she have affairs with so many men at the same time? Top Hat, Paredes, and now Chandler. And with such a handsome husband. Edouard certainly had every reason to be jealous."

The Duchess agreed. "You know, Aline, these Europeans are different from us Americans. Whenever we have a flirtation, we feel obliged to get a divorce and marry. As you can appreciate, I'm an expert at that."

"And Europeans consider divorce shocking. In their opinion the family must remain intact, especially if there are children. Remember, Claudine has a daughter. Affairs are accepted here if they are carried on discreetly, without scandal. But don't you think that even Europeans would consider Claudine's behavior appalling, if all this is true?"

"No doubt about it. I don't think it's possible that Claudine had so many lovers at the same time. Michael Chandler doesn't strike me as a man that would be attractive to anyone. And affairs are so time-consuming. Arranging hidden restaurants where one won't be seen by friends, getting messages back and forth." She threw her hands in the air. "Making excuses." She laughed. "No, no. In my opinion, impossible."

"Remember," I said, "when we lunched with Maureen at Maxim's? She said she didn't like the woman at that table? One was Claudine and the other Chandler's wife. Perhaps you could get her to tell you why."

"I can try."

We reviewed the clues we now had for both missions. There were reasons to suspect the Joranses in regard to Operation Safehaven, and, in my opinion, Enrique Paredes had probably been the head of Safehaven in Spain during World War Two. But Operation Magic was a mystery. Through Maureen, the Duchess had met two other NATO officers and had later invited both couples to lunch at the Pavillon Albert, the place Magic had been observing the night of her death. Neither couple had been there before and the maître d' confirmed it. Until Top Hat's message and this last news about Claudine and Colonel Chandler, no one we had investigated had shown any sign which could be considered suspicious. However, if Claudine was the "link," as Top Hat had advised, and if he had suspected Michael Chandler—there was no doubt that the Colonel was our best bet for Operation Magic.

"Oh, and I did hear more gossip about Edouard de Jorans," the Duchess said. "During the luncheon at the German embassy yesterday, everyone was discussing Claudine's death again. An old friend from the Académie Française said that he had known Edouard since they were both students together before the war. He said that there were rumors Jorans had joined the Communist party in his youth."

"Well, he certainly doesn't act or talk like a Communist today."

"He's not," the Duchess went on. "My friend said that was just a passing fancy. Edouard enjoys luxury more than anyone. But he obviously has no qualms about changing sides, much less political parties."

"At any rate the fact that Claudine has died is not only sad, but disastrous for our investigation. She could have cleared up everything."

"Can't you ask your spies to investigate Edouard de Jorans more thoroughly?" The Duchess had her own ideas and I wondered if there was something she had not told me. "Also Enrique Paredes. It seems that he had something to do with the Spanish side of the Nazi-looted art. We should be careful. You said several people died during that period."

As she spoke, I wondered again about Stanley Baker. Was he completely reliable? He seemed to give so little importance to Top Hat's warnings. And I remembered again that Chandler had accosted me just after leaving him. I wasn't even certain that Stanley had passed on all my messages to Jupiter.

"In London," the Duchess said, "there's a new play everybody's wild about called *There's a Girl in My Soup*. Well, Claudine appears to be the girl in our soup. Too bad we didn't realize it sooner."

"Jupiter will never believe that the two missions are connected," I said, "until we find proof. From the beginning, he didn't want us to pursue that yellow dog painting."

"You know I'm seriously anxious to buy it, fake or not, but I do hope your friend Top Hat was not murdered because of it. That would spoil my pleasure in owning it," continued the Duchess. "The painting was here on approval, hanging in an obvious place, the night Michael Chandler and his vulgar wife came to dinner. He passed right by it and never blinked an eye, nor looked at it again during the whole evening. I was most observant about that. When

I mentioned the Pavillon Albert, he said he disliked the location and had never been there. I repeat what I told you on the telephone: nothing I noticed that night could implicate him." From another room, a clock chimed the half hour.

I looked at my watch. It was already two-thirty and I had to be in the Louvre in forty-five minutes. From the airport, I had made an appointment there with my CIA contact in Paris. Martin was at the door waiting and drove me to Dior. Like my CIA contact, I had to be careful I wasn't being followed. For him, dodging the KGB agents that swamped the city meant he would do the usual going in and out of crowded department stores, movie houses, and subway stations. I left Dior fifteen minutes later and did a bit of the same, just in case.

As soon as I walked into the huge entrance, I had the sensation someone was shadowing me, probably the young man in the gray raincoat, hat, and glasses whom I had noticed standing on the steps as I entered. Yet I wasn't certain, and proceeded through several rooms before going to my rendezvous site in the Reubens salon. When I arrived, my colleague was seated on a bench, engrossed in ogling a painting of a lush nude with reddish hair and an ample milk-white bosom. Casually, I wandered around the salon. The man I had suspected of following me had not come into the room. Perhaps I had been mistaken.

I waited five minutes before considering taking a seat on the same bench. Just in time, I noticed the gray coat coming through the door. The fact that he was there, despite my deliberate intricate route, made me certain that the fellow had been observing me since I'd entered the museum. Perhaps he was part of a KGB surveillance team, working in tandem with another agent. That was the easy way to do it. The other agent might already be in the salon, and might have tailed my CIA contact from the moment he had left the embassy.

My colleague and I carried identical art magazines. His information for me could easily have been passed on—we'd each put our magazines on the bench and then picked up the other's—but, after wandering a bit more in that salon and in a few others, I left without making contact.

As I flew back to Madrid, uncomfortable again lest someone recognize me on the plane, I speculated about the information I had missed picking up. I knew it must be information the CIA had requested from the DST on Claudine de Jorans, and more useful still, their most recent report on Chandler. Getting this information in Madrid was going to be difficult, with Stanley gone. The new electric coding machines made everybody's messages much quicker, but at this stage it was nerve-racking to have to wait until my contact returned.

Chapter 38

When I walked into the house, Luis received me with a face of stone and later remained silent during the entire dinner. The only explanation was that he knew I had lied about my whereabouts that day. Later, I heard him tell my maid to move his things into a guest room. Maybe it was the tension and uncertainty of trying to do a mission. Maybe it was having been on poor relations with my husband just too long, or maybe carrying around the weight of a guilty conscience. Whatever, there was no way I could any longer keep from telling him about the job I'd been doing for John Derby.

It was hard to begin. I was shakier than when Michael Chandler had grabbed my arm that night in Sevilla. "Luis," I began, "please sit down for a minute and listen to me." Without a word, he came into the sitting room off our bedroom and sat down on the sofa, his face expressionless—something he was good at.

I swallowed. "It's not that I don't love you, Luis. It's not that I don't feel proud to be Spanish, thanks to you. But I'm also American and I feel a sense of patriotism to my country." I looked at him, hoping for a softening in his expression. But he remained frosty. Corraling my courage, I burst out. "I've been doing a mission for John Derby."

Now that the dreadful truth was out, I waited for his outcry. For a moment, he just looked at me. Then he stood up and pulled me down on the sofa on top of him. "I hoped that would be the case." Now he was grinning. "After all, it's bad enough that you go against my wishes, but it's a lot better than the story circulating in this town."

He told me friends had told him not only about my being in

Sevilla in a bar alone with a good-looking man, but also in a parked car on a dark street in Madrid! Scandal spread through Madrid like in a small town.

"I don't intend to be living with a wife who people think is putting horns on me. So you'll have to stop this once and for all." But his tone was far from intimidating.

I agreed not to accept another job, but, encouraged by his affectionate embrace, I asked for two conditions: That he would allow me to continue long enough to uncover the mystery of the yellow dog painting and that he would help.

"Now that you've even dared to get the Duchess involved, I have no choice except to do what I can to get both of you out of this nasty business. But this time has to be the last!" He tried to sound severe, but gave up, and instead began an analysis of Enrique Paredes, who I had told him was undoubtedly the man who had been head of the Nazi business in Spain during the war.

"It's hard for me to believe that Enrique would be mixed up in a dirty business like this. I've known his family all my life. He might have been pro-German during the war, but not pro-Nazi, and never a crook. I think you're completely mistaken there. Investigate him and you'll find out. Those bloodhounds in your agency's office should check his record."

Luis said he would ask Klaus about the antique shop on the Calle Leon. I had intended to do that myself, but had never found the right moment during the fair.

"He might be able to supply information about the man who owned the store," suggested Luis. "At least he's in a good position to ask the niece who inherited the business, since she rents the space from him."

Days passed without results. The Duchess and the Duke were going to leave in a few weeks for New York on their favorite ocean vessel, the *Le France,* and the envelope from Paris did not arrive. When it did, it contained copies of Edmundo's reports to the CIA office stating more or less what we already knew. In his usual arrogant style, he had informed the station chief that he would not divulge his latest momentous discovery. He said that the unprofessional CIA newcomers would not resist tailing the person if he gave the name and stated that he intended to get the necessary proof of the mole's identity without their help. There was a copy of the station chief's report to Washington, declaring that Top Hat had been ordered to concentrate only on Operation Magic, but had continued to work on his previous disinformation mission at the same time. And finally, a copy of Edmundo's last cable to the Paris office from London.

> MAGIC MOLE ABOUT TO FALL IN MY TRAP STOP HEAD OF DISINFORMATION ALSO WILL BE UNVEILED STOP BOTH MISSIONS ARE CONNECTED BY SAME SOVIET COR-RESPONDENT STOP KEEP GUESSING YOU POOR DEVILS STOP LUKEWARM REGARDS.

I could well imagine how much this typical Top Hat cable must have irritated his associates, even those accustomed to the way Edmundo worked—consistently ignoring orders, choosing his own priorities. He had never been popular with colleagues in the central office. Now that he was dead, they would be more critical than ever since he had left no clues, no names.

I had hoped for a report on Chandler and Jorans, but all I received was a note saying that nothing of consequence had been uncovered about them. Luis tried to speak to Klaus Fribourg, but he was out of town. Stanley Baker had gone to Paris to consult with the station chief there. The Duchess called daily, as nervous as I about the time it took to get information from the professional trailers. She was already packing for their sea voyage.

"Everything is discouraging, Aline," she said on the phone. "I've just discovered that Claudine and Michael Chandler were not lovers after all. The pianist was here last night for our dinner music and happened to mention that Claudine and Colonel Chandler shared a mutual love for music. Each had studied to be concert pianists and they sometimes played duets together. Evidently, Michael is quite a composer and often gave Claudine his compositions to take home to study." Her long sigh blew through the line. "Oh dear, Aline. This tension will give me another ulcer attack. David notices I'm keeping something from him, and he's becoming difficult."

I wasn't listening. The reference to Chandler giving Claudine musical compositions, and their both being pianists, had suddenly opened a whole new possibility.

"Do you realize what this could mean?" I said, recklessly disregarding the fact that someone in her house could be on the line.

"Michael Chandler could have been passing documents on to Claudine inside those sheets of music. Magic's KGB boyfriend was also a pianist and played at NATO functions. I don't know if it's possible, but I worked for years in code rooms and I believe one can make codes out of practically anything. Why not music? The orchestration could be accompanied by words. The score could contain the message. Just think: even sharps and flats, high notes, low notes—there's a tremendous number of ways in which a code could be developed so that no one could unravel it except the one who had the key."

"Aline, you never told me that! This makes my pianist a valuable ally."

"Ally! If Michael Chandler is the traitor and becomes aware of what that man told you, your pianist could become a *dead* ally!"

"Oh dear! Do you really think so? How can I warn him?"

"That would be fatal. The best way to help him is to say nothing. And don't have him play at another dinner until we get a report on Chandler. When our people learn your news, I bet they'll do a more sensitive study."

When I hung up, I knew that Michael Chandler was guilty. Maybe Stanley too. I also knew that it was the moment to be wary. If the traitor smelled danger, he would react as he had in the past. He would eliminate anyone who could incriminate him, as he had with Magic and Top Hat. I remembered Niki Lilienthal so many years ago. His assassin had been connected with Nazi loot, the yellow dog painting. Claudine was involved in that. Where was the relationship? Again I was in despair that I hadn't pried more information from Claudine. Now I understood better why she had been frightened. Her fear could have had something to do with her fatal heart attack. Did she know how to decipher the musical code? Did she know who the mole was? Magic and her KGB boyfriend had been killed for that reason. If Claudine had lived long enough, she might have been too.

I rushed to tell Luis. His first reaction was to worry about the Duchess. "If anything happens to her, you would be to blame," he said. I told him that Edmundo had said the mole would never dare kill the Duchess. "Edmundo could be wrong," he answered.

Luis hated my still being involved in these murky matters and wanted the whole mess over the soonest possible. He said that he would visit all the old antique dealers in Madrid the next day. Most were his friends and would talk to him freely. Both of us knew that since Claudine was connected with Operation Safehaven, and that since she was also involved in helping Chandler, tracking down one operation could perhaps lead to discovering a connection with the other.

The next evening around nine, I was writing a letter to my mother when I heard Luis come into the house and rush up the stairs to my sitting room where I was seated. He gave me a kiss and sat down. "Pepe Suarez," he said, "the owner of the shop near the Hotel Palace, told me that during the war important *objets d'art* came into Spain illegally from northern Europe and were offered to dealers by a go-between, who provided lists and descriptions of the merchandise in advance."

Most of this information I had known for years. I shrugged.

"Be patient," he admonished. "I was able to find out who the go-between was." He prolonged my impatience a moment. "None other than the recent owner of the shop you visited on the Calle Leon."

I sighed. "But he's dead, and most likely the niece who inherited the business doesn't know what her uncle did twenty years ago."

"That's where Klaus will come in handy. He'll be back the day after tomorrow, and I'll speak to him about it. Meanwhile, ask those snoops you work with to see what they can dig up. Frankly, I don't think they've been especially brilliant so far."

But the very next day, Luis had more news. "Enrique was at the board meeting of Union Electrica this morning," he said. "He was sitting next to me and I brought up Claudine's tragic death in Sevilla. Do you know what he told me?"

I shook my head.

"He said he was glad he had been able to do her a favor shortly before she died. And wait till you hear what that favor was!" Luis paused. "Claudine asked Enrique to deliver some pictures to Paris."

"Go on. I told you I was almost certain he was the one who delivered those paintings. What else did he say?"

"When I asked him where he got them, he said they had been delivered to his house in Madrid, and he had merely dropped them off at an address in Paris."

"Do you really believe that Enrique didn't know he was transporting stolen paintings?"

"Why would he bring the subject up? I never mentioned paintings to him."

"Then you don't think Enrique is the fellow I'm looking for?"

"I told you before. I never did. He's just not the type."

Luis's information disillusioned me. Now I didn't even have a suspect in Spain.

Then the Duchess called me from Paris. Our calls had become daily, despite our husbands complaining about the telephone bill. "From now on, we'll have to call Paul Ferguson . . . Paulette," she said. I wondered what she was talking about. "My dear," she went on, "he's a pansy! Can you imagine! That good-looking man. Alas! It happens often. My fitter in Cardin confided to me this morning that Paul Ferguson is having an affair with one of the young salesmen in Cardin's men's shop. That explains his absences and his stories about secret trips. Now where do we go from here?"

"We must find out more about Michael Chandler."

"And Edouard de Jorans, also," she answered. "Right now he's trying to get us to attend a luncheon next Tuesday for some rich American friend. Frankly, both David and I are shocked. After all, his wife only died a week ago. I don't think we'll go. I'm also most suspicious of him. If Claudine was transmitting secret reports in sheets of music from Michael Chandler, Edouard could have been aware of it. I hope your people are continuing to investigate him. At any rate, the Fergusons have invited us to a dinner with the Chandlers next Tuesday, and this time I'll let him know that my pianist told me he was a great composer and see what he says."

That same day, Stanley Baker returned and said it was urgent we meet. This time, of course, I told Luis, but we decided it was not advisable to see him at home. Neither of us wanted any obvious connection with the CIA offices in the American embassy until I had finished collaborating on this mission. If Stanley had a business cover and an office someplace else, people would suspect him less. I could have seen him freely, which would have helped us avoid gossip.

Chapter 39

I met Stanley after dark on the same street as the last time. Now that Luis knew where I was, I felt more secure. My doubts about Baker still troubled me, though, as first he gave me a report on Chandler, which seemed to clear the colonel of suspicion, then handed me a report on Edouard de Jorans which had come from the DST. Fortunately, I had brought a flashlight, because the print was small and covered two pages. From the beginning, it was obvious that the French intelligence staff had done a thorough job on Monsieur Jorans.

"Edouard François de Jorans, born Bordeaux May 26, 1916. Parents: François de Jorans, owner of a fleet of fishing boats, and Marianne Fleuve of Bruges, Belgium. Attended parochial school in Bordeaux. In 1933 he attended the Sorbonne, sharing living quarters with two foreigners, Ludwig Diehl from Frankfurt and Klaus Fribourg from Zurich."

When I read Fribourg's name, my heart stopped beating for a moment. I remembered how, that weekend at Ferrieres, Klaus and his wife had deliberately given the impression that they were meeting Edouard de Jorans for the first time.

Stanley Baker noticed my hesitation. "Yes," he said. "We were also surprised about Fribourg."

As I read further, my head continued to reel. "In 1938, Jorans graduated from the Sorbonne with a Doctorate in the history of art. During the occupation, Jorans acted as an advisor for Goering on important collections in Holland, Belgium, and France. Jorans' father's ships transported looted Nazi objects to Bilbao. Both Edouard de Jorans and his father, François de Jorans, were collaborationists. . . ."

"In 1945, Edouard de Jorans married Charlotte Gigot, minor official of the Bordeaux Communist party. Jorans joined party the same year. In 1947, divorced wife, leaving her with their one-year-old son, and went to Paris, where he became columnist for a minor art publication. In 1948, Jorans became art critic for *Paris Soir.* In 1951, he became assistant professor of the History of Art at the Sorbonne. Later that year, KGB contacted him through Paris branch of PCF and Jorans began to mount network of journalists to run articles favorable to Soviets. Jorans became one of KGB's main 'agents of influence,' manipulating political columnists for benefit of KGB department A, dealing in disinformation. . . ."

Here I stopped reading again, remembering Edmundo's references to pursuing enemy disinformation, before taking on Operation Magic.

I took a deep breath and continued to read. "In 1952, Jorans married Claudine Beauregard, the widow of a small wine merchant in Bordeaux. One child was born to couple in 1953. Currently, Jorans directs network for Soviet disinformation in the press, under orders of Active Measures department of KGB, and is in regular contact with Soviet Residency in Paris."

An added note at the bottom of the page in someone's handwriting stated: "Jorans is not being taken into custody for time being; continued surveillance may lead to American double agent."

When I finished reading, I looked at my companion, hardly able to talk. "Well, this report clears up many things. You won't have to continue the exploration of the antique shop, for one. It's pretty obvious that Klaus Fribourg must have been Jorans' partner and the fellow who ran Nazi affairs here during the war."

"Our people are not interested today in who controlled Nazi affairs in Spain twenty years ago, but nevertheless I did investigate that shop on the Calle Leon. Fribourg must be a very cautious fellow. His name was not in their books or papers once during that war period."

"And if we now have proof that Edouard de Jorans works for the KGB, it seems quite obvious that Claudine must have been working for them also."

Stanley nodded. "Could be."

I asked him what the Paris station chief thought about Chandler passing on sheets of music to Claudine de Jorans. He said that they agreed that it was possible to hide a code inside musical notes, but that so far nothing had showed up on Colonel Chandler that could make him a suspect any more than he had been before—not even in his compositions, of which they had obtained more than one. Yet the fact remained that the top secret material was being leaked from a department to which he had access.

"Don't you think Chandler could be the mole, even if nothing has turned up against him?" I asked.

Stanley was skeptical. "There are many Soviet agents in Paris who could be used as cutouts," he suggested. "We're still observing Chandler and those close to him."

"But Jorans' wife would have been the perfect cutout to protect both men, don't you think?"

Stanley insisted that, without proof, no decision could be made. "If your friend Top Hat had not been so egocentric, we might have known what to make of his attachment with Madame de Jorans."

When I arrived home, Luis was upstairs in his sitting room playing a game of solitaire. "At last," he said as I came into the room, report in hand. "I've got news for you." He continued placing one card on another. "Klaus Fribourg returned my call and we met and had a game of golf this afternoon."

My heart flipped. With the startling recent developments, I had forgotten that I had asked Luis to talk to Fribourg about the antique shop. Nothing could be more dangerous now.

"I didn't want to get you involved," Luis continued, "so I told him the Americans had asked me if I knew anything about the late owner of the antique shop in his building on the Calle Leon."

Maybe it was my sigh that made Luis look up. "What's the matter?" he asked. "Klaus was most interested and willing to help. He said he would inquire in his office."

"Luis," I cried. "Fribourg himself is the man. I just found out from this report Stanley Baker gave me." I flung the paper down on the table and flopped onto the sofa as he began to read.

When he had finished studying the paper, he tossed the half pack of cards on the table. *"Caray!* Damn. Who would have believed Klaus Fribourg could be a crook or an assassin? How many times have we invited him to dine and to our shoots?" He went on to say exactly what was worrying me. "Now Klaus will alert Jorans, who will alert whoever else is mixed up with them."

"And," I added, "if Chandler is the mole . . ."

Luis interrupted. "It looks to me as if Top Hat's 'link' is Edouard de Jorans, not his wife, whom he probably used as a cover. Jorans worked with Klaus, robbing for the Nazis and for himself, during the war, and then years later did the same for the Soviets, only this time robbing from the Americans. It looks like that fellow you found so attractive is just a skunk. You'd better warn your colleagues right away that Fribourg is apt to blow the deal, now that he knows he's being investigated."

Before following Luis' advice, I decided it might be useful to show him the message from Top Hat that I had decoded that night at the fair. Maybe I had overlooked something that Luis would pick up. I ran downstairs to my room and found the handbag I had used in Sevilla. Fortunately, Angustias had not seen it when she unpacked my things and the paper was still crumpled in the zippered inside pocket. I had been careless to leave it there.

Luis read it while I looked over his shoulder.

ADVISE WILLY TO ASCERTAIN IF CHANDLER IN PARIS FEBRUARY FIRST BUT WARN HER TO BEWARE STOP CATSMEOW IS LINK STOP PROCEED WITH CAUTION SEVILLA STOP ABRAZOS.

I froze as I read. Luis said what I was thinking. "Looks to me as if Edmundo was pretty sure Chandler was the mole. And he also considered him dangerous. How is it you didn't understand that before?"

I explained that Edmundo sometimes invented wild reports to impress the Agency. That although this cable was for me, he knew I would show it to the station chief. And that I had taken it for granted that Edmundo mentioned Chandler because he was one of Jupiter's suspects.

"Well, Edmundo knew something could occur in Sevilla. Do you realize that guy could have killed you? That may have been his intention." Luis looked at me severely. "You must warn the Duchess. She may be in danger right now. And I suggest you advise your people in Paris about Chandler without delay."

I told him that I was still suspicious of Stanley Baker, that Chandler and Baker could have been working together and planning to contact Claudine or Edouard there, when she died unexpectedly and spoiled their plans.

Luis was thoughtful: "Then you'd better call John Derby instead. Don't take any more chances."

It took half the night to reach Jupiter, but I finally found him in New York. When I told him that Luis had spoken to Fribourg, his main preoccupation was that Klaus might advise Jorans. "But," he said, "that does not necessarily mean that Jorans would think our investigation of Fribourg would connect him to Operation Magic. Let's hope so, anyway. At least that might keep him from alerting Chandler or whoever else might be the mole. I'm not yet convinced it is Chandler. We can do nothing until we have proof, you know."

He said nothing about Operation Safehaven having led us to Operation Magic. That was a feather in my cap, and I intended to tease him about it later on.

Luis and I discussed the case for hours. We figured that Klaus and Edouard had run the operation together during the war and had split the profits. I explained to Luis that since Jorans had organized a press network for disinformation in France for the KGB, he was probably one of their most effective Agents of Influence today. We surmised that perhaps he had accepted the added task of passing on NATO information to obtain another source of income to finance his love of luxury.

"Jorans may feel secure in Paris, since we guess he doesn't know your country suspects him. But Klaus could go into hiding. What will your people do about having him imprisoned?"

"That takes time. I don't think Americans have legal rights in this case. It concerns a Swiss national in Spanish territory, which is still further removed. And I'll bet CIA funds cannot be used to investigate OSS cases of twenty-five years ago. There may be some kind of World War Two reparations laws that apply with no statute of limitations, but if so, I don't know anything about them."

"We may never get him."

Chapter 40

One shock came after another. It turned out I was right about the Americans never getting Klaus Fribourg—but for a reason I had never considered.

The next morning, news greeted us that was hard to believe. Klaus Fribourg had been found by his valet with a shot through the head from his own gun! Everyone, except Luis and myself, was astounded. Madrid's telephone lines lit up. Why would Fribourg, one of the wealthiest men in the country, a man who had everything, a man with no problems, kill himself? It was inconceivable! The consensus of opinion was that he must have had a moment of insanity. Others suggested that perhaps his doctor had diagnosed incurable cancer.

Luis sat on my chaise longue while I dressed. "It was probably the best way to protect his family from scandal," he mumbled.

I looked at my husband. "Do you really think Ada knows nothing of his activities during the war? You should have a good idea. It seems to me you knew her a bit too well." Just remembering my suspicions about Luis and Ada made me furious, and I guess my tone indicated it.

He laughed. "I'm glad you're jealous. Unfortunately, I had no relationship of any kind with beautiful Ada. But it is rumored she's having an affair with someone. Who? Nobody knows. Ada is very smart. She knows how to camouflage her actions."

"If she was so smart, she had to know where Klaus's money came from."

"Not necessarily." He chuckled. "You're smart, and I don't think you know where the money we live on comes from."

I laughed. "You're perfectly right. You've never let me pry into your affairs. But Klaus was weak and I bet she married him for financial security. At least, I don't think she was ever in love with him."

When I was dressed, we went together to the Fribourg house, as was normal when a friend dies in Spain. Since embalming is not customary, according to the law, the deceased must be buried within twenty-four hours. This meant that Klaus's burial would take place before four today. When we arrived at the large Fribourg apartment on the Castellana, masses of people were going and coming from the building. In the street, instead of the open black carriage drawn by four black horses decorated with huge black plumes that had been customary a few years before, a shiny, black motor-hearse stood waiting. Inside, the hallways and salons were banked with floral wreaths.

In the library, with her back to the door, Ada knelt in prayer next to the closed bier where four huge candelabras glimmered at each corner. Flanking her, two black-robed nuns fingered their rosaries and droned a litany. The widow spoke to no one. Visitors chatted with friends, who, if they had not already done so, signed the book at the entrance on leaving. The fact that they had been there and fulfilled their social obligations was thus registered for the family to see. Some stayed on to accompany Ada to the cemetery, also a new custom. A decade before, women did not go to the graveyard.

Not even the slightest rumor of Klaus's murky dealings with looted Nazi assets was mentioned. Luis and I left the house no wiser than when we had entered. A man who was not only a crook but, very possibly, an assassin, was going to receive an honorable burial. By now we suspected that Klaus could have been responsible for Lilienthal's death, and maybe other deaths that we didn't know about.

When we drove away, Luis was still thinking about our old friend. "Klaus probably thought this was the way to avoid an investigation. It looks as if he was right. What do you think your people will do now?"

"Not much," I answered. "The looted objects are probably long since disposed of, and according to what Mazerolle says about the South American market, Klaus may have sent copies or fakes there and kept the originals to sell in Europe. Only Edouard de Jorans can incriminate Klaus. At this point, I doubt he would try to do that."

Late that afternoon, when Angustias came into my dressing room with my evening clothes, she began to talk about the funeral. In a particularly rhapsodic mood, she flung her arms in the air as she described the details of the burial. Her eyes rolled from side to side. She would have made a memorable actress, I thought, as I continued to arrange my hair. One of her few sources of entertainment were the weddings and baptisms and funerals of our family and friends. She never went to the movies, and refused to take days off. The household dramas interested her more than anything outside.

"What a sad day, Señora Condesa!" she said, beaming. "A beautiful burial! At least two hundred friends went to the cemetery." She smirked in satisfaction. "Very important people, too."

"Angustias," I said, "don't tell me you went all the way to the cemetery of San Isidoro?"

"Most certainly, señora. Amparo, the Fribourgs' housekeeper, is my friend and, of course, I knew Señor Fribourg. He was always kind to me. Many times he came into the butler's pantry to shake my hand. A really great señor."

I waited impatiently, knowing that Angustias would have to talk about the burial and that nothing would stop her. "Amparo says the Señora Fribourg has taken good care of her husband's favorite belongings," she went on. "As soon as he died, Señora Fribourg ordered the gold plates and paintings in his private rooms upstairs to be put in a locked vault in the basement. Do you know, Señora Condesa, he has many valuable belongings—real gold bars? Now, who in this city has such wealth! And paintings and, oh, many precious objects. Amparo says he's the richest man in Madrid. And she says he has storerooms in the cellar where he keeps valuables for which there is not room enough in the house. A really important man, he was."

Later in the car on our way to the dinner, I told Luis what Angustias had said about Fribourg's valuable belongings. We looked at each other. How much did Ada know about the source of her husband's wealth? Fribourg was famous for his good taste. Their apartment was filled with signed pieces of furniture, magnificent porcelain, and paintings. Whenever friends complimented his collections, he said that he had been an assiduous collector of *objets d'art* all his life. I remembered how obsessed Ada had been about the objects the Nazis had looted from her husband. Had he managed to keep secret from her all these years, the truth about his work for the Nazis?

"Well, we should know some of the answers soon," I told Luis. "Jupiter told me he would request a thorough report on Klaus Fribourg, to be made with the collaboration of the Swiss, French, and West German services."

By now we were in front of the house of Senor Pinto Coelho, a famous decorator friend, where we were dining. We parked and got out of the car. "And," I added, "he told me Jorans is being watched by our people and by French intelligence, too. Do you know, now even Jupiter has doubts about Michael Chandler. He says Chandler did three years' service in the military attaché's office of the American embassy in Moscow just after the war. There was nothing suspicious about Chandler's friendships and activities there during that time, but that post could have marked the beginning of his relationship with the KGB. At any rate, Jupiter insists that for indictment, Chandler has to be caught actually loading a dead drop or passing on information some other way. This case isn't over yet."

Chapter 41

The next day was Wednesday, and I called the Duchess early to find out about her dinner the night before at L'Orangerie with the Chandlers and the Fergusons.

The Duchess' voice was crisp. "What do you think? I'm so disappointed. Maureen's dinner was a flop. Our friends"—she was being wary and at a loss for code names, since the Chandlers were the only ones she had not baptized—"well, they just never showed up. Lockjaw and his wife were mortified in front of David. The missing guest seems to be out of town. Even his wife doesn't know where he is. And on top of that, my romance was furious that I had accepted such a boring evening. There were only two other dreary couples there. One French couple who did not speak English. Can you imagine! You know David cannot speak French. I can barely order my bath in that language. Well, we each had a non-English–speaking Frenchman at our side. Of course, we left early."

I hung up abruptly and called Jupiter. Fortunately, I got him on the line right away in New York.

With so many professionals working on the case, it was ironical that the first inkling that Chandler had skipped came from the Duchess. The fact that he had disappeared from Paris, that even his wife claimed she did not know where he was, made Jupiter quite certain Chandler was the mole. Jupiter said very little. He was obviously annoyed that Chandler had discovered he was being investigated and had skipped without our people knowing.

Pandemonium broke loose when the news reached the CIA headquarters in Paris. Airports, railroads, and bus stations were checked. But it was not until two days later that word filtered from a small Austrian border town that a man fitting Michael Chandler's description had left a rented car there and had proceeded on into Hungary. We knew we had lost him inside the Eastern Bloc. But at least the mole had been uncovered. The leakage of top secret documents would come to an end.

It was Monday. I called the Duchess and told her that, thanks to her, we had learned that Michael Chandler had defected, and that he was undoubtedly the mole. I also told her the other latest news wired us from Paris, that Edouard de Jorans had been taken into custody by the French Sécurité.

For a moment, there was silence. Then a long sigh. "I don't know what to say. I'm shocked. I don't care about Chandler at all. And it is nice to know I've helped to eliminate a traitor. But Edouard seemed so decent. And he was so good-looking. It's just incredible to think he could have been such a double-crosser. Somebody must have led him astray when he was very young. How do those things happen?" We said good-bye and both hung up.

A few minutes later, she called back. I was amazed. Two long distance calls in the same day! "Aline, now that it's all over," she began, "instead of experiencing the pleasures of success, I feel deflated." Then a burst of her sharp laughter came through the line. "When do you suppose you can get us a new job?"

"If you would be willing to meet Jupiter, he may take you on permanently," I teased. "Seriously, I think you deserve to hear the inside story firsthand. Jupiter would love to meet you and I'm having lunch with him in Paris next week. He's promised to give me all the details. How about it? No one would suspect you to be involved in such things just because you lunch with an American businessman and an old friend like myself. Nobody knows about Jupiter's undercover work."

A moment's silence. "If Luis comes along," she answered, "I'll do it. But we're leaving on Sunday, so it'll have to be right away."

A few days later, Stanley Baker, who had just been in Paris, came home to tell me the details about Edouard de Jorans. It was a sad story. President de Gaulle had not attended the luncheon Edouard had arranged for Mr. Worthington, but the forty people present were outstanding government officials, famous intellectuals, and a few respected aristocrats—just the group Edouard most wanted to impress. During the luncheon, Edouard had made a dramatic speech, extolling Mr. Worthington's contributions to French culture. Mr. Worthington had answered with charming reminiscences about Edouard having saved his life thirty years before. The usual amenities were mentioned, and medals were exchanged. While these activities were taking place, French police agents were waiting in Jorans' entrance hall until the ceremonies were over, in deference to the high officials present. When the guests began to depart, however, the police entered and arrested Jorans. In front of everybody, Edouard made an attempt at suicide by trying to jump out a window. At this point, it seems, Mr. Worthington interceded on Jorans' behalf, insisting that a grave mistake had been made. The American ambassador, who was also present, backed him up, and they were ready to make trouble, until the DST agents produced a copy of the accusation. Mr. Worthington and the ambassador were convinced and Edouard was taken into custody.

Chapter 42

Our luncheon with Jupiter took place on Friday. Luis and I went to Paris especially for the occasion. Seated in Maxim's, Jupiter's manner was calm and quiet, and we had no idea of the sensational surprises in store. He began by suggesting that to commemorate the occasion, we all order something special.

"I'll celebrate with my favorite," said the Duchess, "a hamburger. They're so good here."

I was studying the menu, wondering if I dared to order caviar and blinis, when I heard Luis say, "What's Ada Fribourg doing here in Paris?"

Looking up, I saw Ada sitting on the banquette in a far corner. The man lunching with her simply added to my astonishment. When she saw us looking in her direction, Ada lifted a graceful hand and waved.

The Duchess lifted her lorgnette and pretended to be engrossed in her menu, while addressing Jupiter. "Mr. Derby, just in case you are unaware, that man with Señora Fribourg is Monsieur Mazerolle, the owner of the art gallery where Aline found the yellow dog painting."

"I'd say Mrs. Fribourg still has a few paintings left," commented John Derby wryly.

"Do you really think that Ada knew all along about the looted artworks? Do you think she helped her husband?" I asked stupidly.

Luis grinned, looking at me. "It's difficult for a man to do anything that his wife doesn't find out about, isn't it?" Then he added, "It's my bet that Ada's business luncheon is proceeding quite successfully for her. She appears extremely happy and pleased for a woman who lost her husband only ten days ago."

John Derby put down his glass of Lillet. We had all copied the Duchess' favorite before-lunch drink. "The reports we have received this past week," he said, "thanks to West German intelligence, state that Ada Fribourg, formally Princess von Lowenstein, born Adalberta Grundig, knew two men in Hitler's high command rather intimately. She had every opportunity to put Fribourg and his school chum, Jorans, in touch with Goering's group. In fact, the report shows that she knew far more about art than Fribourg. Her first husband's profession was restoring classic paintings."

I was stunned. Luis smiled. "It was always obvious to me that Ada had a greater appreciation of art than Klaus. I never heard him make an especially brilliant comment during the *vernissages* in San Jorge." San Jorge was an art gallery Luis owned near the Fribourgs' apartment on the Castellana.

We all tried not to look in the direction of the table where Ada and Monsieur Mazerolle sat.

"For the time being," said Jupiter softly, as he looked at the Duchess, "I thought you might be interested in the latest news about your late friend Claudine de Jorans."

"Is there something new?" questioned the Duchess.

"Yes, but let's leave that until later. First let's talk about her husband." Patting his pocket, he said, "I've just received a full report on Jorans—a combination of information the French authorities obtained by questioning Edouard the afternoon of his arrest and from studying records that date back to the war. This is information we never could have obtained on our own. Thanks to these proofs, they were able to get Edouard de Jorans to confess.

"For example, Jorans admitted to having been a partner of Klaus Fribourg since the beginning of World War Two. Jorans said Fribourg consistently cheated him out of his share of the Nazi assets, which, in great part, he had helped requisition. Jorans said that during the last year of the war, Fribourg claimed that sales would incriminate them both and advised keeping the looted art in Spain. Later, Fribourg refused to provide Jorans with a complete account of the art objects in his possession. This situation existed between the two men for many years, until a few months ago, in fact, when Jorans was in urgent need of cash. He said he demanded that Fribourg send to Paris the Impressionist paintings he had had one of his father's ships deliver to Bilbao in the spring of 1944. Fribourg stalled again, suggesting the paintings could be sold more safely in America. But Jorans insisted. Fribourg then used the excuse that it was difficult to get art treasures out of Spain.

"Edouard got Claudine to ask a friend who came to France frequently by car, to bring in a few paintings. According to Edouard de Jorans, his wife did not know these were illegally owned paintings. He says he told her only that he had bought the paintings years ago. When they arrived in Paris, Jorans discovered that Fribourg was sending him copies or imitations. That's when he decided to go to Spain to see for himself what remained of the loot he had sent to Klaus Fribourg during the war.

"Fribourg had told him then that the larger portion was in a storehouse in Sevilla . . ."

Waiters were passing by. A friend approached our table to say hello. The Duchess, with great tact, managed to dispatch him in a minimum of time. While the waiter refilled Luis' and John's wine glasses, we made efforts to conceal our impatience. As soon as they had left, even the blinis and caviar were not enough to distract the Duchess and me. We urged Jupiter to continue.

Slowly, quietly, enjoying our intense attention, he proceeded. "Jorans also admitted to assisting KGB double agent Michael Chandler in 1965 to pass sensitive military information on to the KGB. The Soviets used Jorans for this because he had a chain of reliable agents working for him from many years before. In this endeavor, Edouard de Jorans also used his wife as a cutout. Claudine de Jorans' friendship with Chandler, through their mutual interest in music, facilitated transferring coded messages relating to the location of the dead drops. Jorans indicated that his wife was unaware what she was transmitting. He said he told her that it was confidential material for his press articles and instructed her to act with secrecy."

Derby said they surmised that when Fribourg learned he was under investigation, he immediately advised Jorans. Since Jorans was working with Chandler, he in turn warned Chandler to cease sending information. Jorans' intention was to paralyze transference of all messages until he was certain he was not being shadowed. Jupiter paused, breathing heavily, as if he'd been running. I sensed that my old friend was reliving the drama as he retold it. This business of pursuing traitors was like a drug for Jupiter. "You see," he went on, "it was usually Jorans himself who unloaded the dead drops and then passed the information to a Soviet officer from their *rezidentura,* the KGB office here. Although now and then he was forced to send one of his agents." Here, Jupiter sighed and grimaced. "Unfortunately, one of our own agents was careless in tailing Jorans. Already on guard, he became aware he was being watched. Jorans and Chandler consulted with each other again. They both decided to defect. Chandler's defection is what proved to us that he was guilty. But fortunately for us, Edouard de Jorans postponed his own defection until after an important American friend had terminated his visit to France. That was his downfall."

I interrupted. "Yes. I know all about that fellow."

Derby explained. "You see, no one had yet seen Colonel Chandler in the act of passing on a message or loading a dead drop. He might have gotten away with it, but he must have suspected that Jorans would squeal on him."

John Derby was quiet for a moment, but none of us spoke, knowing he had much more to tell.

"There is one more relevant fact about Edouard de Jorans," he said with a wry smile. Again, we waited. "He admitted to having had an affair with Ada Fribourg for many years."

Instinctively, we all glanced at the table in the corner. I don't know who was the most amazed. Probably myself. Then I remembered the day I had seen Ada in the air terminal waiting room. She had been seated on the side where passengers waited to go to Barcelona, but maybe she had actually been waiting for the plane I had come in on from Paris.

"She doesn't seem to be especially upset that her paramour is in jail at the moment, does she?" the Duchess quipped.

Derby continued to tell us what had occurred with Top Hat. According to him, Edmundo became interested in Claudine because he suspected her husband was the head of the KGB disinformation operation in France. "This meant that Edmundo had discovered Edouard de Jorans was a Soviet agent of influence, which, to a professional like Edmundo, also indicated that Jorans was the obvious person to be in charge of passing vital military information for the KGB. Edmundo had been following the Jorans couple and when he saw Claudine play a duet with Michael Chandler, who, of course, he knew to be one of our military officers, he decided to attempt a flirtation with the lady. And he was successful.

Claudine did not become suspicious of her husband's work for the KGB until her weekend in London with Top Hat. We suspect that Top Hat warned her at some moment during that weekend."

John Derby proceeded to tell us how the Soviets had killed Top Hat. "It's a new trick employed recently by the KGB. It identifies the work as theirs." He took his newspaper in hand and rolled it into a funnel with the wide opening facing across the table. "A shot of poisonous gas directly into the face, from a small spray can. In this case," said John Derby, "Top Hat was returning to his apartment. The fatal spray entered his lungs and he was dead in the space of seconds. To make the death appear like suicide, he was then placed with his head in the oven and the gas vents turned on. The autopsy could prove nothing. The KGB gas leaves no traces in the body. Fifteen minutes after use, the chemical is dissolved in the air and the blood. We managed to find a witness who had observed the attack, but we had to keep it out of the press to protect the man."

As we were having coffee, the Duchess took her lipstick out of her handbag and lifted it to her lips. Jupiter raised his hand. *"Cuidado,"* he said. Derby's Spanish wasn't good, and his accent was not the best either, but the Duchess seemed to understand. Startled, the lipstick remained poised in midair.

"I forgot to tell you . . ." He looked at us both. "Think twice in the future before you paint your lips." His face was solemn. "Claudine did not die of a heart attack, as we originally thought." His voice became almost a whisper. "She was murdered!"

With a forceful gesture, the Duchess put her lipstick back into her bag. "Don't tell me . . ." she started to say.

"Yes," said Derby. "The thick coating of red grease on her lips was embedded with a lethal poison. The poison was in her lipstick."

We looked at each other, not knowing whether Jupiter was joking or serious. Not even the Duchess dared to ask. I knew from years of experience that he would never tell us the full or exact story of any operation. There were always details that had to remain top secret. Jupiter's manner, although charming, was not cozy and didn't invite questioning. The Duchess understood this instinctively. Was Jupiter suppressing just the slightest shadow of a grin? Maybe not. I recalled Claudine rubbing the stick across her lips only seconds before she fell to the floor. No, I decided, this time Jupiter was telling the truth.

Then all of a sudden I remembered something to which I had

never attached any importance. "When Claudine took her lipstick out of her bag that night, she dropped it," I blurted out. Now I had everyone's attention. "It rolled on the floor under our chairs. I looked down and was going to pick it up, but Ada had already done so." I looked around the table. "I never gave it a second thought at the time. My attention was concentrated on the flamenco." I breathed deeply. "But now that I think about it, it was just after that, that Claudine collapsed."

"Your friend, Ada, probably knocked the lipstick out of Claudine's hand, so she could replace it with the poisonous one," suggested the Duchess. Then she shuddered. "Just think, we're having lunch with an assassin right now. She's not very far away."

"Maybe they should put a sign at the door. 'No killers allowed,' " joked Jupiter. "But wait a minute. Your deductions may not be correct. Others could have placed a poisoned lipstick in Madame de Jorans' bag."

The Duchess was fascinated. "Who?"

"For one, Chandler." John Derby was enjoying our rapt attention. I wondered again if he was kidding us all at the same time. "Why do you think Chandler went to Sevilla?"

No one answered his question.

"Couldn't it be that Chandler, who had a top Soviet surveillance team at his command, had uncovered the affair between Edmundo and Claudine? And was aware that Edmundo was a CIA agent?"

The tension at our table had completely replaced our interest in food or drink.

Jupiter spoke lower than ever, and anyone watching would have laughed to see the three of us lean closer to him. "Chandler could have easily paid any number of maids or waiters or employees at the Hotel Alfonso XIII to replace the lady's favorite lipstick with another."

We looked at each other. Nobody spoke. We sensed Jupiter had not finished theorizing. "The Chandlers were staying at the same hotel." He looked at each of us in turn. "Interesting, don't you think?"

At that moment, the waiter appeared with another cup of coffee for Luis and John Derby. We spoke of other things until he left. As soon as the waiter was out of range, Luis addressed Jupiter.

"Then it's anybody's guess who did the dirty work on Claudine?"

"That's about it," Jupiter said. "Your good wife knows that we often do not have all the answers. Who could prove a thing like that? And don't leave the lady's own husband out of the running. He could be the killer, too." Derby shrugged his shoulders.

The Duchess sat back in her chair and sighed with pleasure. "This is just too exciting, Mr. Derby. But I'm so afraid you'll be leaving for your plane before I can ask you some of the questions running through my head."

Jupiter looked at his wristwatch. "You're right. I'll be on my way very soon, unfortunately. I'm enjoying this, too, you know. But I want to answer all your questions. I have quite a debt of gratitude to you."

"Mr. Derby," she went on. "And to think I haven't yet been able to buy that lovely little painting of the yellow dog, fake or not. If the price is not too outrageous, I want it."

Jupiter was smiling. "I suppose you blame me for that. If there's any way I can find it, I would be delighted to make you a gift of it, but I fear that will be difficult," he said. "I'm afraid I can't help you there. Why don't you speak to the owner of the gallery again?"

"If he has a reliable business, he would probably refuse to deal in anything that was not authentic," said Luis.

"Oh," said the Duchess. "I don't believe for a moment he's reliable. Just look who he's having lunch with." Her tone and expression changed. "The whole affair about those people—Edouard, Klaus Fribourg and that Ada, and the art dealer—reminds me of my wonderful mother. So many things in life do. She was so clever. She could see through people better than anyone I ever met. Do you know what she would have said?"

We all waited.

"She would have said, 'Wallis, you shouldn't be surprised. What difference does it make who is the assassin? Colonel Chandler, Edouard de Jorans, Klaus and Ada Fribourg, or Mazerolle? They're all the same. Birds of a feather flock together.' "

Instinctively, I glanced at Ada and Monsieur Mazerolle. Did Ada know or care that our entire luncheon conversation had been about her? At that moment, the waiter was pulling back their table from the wall, and they were about to leave. I watched as they stood up and moved toward the door. Jupiter had seen they were leaving also, and kept the conversation at our table going so we would not all look their way.

When Ada got to the door, she turned toward us and smiled. Monsieur Mazerolle made a slight bow in our direction. At our table, a pregnant silence reigned. I don't know if any of the others smiled. I didn't. When the door closed behind them, the Duchess and I started to speak at the same moment. We all laughed.

"Yes," said John Derby. "You are probably right in your assumptions. But what can we do? Undoubtedly, Madame Fribourg began masterminding a plan even before she married Fribourg. In fact, maybe that's why she married him. The person behind Operation Safehaven in Spain was in all likelihood Ada Fribourg, although she used her husband as her instrument. But it was Klaus Fribourg who paid with his life—and who probably took the lives of a few others. When so instructed—by her."

Memories and scenes of some of those moments flashed through my head. Glamorous, beautiful Ada seated next to Claudine in Sevilla during the flamenco. Then I remembered how she had taken a dislike to Claudine from the beginning. Maybe that was because she had been in love with Claudine's husband. But the day of the big game shoot in the mountains of Toledo, I remembered that Ada had remained in the house. Had she ordered Klaus to shoot Lilienthal? These were questions to which we would never know the answers.

Luis lit a cigarette. "And I thought being married to an American woman was an act of bravery!" He looked mockingly at the Duchess and me. "I never thought a European woman would outdo either of you!"

Jupiter grinned. "All I can say is that the Duke of Windsor and the Count of Quintanilla are very lucky men." He looked at his watch. "Oh, I've talked too long. Unfortunately, now I must rush to the airport."

Luis had some business in the same direction and left the restaurant with Jupiter. The Duchess and I proceeded on to the house in the Bois. Once we were installed in the car, we both were silent for a while.

"Aline, a penny for your thoughts."

"I was thinking that now I'd never find out what really happened at the Rothschilds' ball. That man who chased me—who was he? They were all there together—the Fribourgs and the Jorans. Edmundo would have told me, if he'd lived long enough. You never recognized Chandler there that night, but now I suspect somebody was trying to kill Claudine, thinking I was she. I suppose it was Chandler. He could have entered in disguise. Or he could have hired a paid killer to get inside in the guise of a waiter. Goodness, but one feels so let down when it's all over."

The Duchess started to laugh. Rarely had I heard her laugh so heartily. Finally, in a low voice, so Martin couldn't hear, she quipped:

"You're perfectly right. But just think of my position. Besides being among the unemployed now, which I find depressing—I've just lost two of my most amusing dinner guests!"